PORTRAIT OF WILTSHIRE

THE *PORTRAIT* SERIES

BY THE SAME AUTHOR
My Father A. G. Street

Portrait of
WILTSHIRE

PAMELA STREET

ROBERT HALE · LONDON

© Pamela Street 1971

First published in Great Britain 1971

ISBN 0 7091 2109 1

Robert Hale & Company
63 Old Brompton Road
London S.W.7

PRINTED IN GREAT BRITAIN
BY RICHARD CLAY (THE CHAUCER PRESS), LTD.,
BUNGAY, SUFFOLK

CONTENTS

ILLUSTRATIONS

PICTURE CREDITS

Mr. A. F. Kersting, London: 1, 5, 10, 13b, 14a, 18a, 18b, 19, 20b, 21b; Mr. F. G. Miller, Salisbury: 2; Mr. David Robson, Salisbury: 3a, 6; Ministry of Public Building and Works: 3b, 22; Mr. John Tarlton, Christchurch: 4b, 8a, 9a, 12a, 13a, 15a; Mr. Anthony Miles, Salisbury: 4a, 21a, 24; Messrs. Wills, Horne & Smith, Salisbury Times & Journal: 7, 9b, 11; Mr. Austin Underwood, Amesbury: 8b; Mr. J. O. Thomas, Lackham: 12b; The British Broadcasting Corporation: 14b; The Forestry Commission: 15b; Wiltshire Newspapers Ltd: 16; Country Life Ltd: 17a, 20a; Swindon Borough Council: 17b; English Life Publications Ltd: 23.

Jacket colour photograph by Mr. Anthony Miles.

To All Moonrakers,
Past, Present, and Future

REGIMENTAL MARCH 'THE WILTSHIRE'

'Twere on a jolly zummer's day, the twenty-fust o' May,
John Scroggins took his turmut-hoe, wi' thic he trudged away:
"Now zome volks they likes haymakin', and zome they vancies
   mowin'—
But of all the jobs as I likes best, gi'e I the turmut-hoein'."

Chorus
The vly, the vly,
The vly be on the turmut—
'Tis all me eye
Fer I to try
To keep vly off the *turmut.*

"The fust place as I went to work, it were wi' Varmer Gower:
Who vowed and swore as how I were a fust-rate turmut-hoer;
The second place I went to work, they paid I by the job—
But if I'd knowed a little 'afore, I'd sooner a' bin in quod."

Chorus
The vly, the vly,
The vly be on the turmut—
'Tis all me eye
Fer I to try
To keep vly off the *turmut.*

"The last place as I went to work, they sent fer I a-mowin',
I sent word back, I'd sooner take the zack, than gi'e up turmut-hoein'!
Now all you jolly varmer chaps wot bides at home so warm—
I'll now conclude my ditty wi' a-wishin' you no harm."

Chorus
The vly, the vly,
The vly be on the turmut—
'Tis all me eye
Fer I to try
To keep vly off the *turmut.*

Old Wiltshire ditty,
adopted as a marching song
by the 4th Battalion, T.A., of the Wiltshire
(Duke of Edinburgh's Royal) Regiment.

INTRODUCTION

MEN have now set foot on the moon and become, quite literally, moonrakers. Yet many years ago, other men with their feet still firmly planted on this planet, also became moonrakers.

One night when a full moon was shining down on the very heart of the Wiltshire countryside, a few local inhabitants from the village of Bishops Cannings were engaged in smuggling some kegs of brandy which they had concealed beneath a wagon-load of hay. On hearing the sound of horses' hooves, they hastily extricated their illicit goods and dumped them in a nearby pond.

The two excisemen who arrived on the scene searched the cart and rode away but, evidently still suspicious, decided to double back on their tracks where they found the smugglers performing the curious task of trying to recover the booty with their hay-rakes. When asked what they thought they were up to, one of the culprits pointed to the splendid reflection of the moon in the water and said, "Zomebody 'ave lost thic thur cheese and we'm a-rakin' for 'un in thic thur pond." The excisemen smiled and went on their way to Devizes, having been completely fooled by these 'simple rustics' who had so successfully pretended to be fools themselves.

There may seem little in common between these eighteenth-century moonrakers (to whom the Wiltshireman owes his nick-name) and the men who have set out to scoop up some of the real moon's surface today; yet there is a connection. They all seem to have had their wits very much about them. Deep down inside each moonraker there must have lurked the same sturdy independence of spirit and the ability to pit themselves against all odds. They could all have joined together in that old Wiltshire expression, "There bain't no vlies on we."

Unfortunately, the fate of this splendid moonraking county is now in the balance. The proposals for reorganizing local government may mean that the whole entity of the Wiltshire which I have known and loved since childhood will be altered. I hope

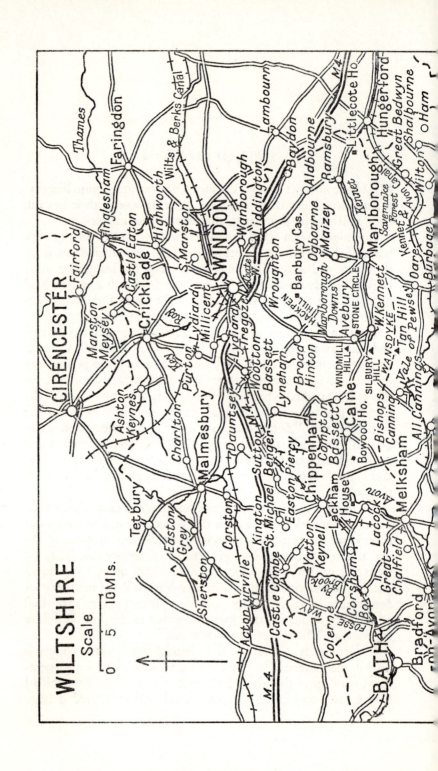

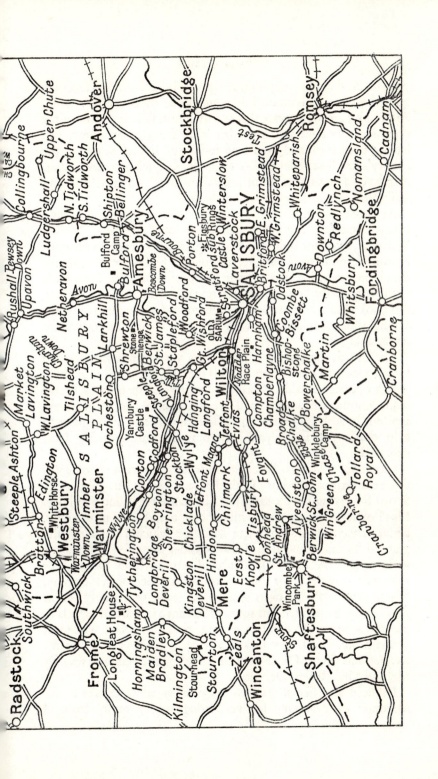

very much that this may never happen, but, if it does, I feel the quintessence of this invincible countryside must surely remain. Although I am well aware that my own wits fall very short of the typical native kind and my spirit is far from independent, yet, having been born and bred (and today still living) in one of the county's loveliest valleys, I like to think of myself as a moonraker, if only of a lesser sort. I am not ashamed of provincialism, and Wiltshire, to me, means a very great deal.

As I grow older, I find my roots growing stronger and deeper. I have therefore become a bad 'goer-away'. I dislike leaving Wiltshire, even for holidays. Although this tendency might well be considered narrow-minded and one to be fought against, the simple fact remains that I never feel quite safe until I am back within my native boundaries; whereas the realization that writing this book would keep me securely ensconced inside them for quite a long time provided me with one of the best incentives for undertaking it.

The British character is said to be not very communicative and to 'keep itself to itself', but, if this is the case, I feel it is something which operates outside Wiltshire. During recent months I have made innumerable journeys all over the county and, without exception, have been greeted by a friendliness and willingness to help that went far beyond anything I could possibly have expected.

I am indebted to Dr. Elsie Smith for her wise counsel on everything concerning Salisbury Cathedral, and also to Mr. Hugh de S. Shortt for giving me the same kind assistance regarding Salisbury. Miss Penelope Rundle bore with my countless queries most nobly, besides checking my complete MS., for which I am especially grateful. In this connection, I also consider myself very fortunate to have had the expert guidance of Mr. Richard Sandell, the Honorary Librarian of the Wiltshire Archaeological Society, whose skilled observations seemed to make the county 'come alive' when he pointed out some of its more important aspects to me on a privately conducted tour round Devizes Museum; furthermore, I feel very lucky to have been escorted down the Kennet and Avon Canal in such a highly entertaining way by Mr. and Mrs. Robert Dunsdon.

I should also like to express a special word of thanks to the Marquess of Ailesbury for permitting me to quote from *A*

History of Savernake Forest. The information in this splendid book has enabled me to write much more fully on a particularly lovely part of Wiltshire, and I am indebted to its author for kindly offering to vet my chapter on "The Vert and the Venison" before going to print. Likewise, I have greatly appreciated the co-operation shown to me in a variety of ways by the owners of many historic Wiltshire homes, not forgetting the tenants of those other houses belonging to that less personal but nevertheless conscientious landlord, the National Trust.

My sincere thanks also go to Sir John Betjeman for allowing me to quote one of his inimitable verses, to Mrs. George Bambridge for permission to use the lines from Kipling's "McAndrew's Hymn", and to Mrs. Frances Gay, the Chairman of the Richard Jefferies Society, for her invaluable advice relating to Chapter XIV. Moreover, I cannot think what I should have done without the aid of Swindon's exceptionally talented Town Clerk, Mr. D. Murray John, and his able assistants, Mr. J. H. S. Masters and the Borough Librarian, Mr. T. S. McNeil, who did everything possible to provide me with a picture of the place, past, present, and future.

With regard to Wiltshire industries, Mr. K. G. Ponting gave up much of his valuable time in 'putting me straight' about the West of England cloth trade with the same goodwill as the Managing Staff of Harris's bacon factory, who spared nothing (not even a pig's trotter) in showing me round their entire firm; while Mr. J. O. Thomas, the Principal of the Lackham College of Agriculture, gave me a 'free run' of the whole establishment, for which I should like to thank him most sincerely.

I also wish to acknowledge the assistance of the Editor, Mr. W. Sanders, and staff (especially Mr. E. Pearce) of the *Salisbury Times and Journal*, who, together with Mr. F. Hazel, Editor-in-Chief, and Mr. H. Clayton of the Wiltshire Newspapers at Swindon, kindly allowed me to burrow through their archives; whereas at the same time Messrs. Wills, Horn, and Smith at the former offices went to no end of trouble in procuring certain photographs for me, as did their Swindon counterparts. Messrs. Kersting, Miles, Miller, Robson, Tarlton, and Underwood also helped me greatly in this particular field.

Then there are countless moonraking friends who went out of their way to lend a hand over tricky little details. In this respect

I am especially grateful to Mr. E. G. H. Kempson for the benefit of his limitless knowledge of Wiltshire and to all those who so readily came forward with the answers to unexpected problems: Mrs. Abnett, Sir Noël Arkell, Mr. Alan Barker, Lt.-Col. Boggis, Mr. and Mrs. C. Down, Lt.-Col. Floyd, Mr. K. D. D. Henderson, Mr. R. Lovett, Mr. Pike, Mr. Quine, Major and Mrs. R. M. Scott, Mrs. Speak, many members of the Stratton family, and the entire staff of the Salisbury and Wilton Public Libraries.

Lastly, my debt is enormous to the following two people: Annemarie Austin of Robert Hale & Company, for the kind and efficient way in which she shepherded the county into print; and my late father's secretary, Beryl Davidge, who once again not only typed and corrected my original MS., but encouraged me all the way along. When I think of these numerous benefactors and the many others without whose moral support this book could not possibly have been written, I am reminded of a toast proposed over thirty years ago at the annual dinner of the former Wiltshiremen in London Society, to which my father was asked to reply. Ladies and Gentlemen, I give it to you now: "Wiltshire, Our County. THE County."

I

THE FOCAL POINT

HOWEVER good or bad a would-be portrait painter may be, it is always an advantage to have the co-operation of a good sitter, and Wiltshire sits beautifully. Secure and solid, there she is, all 1,345 square miles of her, enthroned in the heart of Southern England. She has no fussy coastline to distract her, no awkward scraggy contours to be reckoned with, and none of those depressing areas to be shaded grey in order to prove they are in need of government assistance. As a model she can hardly be bettered, with her comfortable rolling downs divided by gently flowing rivers and that broad undulating sweep of Salisbury Plain thrown in, as it were, just for good measure.

Moreover, Wiltshire has a singularly pleasant attribute compared to many other counties. She has an all-important factor, a highlight or focal point. The necessity for this sort of thing is something which is often underestimated but was once made very plain to me when, for a short period, I lived away from Wiltshire and became the unfortunate possessor of a sitting-room without a fireplace. However many times the furniture was rearranged, the room seemed to lack cohesion and meaning. There was no welcome, nothing to sit round, no unifying feature from which our ancestors drew comfort and cheer in much the same way as we do ourselves, despite the rival claims of the modern television set.

Wiltshire, to me, appears to possess this *sine qua non* to such a degree that it gives her almost an unfair advantage over other counties. Salisbury Cathedral, with its spire pointing so majestically to the sky, radiates a powerful influence, albeit hard to define. Although I realize it is something which is felt much more strongly in the south of the county, before the high chalky barrier of the Plain proper has naturally weakened the magnetic force, yet I still feel that all true moonrakers tend to belong to the Cathedral as it does to them. Some may never have set foot inside it but, nevertheless, they are justly proud of their great inheritance because, like themselves, it has been 'local grown', having been built of stone from the quarries at Chilmark only 12 miles away.

There is, perhaps, a quite subconscious relationship between the Cathedral and the county. It is not only a symbol of faith but a representative and mother-figure all rolled into one. It has that reliable although sometimes undervalued quality of always being 'there', dignified and reassuring. It is not going to take off like a rocket; neither is it going to pretend to be less than its age, which is now some 700 years. Maybe the spire *is* leaning a little, but few of us stand really straight, especially as we get older; and this particular and much-loved antiquity has a whole army of friends and relations willing to subscribe towards its well-being, in the hope that its beauty may be preserved and its spire continue to write Wiltshire's signature in the sky throughout the centuries to come.

There is an illogical but totally endearing legend about how the site for this new church was chosen. In the twelfth century a great many squabbles were going on in what was then the ancient town on the nearby hill-top, which is now known quite simply as Old Sarum. This one-time fortress of Ancient Britons has had a variety of names. There was Roman Sorbiodunum, Saxon Searisbyrig, and Norman Sarisberie, while Sarum was merely a shortened version of the latter coined as a labour-saving device by medieval scribes. From time to time tentative suggestions have been made as to the original meaning of the word; some theorists declare that the name of Salisbury has been derived by a process of folk etymology from 'river-fort', 'trick stronghold', or simply 'dry city' because the inhabitants on the top of Old Sarum were for ever short of water which disappeared so quickly into the chalky subsoil.

William Cobbett, in his famous *Rural Rides*, gave it yet another connotation. He referred to it as the "accursed hill" because he considered it to be the rottenest of rotten boroughs, although his subsequent graphic description of its topography was much more pleasing. He likened the elaborate fortifications to three cheeses laid one upon the other, the bottom one a great deal broader than the next and the top one resembling a Stilton cheese in proportion to a Gloucester one.

At the beginning of the thirteenth century this heavily populated pyramid had evidently reached overspill point. Added to this, there was constant friction between the ecclesiastical body in charge of its Norman cathedral, established by the great Bishop Osmund, and the military authorities in charge of the castle. At rogationtide one year, the clergy, as was their custom, went in procession singing litanies through the fields belonging to their present bishop's manors of Milford and Stratford. On their return, they found the soldiers had played them a dirty trick and locked them out of the city gates so that they had to spend the night outside. Bishop Richard Poore is said to have been away at the time or this could hardly have happened, but when he heard about it he was, quite naturally, consumed with righteous anger and vowed to build another church and abode away from the castle and removed from royal power. "Let us, in the name of God, descend into the meads," one of his canons is quoted as having said, which seems a very understandable, human remark and, had it not been uttered by so devout a man, not far removed from the twentieth-century cliché, "Come on chaps, let's get to hell out of here."

And they did; or rather, perhaps, the building of Salisbury Cathedral brought them a little nearer to heaven. The legend goes that having obtained permission from the Pope, Bishop Poore stood on the ramparts at Sarisberie praying for guidance as to a favourable site, while an archer drew a bow at a venture. The notorious arrow happened to fall nearly 2 miles from where they were both standing which would make it appear to have been assisted by an uncommonly strong following wind. Its actual landing-point was on part of the Bishop's own estate at Myrfield or Maryfield, a low-lying marshy place that was completely unsuitable for any building whatsoever. Nevertheless, it seems certain that whatever made that good man and his "Incomparable Artifex", Canon Elias de Dereham, start to build Salisbury Cathedral in a meadow, they never doubted the decision was prompted by a Divine Hand. The possibility of flooding was but a trifling matter and certainly not one to be allowed to stand in the way of the House of God.

What faith! Seven hundred years later here stands the glorious testament to that faith. What stuff they must have been made of, those men who were responsible for the Cathedral as we see it today. Sadly, Bishop Poore, who was evidently as capable as he was saintly, was transferred long before his plans were completed to the see of Durham, where his obvious talent for organization was badly needed to improve another kind of unsatisfactory situation. After the foundation stones of Salisbury Cathedral were laid in 1220, it was thirty-eight years before it was finally consecrated, by which time Bishop Poore was dead and buried; and almost another 100 years were to pass before the spire was added, an act of unexpected daring but incredible success.

The spire seems to secure the unity of this classic piece of Gothic architecture in much the same way as it secures the unity of Wiltshire as a whole. Perhaps, having lived so closely within its protective orbit all my life, I am prejudiced. Those who live farther away may lay claim to other rallying points; but for me this seems hard to envisage. Salisbury Cathedral, standing in its green, still Close, is so splendid, so English, and so *unable to be ignored*, whatever faith or lack of it a person may have.

From whichever direction a traveller comes to Salisbury, the Cathedral spire is the first thing he or she sees; and each time it seems to take on a different hue. Driving in from the west on a summer evening, the sun tints it a warm golden colour; another day, coming over Pepperbox Hill from the south-east, this same spire can look grey and austere as it dominates the Wiltshire landscape for miles around; then again, returning late at night from London, its dark form may just be distinguished with its little glowing red night-cap perched high in the sky, a warning to low-flying aircraft and a welcome beacon that tells many a moonraker he is 'nearly home'.

This is only a recent innovation which has taken place since the last war when, naturally enough, the Cathedral was enveloped in darkness like the rest of Salisbury. Occasionally, the sinister throbbing sound of a lone German reconnaissance plane could be heard circling over the city; sometimes the more persistent drone of several enemy bombers gradually became louder and louder as they passed overhead on their way to more strategic targets such as Bristol or Cardiff. Alone each night, surrounded by the Wiltshire Downs, Salisbury Cathedral stood guard, unafraid and unharmed, waiting to challenge the coming day. Its secrets and treasures remained safe, even though that priceless symbol of liberty, the best-preserved of the four original copies of Magna Carta, had been carefully removed, according to instructions from Winston Churchill, to a local quarry where it remained for the duration.

The person who knows more about the Cathedral and its priceless treasures than any other living soul is the librarian, Dr. Elsie Smith. Dr. Elsie is a very great, very wise, and very old lady. She lives down Rosemary Lane, just off the North Walk, and she actually has a bush of rosemary growing in her garden. Nearly every day her figure, bowed but indomitable, passes slowly across the green and into the Cathedral through the Dean's door, which is courteously unlocked for her by the Chief Security Officer in the Close. She then crosses over into the south transept and somewhat laboriously climbs the thirty-eight steps of the long circular stone staircase to the library. If ever an expression "where your treasure is, there will your heart be also" applies to anyone, it applies to Dr. Elsie. The treasures in the library may belong to the Cathedral, but the reverent and loving way in which they are handled and cared for by this particular librarian makes them appear to have a much more personal owner.

For despite all its fame and beauty, there seems to be something extraordinarily simple and human about this cathedral and its history. It is a perfect example of illogicality over reasoning, genius over madness. In the first place who, other than madmen, would start building in a marsh? None other, it seems, but good Bishop Poore and the indefatigable Elias de Dereham. Nearly 100 years later, who would have had the temerity to add a spire, 404 feet high weighing 6,400 tons, on four pillars that were never intended to carry any such load? Evidently small but bold Bishop Wyvil and his architect, Richard of Farleigh. Lastly, who would have dared to upset the city fathers of the eighteenth century by removing the gravestones of their ancestors, in order that the Close might become the lovely flat green sward which we know to this day? Merely Bishop Barrington and James Wyatt, that very famous architect and iconoclast, whose advice was so sought after at that time.

Wyatt has been held responsible for many less pleasing acts during his so-called 'improvement' of the Cathedral, such as the removal of the remainder of the beautiful thirteenth-century stained glass which had already suffered great destruction at the time of the Reformation. There are certainly many people today to whom the interior of the Cathedral comes as something of a disappointment, because they consider the clear glazing casts an altogether too cold and modern light on the tall Purbeck marble pillars and the ancient tombs lying between them, which Wyatt so neatly rearranged at the cost of disturbing human remains. He also did away with the detached bell tower, the two fifteenth-century chantry chapels in memory of Bishop Beauchamp and Lord Robert Hungerford, together with the High Altar (which was later restored); furthermore, he engendered violent criticism for limewashing the high vaults to hide their faded medieval colour, and also for transferring to the 'morning chapel' the delicate stone screen which once divided the choir from the nave.

But on the credit side, Wyatt accomplished valuable work of maintenance and restored the effect of simplicity and unity which the original builders of the Cathedral undoubtedly intended. When his work was completed in 1792, to do honour to the occasion "on Friday morning, soon after eleven o'clock, the King* and Queen, with the Princess Royal and the five other Princesses Augusta, Elizabeth, Mary, Sophia and Amelia . . . after partaking of an elegant refection with the Bishop and his Lady, visited the Cathedral Church, now quite finished, accompanied by the Bishop, the Dean and Chapter, several Prebendaries, the Earl of Pembroke and Mr. Wyatt . . . and expressed much satisfaction at the boldly striking yet simple and singularly beautiful effect of the 'tout ensemble'."

How much responsibility for this work really rested on Wyatt's shoulders and how much on Bishop Barrington's has always been a matter for conjecture; it is said that probably most of the drastic steps were undertaken at the express wish of the latter. It is also asserted that his successful 'coup' regarding the raising and levelling of the churchyard was carried out overnight so that the citizens of Salisbury were presented with a *fait accompli*, even if the ensuing rumpus did mean the Bishop's removal to another diocese.

Somehow, it is impossible not to feel admiration for men of such calibre. I have always had a very soft spot in my heart for bishops, especially since being billeted on the assistant Bishop of

* George III.

Sherborne during the last war. He lived in a house just outside Sarum Close, secluded behind its own solid oaken gates in which there was a smaller door, similar to the sort of things cats use after a night on the tiles.

My bishop, as I used to think of him, was nearing retirement and one of the kindest and most genial men one could ever wish to know. The only cloud that ever appeared on his otherwise cheerful countenance was on the day I asked permission to stay out later than 9 p.m., the time he usually locked up for the night. His concern for my safety was endearing. Where was I going? Who was escorting me? And paramount in importance, *when was I coming back?* We settled on what, in these permissive days, would seem to be the ludicrously early hour of 10.30 p.m. Dead on time, I returned to the fold. He was too nice a man to let down and there he was, waiting to greet me in his hall with a thermos of hot milk in one hand and a glass in the other, beaming with pleasure at my safe return from the perils of Salisbury in the black-out and the possible advances of the licentious soldiery who had descended from the Plain.

To this day, two main gates of the Close are shut and locked at 9 p.m., while a third remains open until the circumspect hour of eleven, after which a night-watchman takes over until 1 a.m. Only the Bishop and a highly respectable doctor appear to be allowed their own keys, and should any inhabitant want to go howling about at night, he or she must make arrangements with the Chief Security Officer or the Close Constable. Judging by the cheerful and healthy appearance of these astute gentlemen, it seems as if the Close must have a sobering effect on most of its inmates because their guardians do not look as if their sleep is disturbed very often.

The Close was walled in about 1331 when Edward III gave permission for all the stones from the old cathedral and canons' houses at Old Sarum to be removed for this purpose. Together with the assistance of the River Avon they protect what can only be thought of as a closed community. Although all sorts of people live in the Close, it is difficult not to think of them as somewhat set apart, as having a kind of privilege not accorded to other Wiltshire moonrakers. "You live in the *Close*, do you?" is a remark often overheard, and the way in which it is said seems to brand the Close-dweller with a certain respectability and confer on him or her a status not be found anywhere else in Wiltshire.

The whole story of English domestic architecture is told within its walls. The houses, from the outside, are all as lovely as they are varied. Each one is quite unique with a history all its own. Some were built at the same time as the Cathedral itself, such as the old Bishop's Palace (now the Cathedral School) and Leadenhall, said to be the oldest of all, nowadays also a school but once the home of that zealous innovator, Elias de Dereham. Nicholas of Ely, the master mason in charge of all the others when the Cathedral was being built, is said to have lived in an especially attractive small house facing the North Front, from which he could spy on his workmen at all hours as they inched this glorious building from the ground. A hard taskmaster perhaps? Or a man with a vision? Who was it who said that nothing worthwhile is ever done without enthusiasm? Judging by Salisbury Cathedral, its creators had plenty of that.

Just inside the High Street gate stands the Matrons' College, built by Christopher Wren at the instigation of his good friend, Bishop Seth Ward. This was to provide dwelling-space for eight widows or spinster daughters of departed clergy. It was rumoured that the hand of the bachelor bishop was once refused by a certain lady who subsequently married another cleric. This gentleman later left her widowed and in poverty. In order to provide for her, Seth Ward built the Matrons' College. There can surely have been few rejected suitors willing to found a home for eight women so that his lost love might be accommodated.

Between them Seth Ward and the Wiltshire-born Christopher Wren were responsible for many of the Close houses, as well as as for the enormous task of trying to repair the Cathedral itself well over a century before Wyatt got to work, owing to the deplorable state into which it had fallen at the Reformation and during the Commonwealth. It was Wren who, in 1668, also determined the exact extent of the spire's declination and his original survey is another of the treasures that is preserved and now kept so safely by Dr. Elsie Smith.

Facing the Choristers' Green stands a home of a later vintage. Built in 1701, and now the property of the National Trust, is the famous Mompesson House, which is open to the public. Then in splendid succession facing the West Front, with their gardens backing on to the River Avon, lie some of the most graceful-looking houses in the whole of Wiltshire. Here come Wren Hall, the Wardrobe, Arundells, the North Canonry with its medieval gateway, the Old Deanery, and the King's House, where Richard III and James I both stayed but which now, somewhat unfortunately, has taken on modern accretions to itself to become a teachers' training college. The new red brick result seems to strike the only discordant note along the harmonious façade of the West Walk.

Farther still, lies the Walton Canonry where once the son of that lovable fisherman, Izaak Walton, lived; and past Elias' Leadenhall right down at the farthermost south-western corner of the Close is the South Canonry, the home of the present Bishop. This modern generation of bishops has 'moved out' of the big house; the palace is perhaps no longer in keeping with the times; and now that it has become the flourishing Cathedral School, housing the original choristers, maybe it suits everyone better. At the end of this little lane leading nowhere except to a quiet bend of the Avon, the Bishop lives in less exalted style but still in near-perfect seclusion.

It would be difficult for anyone to visit the Close without gaining a feeling of tranquillity, or at the very least a slight easing of tension, the more pronounced nowadays perhaps, owing to the contrasting pace of everyday living. Even though the twentieth century is evident in the form of a recognized car-park inside the High Street gate, this itself seems to aid the 'slowing-down' process. "Ten m.p.h. sir, please," says the uniformed attendant as the young man in the red sports car, still full of frustrated acceleration, corners a little too quickly into the North Walk. "Sorry, was I doing more?" asks the youth innocently. "Just a little, I think, sir." Nicely put. No offence taken. A pity more speed limits are not enforced and in so satisfactory a manner.

The overall effect of peace is undeniable, but everyone on leaving the Close must retain his or her individual impressions. Although still a frequent visitor myself all the year round, the pictures of it most firmly planted in my mind's eye are all to do with summer. Maybe this is because during childhood, when memories are vivid and lasting, we were marched in crocodile formation down to the Close from the Godolphin School on the hill, which once started its life in a far humbler fashion in Dr.

Elsie's very house. We came, wearing our straw boaters, clutching our little camp stools, sketch-books, pencils, and rubbers (which were usually left behind on the grass), to spend the morning drawing. It seemed for ever June, sunny and hot as childhood summers always are in retrospect.

The more ambitious of us chose the West Front for a subject; the fast workers tried to sketch the flying figure of some minor canon as he hurried across the grass, possibly late for service. I rather fancied the houses. They made me think of afternoon tea and cucumber sandwiches and nobody saying anything very much at all. I used to wonder whether they really were as gloomy inside as some people said. Did they really have the curse of the 'four Ds': darkness, damp, drains, and death-watch beetle? It seemed impossible to imagine such sinister interiors when confronted by their serene faces and their gardens full of roses, honeysuckle, and bumble-bees. The Close was a wonderful place in which to day-dream until the voice of the art mistress, creeping up on us in her sensible rubber-soled sandals, cut in sharply, "That doorway looks out of proportion. I'm sure the Dean would have to be a contortionist to get through it."

A world war and a social revolution has taken place since those far-off days, yet their effect on Salisbury Cathedral and its Close seems minimal. The peace and permanency of this unique focal point of Wiltshire enables visitors and inhabitants alike to go out refreshed and ready for the city around it and the rolling hinterland beyond.

II

A CHILD OF THE CHURCH

VENTURING forth from the Close into the High Street of Salisbury is rather like walking down a narrow passage leading from a quiet drawing-room into a noisy cocktail party. Salisbury may be a cathedral city but it is also very much a market town, besides having strong military associations. In the immediate vicinity of the North Gate, the church-like aura still clings; houses and shop fronts are medieval, but gradually, here and there, the twentieth century takes over and modern innovators have been at work, doing their best, perhaps, to let the older inhabitants down as lightly as possible.

Bishop Poore was evidently a man of many parts, because he gave as much thought to the lay-out of the city as he did to the design of his new cathedral. Although there were already a few humble little communities in the meadows at Milford, Fisher Town, and Harnham, once the exodus from Old Sarum had begun on a larger scale, the Bishop realized the necessity, even in those far-off days, for good town planning. Therefore the date he helped to lay the foundation stones for his new church, 28th April 1220, was also the birthday of New Sarum.

Salisbury (as most people now call it) grew in tidy rectangular chequers or blocks giving a solid, four-square appearance which, a century later, must have been clearly discernible to the steeple-jacks as they made their perilous sky-scraping ascent during the building of the spire. In the centre of Salisbury to this day it is still possible to 'take a walk around the block', as it is so many thousands of miles away in modern New York.

At the first busy cross roads in the High Street, once known as Florentine corner because of all the Lombard merchants who

came to do business there, stands Mitre House. This has replaced
an inn and, long before that, a simpler dwelling where Bishop
Poore lived while the Cathedral was being built. The lease of this
house, which is now a dress shop, still provides for the robing of
each new bishop to take place within its walls just before his ordi-
nation. An embryo broad-minded bishop may be ushered into a
little back room among all the latest tops and trouser-suits, to
emerge shortly afterwards, clad in gold lamé and most likely con-
ducting himself with a dignity and grace far exceeding many a
fashion model's highest aspirations.

It is perhaps this incongruous mixture of church and civic life
which makes Salisbury what it is, although the two have not
always gone well in double harness. At the beginning of the
fourteenth century, after a spell of initial prosperity, the citizens
rebelled against the control of the Bishop and particularly his
power to levy taxes. They applied to the King for exemption from
this which was granted but only at the cost of forfeiting the liber-
ties their charter had given them, such as their weekly market and
annual fair. Within a year the trade, comfort, and importance of
the town had visibly diminished, and the citizens were on their
knees begging for the patronage and protection of their overlord,
the Bishop.

The church authorities have always been very well aware of the
potential prosperity of Salisbury, especially as a trading centre.
Throughout the centuries many a bishop would have put a
modern-day economist to shame. After Bishop Poore had seen
Salisbury given its first charter by Henry III, it was left to the
entrepreneurial qualities of two of his successors, Bishop Bingham
and Bishop Giles of Bridport, to show their individual business
acumen. Bishop Bingham built a bridge and Bishop Giles created
a college. At first glance, in themselves neither of these innovations
seems unduly important, but those two astute gentlemen knew
what they were about. The bridge over the Avon at Harnham
gave Salisbury access from the south and diverted much of the
western traffic from the neighbouring rival town of Wilton. In
fact, it sounded Wilton's death knell. According to that sixteenth-
century antiquary, Leland, "the chaunging of this way was the
totale cause of the ruine of Old Sarisberie and Wiltoun. For afore
this Wiltoun had 12 paroch churches or more, and was the heade
town of Wileshire."

A little later on Bishop Giles was not slow to perceive two things. Firstly, the rapidly rising suburb to the south of the city due to the opening of the new route; secondly, the attraction which Salisbury now held for students fleeing from the educational centre of Oxford. It appears that student riots and unrest were nothing new in those days, except that the possibility of dire punishment was very much greater. Therefore shrewd Bishop Giles founded the first university college to be set up in England, the College of St. Nicholas de Vaux, and Salisbury became something of an educational centre in its own right. The name of the city was well known to every medieval scholar, and for those fortunate to reside in the town there were lectures by many qualified individuals. The precious manuscripts of Bishop Osmund, that wise and learned man responsible for the first cathedral at Old Sarum and who later became Salisbury's patron saint, formed the nucleus of an ever-growing library. From early on Black and Grey Friars took root in the city, teaching, preaching, and ministering to the poor, and an area near the Close is still known as the Friary.

Although many of the city's oldest and loveliest buildings still stand in this area, such as the seventeenth-century Joiners Hall (now appropriately an antique shop), many modern developments have infiltrated almost, it seems, overnight. A glassy new college of Further Education stares out somewhat balefully on to a noisy new roundabout so that the voices of teachers and the ears of students suffer accordingly. Next to it is a red-brick house with the singularly unlovely name of Bugmore. This seems hardly credible until one remembers that the Grey Friars once lived at Bugmore Priory. More strategically tucked away, a flourishing Friary Laundry now sends out its vans daily in order to keep the twentieth-century citizens clean.

There have been somewhat conflicting reports on the cleanliness of Salisbury throughout the centuries. It has been said that in comparison with other towns during the Middle Ages its standard was good, in spite of the fact that in the street now known as New Canal butchers were apt to cast entrails of slaughtered animals into the ditch which ran through it, until this insanitary habit was stopped during the reign of Henry VI. The town suffered severely when the Black Death ravaged the country in 1348 and from other subsequent outbreaks of plague. There is a heartening account of

a mayor called John Ivie who, during the reign of Charles I, fought
the scourge that was sweeping the city almost single-handed. As
recently as 1932 his efforts were rather touchingly commemorated
by a plaque in the Guildhall with the inscription

In lasting memory of
John Ivie
Goldsmith
Mayor of the City of New Sarum
In the year 1627
When the City was sorely stricken
with plague
So that many citizens fled
For safety leaving him to bear
The burden of his office alone
Aided by two petty constables

Christopher Brathat and John Pinhorne

"You have done your countrey good service
For which we are all beholding
To God and you."*

It would seem that John Ivie, whose memory is also kept alive
by way of a street bearing his name, was a more conscientious
character than a man called John Halle, a prosperous wool
merchant of the fifteenth century. Besides being a Merchant of
the Staple, he was also a shipowner at Southampton, four times
Mayor, and a Member of Parliament. But in spite of this impressive
list of achievements he appears to have been a man of troublesome
temperament, arrogant and overbearing, always quarrelling with
the Bishop, and even spending a short time in the Tower of
London. However, his lasting and finest contribution to posterity
is a magnificent building called the Hall of John Halle, now a
cinema but once, during my youth, a china shop.

Although Salisbury's history and the said merchant's doubtful
reputation were then quite unknown to me, it always filled me
with foreboding whenever I heard my mother's solemn announcement, seemingly charged with import, "*Today* we shall be going
to the *Hall of John Halle*," and I knew that I should be left waiting
there while the grown-ups browsed around this curious man's

* The words quoted are said to have been addressed to Ivie by the Salisbury
Corporation after his heroic efforts.

possessions. Who was this John Halle? Why did he live in a hall?
Did he not have any other rooms, a bathroom for instance?
Would he, perhaps, pop out from behind the lustre tea-pots and
inveigle us farther into the recesses of this gloomy building, whose
splendid raftered roof and mullioned windows left me unim-
pressed? It seemed certain that, whatever else he was or was not,
he was very rich, considering his hall in which there was such an
array of delicate china that it was a relief to get outside again
without knocking over some piece of Crown Staffordshire.

That Salisbury has always been a comparatively prosperous city
there seems no doubt. Few of its inhabitants ever went barefoot
and clogs were more or less unknown. The people 'walked on
leather', amply provided by the poor slaughtered animals who
ended their days in Butcher Row. There are still some people who
come from London especially to buy good country shoes from the
long-established boot- and shoe-makers in the town.

Three factors made Salisbury wealthy in the Middle Ages. They
were, quite simply, bishops and the intrinsic worth of the respective flocks under them, namely people and sheep. It has been said
that Salisbury Cathedral was founded upon wool-packs.* Certainly, it was Bishop Poore and his successors who had the
perspicacity to see that anything which furthered the wool trade
furthered the well-being of the city as a whole. The vast wind-
swept acres of Salisbury Plain fed sheep; sheep produced wool;
Salisbury, aided by its bishop overlords, provided the facilities for
turning that wool into wealth. The inhabitants washed, carded,
spun, dyed, and cleansed the bulky raw grey stuff, the colour
perhaps of the gathering clouds over Salisbury Plain where those
lucrative wool-producing animals were raised. So many processes
went into the making of a piece of cloth that even when it was
thought to be finished it still had to be laid out on areas in the city
such as the Green Croft, where it was stretched and dried, after
which the nap was raised with teazles and sheared until smooth.

Salisbury Plain no longer confines itself to sheep-rearing. The
industrial revolution turned the wool trade into a manufacturing
industry requiring power not easily available in Salisbury. An
area once thought of as only eligible for grazing sheep now goes
in for army tank tactics and, thanks to an agricultural revolution,

* It has been estimated that the cost of building the Cathedral was about
40,000 marks or £27,000, an immense sum for the times.

corn crops. Gradually, sheep have lost their importance, although the prestige of the sheepfarmer still held good in Wiltshire even at the beginning of the present century. The select community who kept sheep or beef cattle travelled by train to Salisbury market each Tuesday in a separate coach from so-called lesser breeds of farmers who were the daily slaves of those animals demanding such constant attention, cows.

There are still subtle undercurrents at work on market days in Salisbury. There are, for instance, the farmers who always go to market and the farmers who never go, the latter type gaining in predominance. The distinction between the two is not always easy to define. It is not just a question of age or class but more a sign of the times, the result of technological developments that have taken place during the last twenty years.

Although many of the older farming brigade still go to market through force of long-standing habit, there are now in Wiltshire a great many men who have taken up farming since the last war. Many of these are not primarily countrymen; they run their farms (often of 1,000 acres or more) with great efficiency and a kind of dedicated interest. But market day in Salisbury has little to offer them in return for a personal visit. They bear no resemblance to those "brown-faced farmers, in their riding and driving clothes and leggings, standing in knots or thrusting their hands into sacks of oats or barley", described by W. H. Hudson at the beginning of the century. These non-countrymen communicate mostly by telephone, or by letters dictated to a secretary. The face-to-face relationship has gone from their transactions. Their samples of wheat or barley are sent off by post in specially prepared envelopes to be scrutinized by some merchant near Bournemouth or Hull. They consider it waste of time to watch their cattle being sold. Tuesday mornings find them filling up forms in their offices or supervising the work on their farms. Market days may even find some of the more affluent shooting during winter or occasionally sailing in summer; but wherever they are, they are certainly nowhere near Salisbury market.

Not that the city lacks numbers on those days. There are still enough farmers and other folk to make market-day not only a 'must' but also a 'madding crowd', despite the fact that the cattle market has been successfully removed to a well-planned site on the outskirts of the town, thereby removing the possibility of a

The Focal Point

"bull in a china shop" which, until a few years ago, was not so improbable in Salisbury as it might seem.

On Tuesdays and again on Saturdays traders ply their goods in the city centre; streets and shopping-bags overflow. Of the four original spots where once cheese, cattle, wool, and poultry were sold, only the last survives under a curious edifice known as the Poultry Cross. There is a story which alleges that this was initially built by a Wiltshire knight who, having incurred the censure of the Bishop, was made to come there every Friday, bareheaded and barefooted, to do penance for his misdemeanours. Nowadays, vendors of bric-à-brac, bananas, and home-made paté cluster around its arches, undercutting the less volatile though more permanent shopkeepers in the nearby vicinity of Butcher Row.

In the summer, sightseers and travellers to and from the West Country add to the confusion as they "pussyvanter"* about. Some years ago, in a desperate attempt to keep the traffic on the move, many streets became one-way only and many which were already one-way became the opposite-way. Disorder reigned; citizens swore; the town, it was said, was ruined. But now no one remembers very much about it, such is the healing quality of time.

Far more drastic changes have taken place in the shape of new by-passes which have been bull-dozed through the suburbs, while underground passage-ways or smart shopping arcades have suddenly opened up, as if moles had been busily at work under cover without anyone knowing what was going on. One of these arcades, complete with stone-enclosed flower beds and seats for the weary, goes by the somewhat pretentious name of Old George Mall, and leads out into the High Street under what was once the lovely Old George Hotel. It was here that Samuel Pepys stayed when he visited his friend, Bishop Seth Ward, and where he reported that he "lay in a silke bed and had a very good diet", but went on to add that on finding the reckoning so exorbitant he and his family moved to a small place just outside Salisbury where "the beds were good but lousy, which made us merry"; and just exactly what he meant by that is anybody's guess.

If Pepys were to return today he would find no Old George, no silk sheets, and no entertaining bed-bugs either. But he might still

---

* Old Wiltshire word originating from the French *poursuivant*. Used to describe making a lot of fuss and bother without getting anywhere in particular, i.e. ineffective bustle.

C

The Wilton Foxhounds coming through the Close via the High Street Gate enjoy the famous dish served by the ancient hostelry of the same name, the 'Haunch of Venison', where he could look out on to St. Thomas's Church, the origins of which date back to the time when the Cathedral itself was being built. If he were still worried about his financial situation, however, he might prefer a sandwich and a glass of beer at the Pheasant Inn on the site of the Shoemakers old Hall. Should he require further entertainment he could play Bingo at the Regal Cinema, watch *The Seven Year Itch* well-acted at the Arts Theatre, and write a shocking account in his diary of an X film at the Hall of John Halle. For a more edifying diversion, he could marvel at the latest excavations in the museum, soon to be housed in larger and far more ambitious surroundings.

As for board and lodging, he would have a number of alternatives; if really concerned about the cost he could get it all free at the Common Cold Research Unit, provided he was prepared to be a guinea-pig; on the other hand, he might decide to put his hand in his pocket and lie in bed looking at the Cathedral, like any American tourist, from a room in the new annexe of the 'Rose and Crown' in its perfect setting by the river close to Bishop Bingham's famous bridge.

But possibly the place where Pepys might feel most at home would be in the fourteenth-century Red Lion Hotel, now run by the son of the grandame of Salisbury. Mrs. Thomas (or rather Mrs. Speak, as she now is, having remarried after the death of her first husband) is one of the city's hardiest and gayest perennials. In providing local colour she has no equal. The sight of her walking along the Canal in one of her broad-brimmed cavalier-style hats is enough to cheer the greyest December morning. A lady with charismatic qualities, splendid and smiling, she seems part of the very life-blood of the city. Nowadays, she lives just outside the town and unfortunately is not seen quite so often as when she and her first husband presided personally over the patrons of the 'Red Lion', but it will be a sad day indeed when the citizens no longer catch sight of her well-known figure in their midst. One cannot help feeling that Pepys would have enjoyed staying at the 'Red Lion' if Mrs. Thomas had been in charge.

Finally, after so interesting a visit to Salisbury, he could go off into the surrounding neighbourhood to take part in something, the name of which had not yet been invented in his day, the so-called 'country week-end'. This is now a very flourishing institution in Wiltshire. On Friday evenings the down trains from Waterloo are packed, in spite of the ever-increasing amount of road traffic. Mothers driving minis sweep up to the station to collect flat-sharing daughters from the metropolis, who have been existing on cheese and cornflakes all the week; Cecil Beaton comes through the gangway wearing a cloak and sombrero-type hat *en route* for his home at Broad Chalke; weary bread-winning fathers heave sighs of relief as the train loses speed after emerging from the long tunnel cut through the chalk in the nineteenth century by Brunel's navvies. Some foolhardy fathers tried commuting to London daily but the majority of them found they had to give up. An hour and forty minutes each way with another journey at either end proved too much. The one persevering gentleman who tried for too long died in the attempt.

So on Friday nights at the end of the working week these weary toilers converge on the focal point of Wiltshire. The Cathedral spire, gun-metal grey in the evening light, watches patiently as the train, like a cinematograph picture in slow motion, crawls into the station. Here the travellers spill out, exhausted but grateful. Salisbury and District embraces them, cossets them, and returns them on the up train on Sunday evening, rejuvenated and ready for another five-day battle.

As an assembly point Salisbury is supreme. Her great forte is service. She gathers together a heterogeneous collection of moonrakers, strangers, soldiers, and four-legged beasts, deals with them all, sorts them out, and sends them on their way with the same happy ingenuity with which she marshals the five chalk streams that flow towards her into one broad river, the Avon, before sending it forth over the borders of Hampshire to the waiting sea at Christchurch. If Salisbury Cathedral is the focal point of Wiltshire, it could hardly be encircled in a more pleasing fashion than by this warm-hearted city that grew up around it.

III

SWINGING SARUM SUBURBIA

CLUTCHING on to Salisbury's apron strings, sometimes daring to step outside the city boundaries and sometimes not, there are a whole host of little localities with a life of their own, yet dependent on that vital nucleus they surround. Every day, friendly red buses trailing umbilical cords, go throbbing to and fro transporting people to West Harnham, Odstock Hospital, Laverstock, Bishopdown, Stratford-sub-Castle, Bemerton Heath, and on certain auspicious days during summer, the Races.

Irrespective of whether one is a gambler or merely a horse-lover, a day at Salisbury Races is a rather splendid affair, worth going to at least just once for the feel of it all and the view from the top of the downs where the old Shaftesbury turnpike draws to an end. Originally, this was inaugurated on a point-to-point basis by a sporting Earl of Pembroke as long ago as the late sixteenth century. At that time the course occasionally ran for 14 miles, beginning on White Sheet Hill in the south-west of the county; although more often the start was 4 miles away above the village of Broad Chalke. A famous horse called Peacock (known as the "bastard barb") which belonged to Sir Thomas Thynne of Longleat, is reputed to have run the latter distance in the questionable time of just over five minutes and was continually the winner of the silver bell, a coveted trophy presented by the Earl.

The Raceplain, as this smaller area is called today, is high, dry, and invariably windy, somewhat like Old Sarum. At the first flat-meeting of the year in May, ladies need close-fitting hats and, if they are rash enough to break out in summer clothes, warm underwear as well, unless they want to catch pneumonia. Recently, great improvements have been made to the old grandstand, which

36

enables members of the Bibury Club and their friends to enjoy lunch in something akin to a ship's dining-room. While eating their salmon mayonnaise or cold chicken, they can float in this glass-enclosed building on a wave of race-day euphoria surrounded by a panoramic view of South Wilts.

The punters proper, red-faced and festooned with field-glasses and all the other paraphernalia peculiar to earnest race-goers, care little for the scene spread out majestically around them. Their attention is focused on matters closer at hand, the food, the drink, and the form-cards in front of them. Later on, their field of vision lengthens a little when they study the horses in the paddock, before placing their bets and returning to the grandstand for those critical few minutes spent in agony, for richer, for poorer.

The not-so-intense race-goers study other kinds of form: the ladies' fashions, the gaudy colours of the jockeys as they flit down the course like fire-flies on their way to the starting post, and the broad green backcloth of Wiltshire behind them. There it all is, stretching away into the distance, the downs, the clumps of trees on top of them, the startling white of a chalkpit or two, and Salisbury spread-eagled in the valley below with the Cathedral spire rising up in its midst. It does not seem to matter so very much if four shillings goes down the drain on an outsider, as long as the sun is shining and Mrs Thomas is wearing her new hat.

A few years ago race-horses would be sent from the famous Druids' Lodge stables, near Stonehenge, owned by the late J. V. Rank. Recently, the closest ones have been those of Mr. R. C. Sturdy at Shrewton, and Sir Gordon Richards, who has just retired from training on the Hampshire Borders, where he rented the lease of bookmaker William Hill's stables at Whitsbury. A little farther afield, Messrs. Blagrave, Marshall, Todd, and Tree provide competition from North Wilts.

There is always hopeful and heavy backing on a 'local' horse. People are 'in the know'. They get it straight from the horse's mouth itself via the stable lad, via the pub, via the retired general's part-time gardener, who tells the daily, who tells the general's wife, who tells the general. If it wins, local pride is vindicated, bursting forth in fitting fashion as the jockey urges his mount past the winning post. If it loses, well, there is always another hot tip from someone who has actually been out in the misty early morning on top of the downs, witnessing the phenomenal staying-power of some horse few people have heard about.

Then, all too soon for some, race day is over. Cars sweep down from the Raceplain and are directed by extra policemen strategically placed on point duty at the busiest corners. In my youth, the words 'race traffic' used to strike a rather frightening note. Grownups avoided going to Salisbury because of it. "We won't go today," they said, "there will be too much *race traffic* about." Even now it is still possible to hear the same remark made by older people, although the majority have become used to traffic and the jams that go with it. The cunning ones who know the district avoid the worst places. They cut along the 'back' or 'lower' roads and wiggle their way into or around Salisbury via Bemerton, where the road is such that any question of passing is impossible.

At one point, where it is exceptionally narrow, stand two buildings far removed from the worldly pressure and pleasure of Salisbury Races. They are the ancient little Church of St. Andrew * and the lovely Tudor rectory opposite it, where George Herbert, the poet parson and kinsman of the Earls of Pembroke, lived such an idyllic life for the short space of only two years, yet two years which are still green in Bemerton's history.

George Herbert never took holy orders until the age of 33, before which his high birth and intellectual ability marked him out for a far more sophisticated career. His friends included the poet John Donne, the philosopher Francis Bacon, and that great fisherman and Herbert's own biographer, Izaak Walton. But he himself was a mystic at heart; as time went by he felt the increasing strain between his academic, courtly, and religious leanings. His priestly vocation won, aptly described in his own words:

> Whereas my birth and spirit took
> The way that takes the town,
> Thou didst betray me to a ling'ring brook
> And wrap me in a gown.

In 1630, at the age of 38, his brook was the combined water of the Rivers Nadder and Wylye which had joined forces near by,

* In 1860 this little church had become too small for the growing parish and a larger one was built not far away as a memorial to George Herbert.

and his gown the canonical one he wore every day in his little parish church at Bemerton. He had by now married Jane, the much-loved daughter of Mr. Charles Danvers of Baynton. It is alleged that the bride's father had been so taken with Herbert, whom he met while visiting his relative, Lord Danby of Dauntsey, in North Wilts, that he did his best to promote the match. At all events, it appears to have been an ideal union and the only alter-cation that ever occurred between the two was over their respec-tive attempts to incline most to the other's wishes, from which, perhaps, present-day matrimony might well take a lesson. To-gether, they tended the sick, helped the poor, befriended the lonely, and advised the ill-educated. In *The Country Parson* George Herbert laid down in precise terms the duties expected of a parson's wife in those days, and his own appears to have lived up to them admirably.

But this happy marriage was short-lived. In 1632, George Herbert lay dying of consumption in the large bedroom at the rectory overlooking the garden and the way through the meadows which he himself took so many times as he walked to Salisbury Cathedral. Shortly before his death he gave a bundle of papers to his friend, Nicholas Ferrar, with instructions to make them public if he considered them likely to "cheer any dejected soul". Other-wise, they were to be burnt. Many dejected and not so dejected souls were later to appreciate George Herbert's works, some of whom were Coleridge, Cowper, John Wesley, and Charles I, when imprisoned and awaiting execution.

George Herbert has sometimes been called the Laureate of the Anglican Church. In St. George's chapel at Westminster Abbey are two stained glass windows in which he is depicted standing alongside William Cowper, but in the humble little church of St. Andrew at Bemerton there is only a small tablet with the initials 'G.H.' and the date '1632', placed in the wall above his supposed grave. Yet in the stained glass windows above the altar, the words: "Greater love hath no man than this, that a man lay down his life for his friends" seem unusually appropriate.

Bemerton and Bemerton Heath (a large new housing estate on higher ground which, during the reign of Richard I, was the site of a very famous tournament) would appear to be singularly fortunate in its rectors. In the latter parish, which now accounts for a third of the population of Salisbury, a former rector of the new St. Michael's church has initiated a most thriving community centre, complete with licensed bar, hall, stage, skittle alley, and billiard table, an innovation still rare to be found in this country.

Along the lower road leading through Bemerton there are two pathways across the water-meadows that link up with the suburb of Harnham, where supplies of chalk are produced from a seemingly bottomless pit. The longer of these paths starts close to George Herbert's rectory; the shorter one leads straight from the city itself. On a fine Sunday in summer they are both very much in use. Cars are forgotten and the citizens, leading children and dogs, meander like the river itself. There is no other word that describes so expressively that particular form of motion which overtakes most people who find themselves in the Wiltshire water-meadows.

During the last war a musically minded lance-corporal from London shepherded me along the longer route while earnestly explaining his reactions to some concert at the Albert Hall, so that both the beauty of the river and the view of the Cathedral were unfortunately lost. Nowadays, the erection of buildings for light industry has had a somewhat similar effect, although Constable's favourite view from the Long Bridge, which inspired his "Salisbury from the Meadows" or "The Rainbow", is still as lovely; while the Old Mill at Harnham maintains a child's old-fashioned picture-book quality. In front of it the ducks are there on the pond in dozens, and if they do have to share it with a few bikini-clad maidens and half-naked young men from the city on a hot afternoon, there is all the rest of the year in which to have the place to themselves. The Old Mill is now a pottery show-room with an adjoining hotel in what was once a granary, but in spite of this it retains a timeless atmosphere. The Society for the Protection of Ancient Buildings has seen to it that careful work has been carried out on the oldest part, at one time thought to be a monk's hostel, the age of which is dated by the fact that the roof is 'queen-jointed', a method not used after the thirteenth century.

Whether or not it is because of its southerly aspect, Harnham has always been a haven for the old and sick. There is mention of the hospital of St. Nicholas for the succour of poor and infirm persons a century before the bridge-building bishop got to work, and he greatly enlarged it, even entrusting his precious bridge to its care. In the sixteenth century married couples were eligible for admission, but this practice had to be stopped after a certain Nicholas Newton and his wife, "brawled at board and threw bones before all the company". Today, Harnham can boast at least five places for elderly sufferers, as well as the Common Cold Research Unit, and the vast sprawling 'spill-over' from Salisbury General Infirmary, which is high on top of the neighbouring downs towards Odstock and maintains a world-wide reputation for plastic surgery.

To the east of the city, on the far side of Milford Hill, lies the ever-growing village of Laverstock, where the River Bourne winds in to make its small contribution to the swelling Avon. Not so very long ago the name 'Laverstock' was enough to strike terror in many a moonraker's mind because of the old-fashioned asylum which stood there, barred, bleak, and bolted. Today, Laverstock can only be thought of as the swinging suburb. The asylum has been pulled down and replaced by an up-and-coming housing estate, new schools, and new premises for light industry. The village is the home of bank managers, personnel from the Services, and Dave Dee and his one-time pop group. The parish may lay claim to being almost on a par with Old Sarum in antiquity, but the Laverstock of today belongs very definitely to the twentieth century.

So, too, does Bishopdown on the hill at the opposite side of the Bourne, where the trains from London go burrowing through the chalk before reaching Salisbury station. Henry V and his army camped on the slopes of Bishop's Down and Laverstock on their way to Southampton in 1415 and an official account of the Agincourt campaign, written in old French, is still preserved in the municipal archives. It is hard to imagine this event when confronted with all the new neat red-brick, the sterile well-stocked food-store, and the crematorium puffing wisps of grey smoke over the estate, as a reminder that it is doing continual business although the city's death-rate is low.

It is much easier to contemplate the past at Old Sarum on the northern spur of Bishopdown. The boundaries of New Sarum now embrace the mother city in her old age and ensure that this ancient monument is preserved in peace and tranquillity. In an era of society when looking after the elderly has become somewhat of a problem, it is cheering to find Old Sarum so well-respected and cared-for. Calm and benign, it gazes down on its flourishing child sprawling happily on the green carpet below it, perhaps faintly surprised and impressed at its progress and genuinely amazed at the genius responsible for the soaring edifice in its midst.

Old Sarum is mellow now, its turbulent youth and middle age forgotten, but it is not difficult to understand just why Bishop Poore wanted to get away from the place. The castle was so very much top dog; it occupied the pinnacle of Cobbett's pyramid of cheese. The foundations of Bishop Osmund's Norman cathedral (which owing to destruction by lightning was subsequently rebuilt on a grander scale by his successor, Bishop Roger) are now meticulously marked out by the Ministry of Works; but the church was always on the next rung down or 'lower plane', as it were, and obviously in direct line of any fighting which might have taken place on the north-western approaches to the fortress.

In order to obtain permission from the Pope to remove to the meads, the numerous supplementary complaints put forward by the clergy to boost their request were no doubt true. They probably were 'shrammed' (to use that old Wiltshire expression meaning numbed by the cold); the wind may well have roared round the ramparts making it hard for anyone to hear them preach. The cathedral roof most likely was in danger of collapsing, while the lack of water and appalling sanitary arrangements in this overcrowded township must have sorely tried the more aesthetically minded. It is small wonder that when the cockiness and ribaldry of the soldiers became too great, the clergy added the slightly irrational but pathetic lament that the whiteness of the chalk glaring on the bare escarpments was causing some of them to lose their sight.

The peaceful fertile meadows below them must have seemed more than unusually inviting compared to this tower of Babel which, deserted as it was centuries later, caused Pepys to say that it would "affright" him to be alone there at night. Even today, it is one thing to sit on the top of Old Sarum on a warm summer evening with a blue-grey haze covering Salisbury and the district around it, while some noiseless glider swoops and turns in the sky above the nearby aerodrome that was also once a tournament field; but it would be quite another matter to remain there in the dark with the possible ghost of a Roman centurion clanking round the Keep.*

As the shadows fall it is a relief to "descend into the meads" like those desperate clergy of long ago, and slither down the lonely little pathway on the western side of the fortress that leads into the village of Stratford-sub-Castle nestling underneath. Although the long red tentacles of suburbia are creeping up on Stratford, basically it remains one of the least spoilt of the villages close to Salisbury, possibly because, owing to being near an Ancient Monument, much of the land round about is zoned as having 'landscape value'. Stratford still seems old-fashioned and many of its lovely old homes are early seventeenth or eighteenth century.

In a field just under Old Sarum is a sarsen stone to commemorate the spot where the so-called 'election' was held under a tree when the 'rotten' and deserted borough above it still sent two members to Parliament before the Reform Act of 1832. Pitt the Elder once sat as M.P. for Old Sarum, having spent a large part of his childhood at Mawarden Court, a much-altered Jacobean house near the church at Stratford which, at one time, was the Old Vicarage. The name of his grandfather, Thomas Pitt, Esq., is engraved on the outside of this little church with the one word 'Benefactor' after it, a slightly pompous but expressive way of proclaiming the diamond merchant's various services to the village.

Stratford's history is inextricably bound up with the giant hill above it. The first men who started reinforcing this natural stronghold must have been well aware of the power it would give them over the river below which was easily fordable at this point, a point on a route that must have been important long before the road-building Romans arrived to make Old Sarum look like some gorgeous roundabout or Piccadilly Circus; while to those water-starved inhabitants of Norman Sarisberie, the shining Avon must have had a mirage-like quality.

Today the river still meanders along through Stratford past the old Manor House where Mrs. Thomas lives in semi-retirement, past the eighteenth-century Parsonage Farm, past the Old Forge,

* Owing to the paucity of Roman 'finds' on the actual hill, it is now thought that the Roman station was lower down where the village of Stratford lies today.

past the cottages built of flint and cob★ (well-protected by 'good hats' of thatch designed by master craftsmen), and onwards to Salisbury to gather up the tributaries of the Bourne, the Wylye, the Nadder, and the Ebble that are slowly converging in like manner on their appointed meeting-place.

★ Cob is a mysterious mixture of chalk, chopped straw, horsehair and sometimes even dung, all pounded together and mixed with water to form a soft compound, which is easily susceptible to rain unless properly roofed and given firmer stone foundations.

IV

HOME TOWN

WILTSHIRE is a big county but the magnetism of her focal point is so strong that it takes time to move only a little way from it. There is so much to see and so much to portray. There are all the little towns and villages and valleys round and about the Plain; there is the army-commanded part of the Plain itself with the lost village of Imber wiped off its map; and then there are those 'foreign parts' to the moonrakers of Southern Wiltshire, frightening areas of great oolite or heavy clay, 'unknown quantities' as mysterious as those samples of moondust brought back by the moonrakers of the twentieth century. They are all there like pieces of patch-work waiting to be included in the final quilt, but for the moment the Salisbury 'basin' predominates and the town of Wilton in particular.

This is for three reasons. Firstly, because it was once the "heade town of Wessex and Wileshire" (in fact, it is said that the county originally grew out of Wilton); secondly, because it has one of the loveliest and stateliest homes in the whole country which has been in the same family for over 400 years; and lastly, but by no means least in my own mind, for the simple reason that Wilton happens to be my birthplace also.

My impressions therefore are bound to be highly coloured and very personal, perhaps not detached enough for a reasonably clear-sighted view. I think of Wilton with great affection, and my memories of it will always be cherished in my heart. Hardly a week goes by without my revisiting it because I still live only a few miles away, and the narrow high-hedged back road through the Wylye Valley from my present home leads to Salisbury via Wilton and is often the quicker route.

The little town has a long and chequered history, probably owing to its particular position on a peninsula of land thrust out between the Rivers Wylye and Nadder before they join forces. Together with the high downs to the west it had a strong and natural defence in ancient times, which accounted for its importance. Ditchampton Farm, where I was born, stretches up to those downs and was mentioned in Domesday Book as an estate called "Dechementone" where the church owned half a hide of land, which was probably the equivalent of 100 acres or as much as could be tilled with eight oxen and one plough in a year.

But Wilton made its first reputation in a historical sense long before this, in the ninth century, when Egbert, King of the West Saxons, subdued both the Mercians and Northumbrians in their long struggle for supremacy and so, according to some reports, became the first 'king of England'. The treaty bringing this about was signed ceremonially by the 'King' in his palace in the royal borough of Wilton, and the remains of this palace are said to be buried under the present Kingsbury Square. At Wilton Egbert founded a small Benedictine priory, which was made into an abbey fifty years later by King Alfred after victoriously defeating the Danes. The abbey at Wilton was responsible for the education of many a Saxon princess, including Wilton's patron saint, Edith, the daughter of a beautiful abbess called Wulfthryth, and the happy result of this lady's former lapse from virtue with King Edgar the Peaceful.

During the coronation celebrations of a very much later king, those of George VI in 1937, a pageant was arranged in the town by that well-known authoress and highly entertaining Wiltonian, the late Miss Edith Olivier. With her customary gracious magnanimity, she entrusted me with the role of Saint Edith, an honour which I commemorated in somewhat doubtful fashion by making my first daring experiments with make-up, something of which I feel sure the saintly Edith would have disapproved, although history relates that she said she could be just as virtuous in gold thread as filthy rags; which is why, I suppose, I was so delighted with my gorgeous gown specially hired from Moss Bros for the occasion.

Wilton has always had a strong link with royalty. When the West Saxons first moved there they were known as Wilsaetan*

* Dwellers by the Wylye.

or Royal Family and considered themselves a race apart, a characteristic which seems to have descended with the generations and still holds good today. Wiltonians maintain that not only is their town more beautiful than their neighbours', but the fish in their shops is fresher, the cauliflowers sweeter, the meat more tender, and anyone who wants to live anywhere else must need his or her head seeing to. Especially do these sentiments hold good concerning Wilton's close and dastardly rival, Salisbury.

Wilton obtained its first charter early in the twelfth century, long before the upstart infant, New Sarum, was even thought about. When that child began to grow both in size and strength so that it made Wilton look puny in comparison, I am ashamed to say that my home town regressed into somewhat infantile tactics, behaving like a child whose toys and sweets had been stolen. As soon as Wilton found that Salisbury was holding markets every day instead of the statutory Tuesday one allowed by its own charter, the Wiltonians harried and waylaid any merchant travelling to Salisbury and forced him to do business at Wilton. But although the dispute over the respective market days was eventually settled, it was really Bishop Bingham's bridge that dealt Wilton such a blow and made her lose out in the commercial stakes.

It is strange how often that single innovation of 1244 keeps cropping up in any history of Wiltshire. "A mayne and stately thing," as Leland described it, yet it was far more than just that. Harnham bridge, or to give it its old title, Ayleswade bridge, opened up such vast new avenues for Salisbury's trade on the southern banks of the Avon. Wilton by then had suffered many vicissitudes; she had been burnt to the ground by the Danes at the beginning of the eleventh century, fired again in the twelfth by the forces of the Empress Maud; yet she had bobbed up again from both these assaults. It was the ingenuity of Bishop Bingham, probably scheming away as he trotted about his ecclesiastical duties, that sent Wilton on the trading downpath and accounted for her stunted growth. How delighted her own traders must have been when Salisbury was stricken with plague in the sixteenth century so that its market was temporarily transferred to Wilton. There is said to have been a stone half-way between the two towns on which the dreaded citizens of Salisbury placed the money for their purchases in a bowl of vinegar, presumably the best the Middle Ages could do in the way of disinfectant.

Curiously enough, it was always the commercial aspect of the little town that interested me most. As a child, I was often sent to the shops on Saturday mornings to settle my mother's weekly housekeeping account. Armed with basket, money, bills, list, and pencil, I set off with firm instructions always to "cross by the church", where the road was wide and straight ensuring a good view from either direction. The fact that this was a completely out-of-keeping building for a small Wiltshire town, did not strike me as such at the time; although later I came to realize that Wilton Church was, and still is, quite unique.

It is Byzantine-style and was erected according to instructions from the Italian-loving Lord Herbert of Lea in the nineteenth century; it is also one of the very few churches in this country built pointing southwards, because Lord Herbert's mother happened to be Catherine Woronzow, the daughter of a Russian Ambassador. It was her wish that the church should face this direction like those in Russia which look towards the Holy Land. But the actual design was inspired by the Lombardic churches of San Pietro and Santa Maria outside Tuscania. I cannot help feeling that T. H. Wyatt's finished product must have caused quite a sensation among the Wiltonians of 1845, who knew little about Italy and probably cared less.

Yet it seems as if they must all have 'rallied round', because the Reverend Drury, whom I remember well, has written a delightful little account of Wilton Church, in which he says that the altar, principally of oak, was given by "inhabitants of Wilton", and the carpet in the Choir was made by the girls employed in the Wilton Royal Carpet Factory as their own particular gift. As might be expected, the interior of this church, darkened by its tall stained glass windows, is highly ornate. Two recumbent figures on either side of the Choir commemorate its founders, the Dowager Countess of Pembroke and her son, Sidney Herbert, who was Minister of War at the time of the Crimean campaign and also a friend and patron of Florence Nightingale.

But to me, as I dutifully hurried along on Saturday mornings, I simply thought of it as the place one went to on Sundays. It was run by a friendly broad-minded rector who let us bathe in the River Nadder running through his garden and who, on one

The twin forces that have made Salisbury: Trade and the Church
Old Sarum from the air

exciting and terrifying occasion, took us through a small cloister linking his church with the belfry, where we climbed up 108 feet in order to inspect his bells.

It was really the shops that were uppermost in my mind in those days. There was the butcher, the baker, and, not the candlestick maker, but the Misses B. & M. Winters. The butcher lived in a low little shop alongside an alleyway, through which he was for ever disappearing in order to return with stiff pink carcases slung nonchalantly over his shoulder. He himself was red and cheerful as butchers ought to be; but his wife was about as out of place in a butcher's shop as Lord Herbert's church in Wilton. She was pale and drawn-looking with a lot of hair, and I remember being frightened of her when handing up the literally bloody little meat bills.

The baker's was altogether different. Having discharged any responsibility over various payments, I was allowed to spend a little extra either on a Wiltshire 'lardy' cake or on what my father always referred to as 'indigestibles'. There were seven of these for sixpence, gorgeous gooey-looking affairs including a jammy doughnut that only our local baker could make.

Across the road were the Misses B. & M. If one had referred to them as the V. & A. it would have seemed equally appropriate. They were an institution in Wilton, two spinster ladies of uncertain age. Miss Beatrice was the less active but more erudite of the pair; Miss May was the 'Martha' of the partnership. Although the Misses B. & M. were primarily stationers, they sold most other things as well and for many years assisted me over the agonizing problem of my Christmas shopping.

A few weeks before Christmas it was my father who usually escorted me to the Misses Winters, where he himself was ushered by Miss Beatrice into an inner sanctum in which, so I understood, they talked 'books'. Although her nose was invariably red, especially at this time of the year, I cannot believe she ever regaled him with anything stronger than coffee. It was left to Miss May to spread out before me all her fascinating wares carefully estimated to be within my price range. She then left me alone, at least ostensibly. She was an extremely good saleslady. I was never aware of her hovering anywhere near me, although doubtless she was well aware of me and my awful indecision. To this day, whenever a shop assistant tries to persuade me into buying some

D

Wilton House, with the Palladian Bridge over the River Nadder
Dew-pond on the Wiltshire Downs

article, I usually retreat empty-handed and think of Miss May and her far more subtle and successful tactics.

She always seemed to know the exact moment when my mind was eventually made up. Then she would bustle around with high speed and efficiency. The ninepenny lavender sachet for my cousin was wrapped with loving care; the one and threepenny comb in its (surely?) leather case for my father was given equal treatment; and the daring act of forking out one and sixpence on a handbag scent spray for my mother was rewarded by an extra piece of new virginal tissue paper.

The stationer's shop on the corner still trades under the name B. &. M. Winters. It has suffered a slight face-lift and is run on more modern lines. The people who now serve there are kind and obliging, yet I never go in to buy a paper or a note-book without somehow seeing the ghosts of Miss Beatrice and Miss May smiling at me from behind the counter, and I never go out through the door without regretting their passing.

There are two other places in Wilton where once again I cannot but regret the march of economic progress. They are the Felt Mills and the Carpet Factory. My grandmother lived at the Felt Mills and I knew every corner of it. My mother's family was of the real old extended kind and there were always aunts, uncles, and cousins around this hot, steamy, woolly, yet so exciting place. As far as I was concerned, it belonged to the family, although later I came to realize with sadness that the owner was the man who grew orchids in the greenhouse by one of the streams.

My grandmother used the Mill in which to do all her washing, having no tap of any kind inside her house. She was a very clean person, for ever standing on one of the duck-boards and plunging a wooden pole with rubber on its end into one of the huge tubs of hot water. Sometimes she would pass me over to the care of an aunt in another drier, dusty building, who was feeding wool into a veritable moloch of a machine which devoured it greedily and spewed out rolls of felt at the other end; or maybe I would be left with Uncle Charlie, whose finger had been chopped off in another of these machines, and who used to take me roller-skating in one of the empty sheds on Bank Holidays.

Two other aunts were allowed the use of a small honey-suckle-covered shed in which they made their living by dress-making. It was sometimes touch and go whether the horse and cart delivering coal, or the lorries departing with felt, would circum-navigate the narrow corner by their establishment without ending up inside it. Yet even when this excitement palled, there were always minnows to be caught in the surrounding streams, horses' dung to be shovelled up into a toy wheel-barrow for my grand-mother's roses, or the culminating thrill of the annual Pleasure Fair to which these aunts always escorted me.

Although my father sometimes took me to one of the autumn sheep fairs held at the old Fairground field on a day when I had been woken early by the sound of baas and barks, as the various flocks flowed down the lane from Grovely Woods just above our house, it was always the raucous junketing in the market-place which fascinated me most. With Aunt Cecilia and Aunt Edith perilously hitched side-saddle on one of the horses at either side of me, we swung away on the merry-go-round to the tune of "Bye Bye Blackbird" blaring forth only a few feet away from the Old Rectory, where the quiet respectable Misses Rawlence must have been covering their ears in agony.

And lastly there was Grandmother's house itself, one room down, two rooms up, and a long, long attic stretching the whole length of one of the Mill buildings and where, from time to time, various of her seven children were accommodated. In the winter, the house invariably flooded. The great day one had been expect-ing (and secretly hoping for) arrived. "The water is seeping through Granny's floor-boards," one heard. Tension mounted step by step with the rising Wylye. Next day it was "the water is over Granny's skirting-boards" (three cheers, *sotto voce*). The third day it was half-way up the legs of the piano and Granny her-self, fighting a rearguard action, was forcibly removed to stay with us until the river abated.

The Felt Mills in Crow Lane are not like that any more. My grandmother's house has disappeared, and science has done some-thing to the Wylye. It does not seem to flood at that particular point, more's the pity perhaps for the younger generation of Wilton.

My relationship with the Carpet Factory was less intense, al-though it was managed by an uncle who lived there and always took the greatest pleasure in showing us round the creeper-covered buildings. In front of the fireplace in the room where I am now typing is a small square mat that he once gave me. It represents a Red Indian's head, feathers and all, and was a sample of a carpet specially designed and made for the Savage Club in London. My uncle has been dead and buried some years now but, judging by the thickness of the pile, my Red Indian sitting by the fire should have a long life in front of him.

It was the eighth Earl of Pembroke who was really responsible for Wilton being a carpet town. He appears to have been a collector of men as well as beautiful possessions because, having admired the work of some French weavers, he is said to have smuggled two of them over to England in enormous wine casks, which must have greatly enraged poor Louis XIV. The descendants of these Frenchmen still live around these parts, the name 'Dufosee' striking a somewhat discordant note among the Wiltshire moonrakers.

As yet, I have said little about the seventeen Earls of Pembroke and the famous Wilton House that belonged and still belongs to the family, possibly because it is so hard to know how much to put in and how much to leave out; and also there are so many detailed descriptions of this stately home and its owners. Therefore, in keeping with the rest of this chapter, perhaps it is better that my own account of Wilton House shall remain purely personal.

To me, the nicest thing about it is that it needs no lions to entice the hesitant visitor. That is not to say I have anything against lions. They are the greatest fun when well-fed and seen from behind the safety of a closed-in car. But it is just that as a stately home, Wilton House seems out on its own. It really *is* stately. The place which houses a lock of Queen Elizabeth's hair and Rembrandt's portrait of his mother somehow does not need added attractions. Wilton House, with its treasures inside and its lovely garden outside, is really beautiful. It is as simple as that.

During the war, when the Southern Command took it over as its headquarters, I worked there for a time as a registry clerk. Each morning, after bicycling through the Triumphal Arch, I used to run up the front steps, then rush along the corridors and down into the cloisters built by the indefatigable James Wyatt in the early nineteenth century in order to provide easier access between the rooms. In the exact place where I once sorted letters under the surveillance of a jolly sergeant-major, there is now an easel on which is a picture of the Palladian Bridge in the grounds, painted by Sir Winston Churchill and presented to the sixteenth Earl of Pembroke by Lady Churchill in 1966.

On summer evenings, when there was a pause between the arrival of crash-helmeted motor-cyclists with secret messages for the duty officer in charge, I used to stand looking out over the garden at a tree. That it was the largest and loveliest cedar tree in the world there seemed no doubt, and this appeared to be confirmed when I later learned that the fourth Earl of Pembroke had sent his gardener over to the Lebanon specially to obtain the seedling.

There is about Wilton House the same kind of dignity, peace, and permanency that is to be found in the Cathedral Close at Salisbury. It is the perfection of the surroundings of these great buildings which sets them off and creates this atmosphere. Although beautiful in themselves, they would be nothing without their magnificent trees and their all-green enclosures, an English green like no other green in the world.

Wilton House first rose from these green banks of the Nadder when Henry VIII favoured the son of a certain Welsh knight, William Herbert, to whom he granted the remains of the Abbey and its lands at Wilton after the Dissolution of the Monasteries. This lucky young man also acquired a crest and a coat of arms and subsequently married Anne, the sister of Catherine Parr, the King's last wife. He then appears to have lost no time in building himself a house worthy of his new position, one in which he might accommodate any member of the royal family to whom he owed his good fortune.

His son, Henry, entertained Queen Elizabeth I at Wilton, and she is said to have been both "merry and pleasant" during her visit. When he married, for the third and last time, the sister of Sir Philip Sidney, Wilton House seems to have become almost like a college, so great was the number of learned people who came there. Shakespeare, whose statue stands today just inside the main hall, is reputed to have presented the first performance of *Twelfth Night* or *As You Like It*—both plays have been mentioned —at Wilton House not long after the second Earl's death.

With few exceptions, all the Earls of Pembroke have loved and cherished their home, but the twentieth century has wrought even greater changes than the fire which caused it to be rebuilt in the seventeenth. During the Second World War the fifteenth Earl lived in but a small fraction of the house, letting the army have the rest, where he magnanimously left many of his lovely pictures as an inspiration, perhaps, to Winston Churchill and Eisenhower when they came to plot and plan with the General in Command. The beautiful Countess of Pembroke served copious cups of coffee to the soldiers and A.T.S. in a canteen converted from the old stables just inside her gate and where now, as a further sign of the times, paying visitors are likewise regaled, albeit with not so gracious and personal a touch.

But the town of Wilton appears to have taken all these revolutions in its stride. Its twentieth-century inhabitants no longer need to fear their one-time rival. As the last load of sight-seers roars away from the Triumphal Arch at the end of September, Wilton remains to await the winter, still blooming and booming. Around the town, new houses and establishments show the army is still very much in evidence, and, in fact, Wilton is soon to become the Headquarters of the United Kingdom Land Forces. Today, soldiers' wives queue up at the self-service stores; friendly citizens from Salisbury drive out to Wilton to do their shopping because sometimes (although not always) they find it easier to park there; or maybe Wilton cauliflowers really are sweeter and the meat more tender. As an endearing token of Wilton's complete forgiveness of her old enemy, the ruined church in her market-square has been greatly restored thanks to an endowment by an American Ambassador called Bingham, who needs no better tribute than the following words engraved on a plaque by the door:

> Honouring the memory of his ancestor Robert Bingham, consecrated Bishop of Salisbury on this spot 27th May, A.D. 1229 Robert Bingham, Ambassador of the United States at the court of St. James 1933–37 caused the chancel to be restored. The Ambassador who died 18th December 1937 left in this country an honoured memory and many friends.

As for me, as I travel up the back road past Ditchampton Farm, past the stables where my beloved pony once lived, past the whole stamping-ground of my lost youth, I like to think of Wilton lying there safely in the shelter of the downs, perhaps not as peaceful as once I knew it, but still, as Queen Elizabeth was said to be, "merry and pleasant".

V

'GENERAL' COUNTRY

THE area around Salisbury south of the Plain proper is sometimes referred to as 'General' country. This is because, although primarily agricultural, it is the home of such a high proportion of retired army officers. Many of them live here in order to have part-time jobs at Southern Command (or Strategic Command as it is nowadays); others perhaps settle in the district because, having known it during their more active years as a good place in which to relax when off duty, they and their wives have now decided that this is where they would like to spend the rest of their days. But, whatever the reason, summer evenings in South Wilts will find the Generals, Brigadiers, Colonels, and Majors bent double and bottoms up, *gardening*.

The local farmers, on the other hand, never garden. The prosperous ones employ a gardener-handyman; the others leave it to their wives; and when these overworked ladies start wailing about the weeds so that their husbands can hold out no longer, the latter send in reinforcements from the farm staff for mopping-up operations, just like some sort of swift army manoeuvre.

Of the five lovely valleys that have often been likened to the fingers of an outstretched left hand holding Salisbury in its palm, that of the Wylye is probably the best known, especially by keen fishermen. But the inhabitants of each valley regard their own with a fierce personal pride. The south-westerly Ebble-ites sitting along the thumb (otherwise known as the Chalke Valley Tribe) say theirs must be the prettiest, an assertion that is not without justification. At the beginning of this century, the writer, Maurice Hewlett, was a great exponent of its charms and delighted in living at its little "capital" of Broad Chalke; while much longer ago, none other than that celebrated antiquary, John Aubrey, also rather fancied the place, becoming church warden there for several years.

The Ebble nominally begins its life (at this stage mostly a winter one only) near the tiny village of Alvediston or "'Ellofadistance", as it is called by the locals. I am not quite sure exactly where it is a 'hell of a way' from, unless they are referring to the remoter regions farther west, as from "'Ellofadistance" to where the Ebble links up with the Avon just south of Salisbury, it is only a matter of some 13 miles, during which journey there is almost the same number of villages. Each of these is attractive in its individual way, especially Bishopstone, which possesses a fourteenth-century church that is said to have been built at the instigation of William of Edington, Bishop of Winchester, from whom the village acquired its name.

Throughout the entire valley the Ebble barely achieves more than the status of a stream although it is helped along by a slightly grander one flowing down from Bowerchalke, which probably accounts for the greater share of the water, besides supporting flourishing water-cress beds. In fact, many people consider this to be the proper 'Chalke' stream which should, by rights, have named the whole river. But whatever anyone likes to call it, there is little doubt that the Ebble or Chalke Valley is today one of the least spoilt of the five, lying carefully guarded by the high ridge of downs stretching from Cranborne Chase on one side and the old Shaftesbury Turnpike riding high on the other.

The natives by the River Nadder, however, think there is nothing that can compare with their fertile greensand lowlands watched over by the steep northern-facing slopes, especially above Fovant, where the badge of their very own Wiltshire Regiment has been proudly emblazoned in the chalk. Maybe because this valley is the home of the famous Chilmark quarries, it possesses more than its share of beautiful stone houses. At its western extremities it can boast the largest eighteenth-century house in Wiltshire, Wardour Castle (now Cranborne Chase School), which has been built near the romantic ruins of that first castle, so gallantly defended by the spirited Lady Blanche Arundell during the Civil War. Moreover, close by, the natives may also lay claim to Pyt House, Hatch House, and the particularly lovely medieval

Place House at Tisbury, the latter standing beside one of the most magnificent tithe barns in the country.

Tisbury is a large village that was once considered inferior to its attractive neighbour, Hindon, because it boasted neither market nor fair. In the last century, however, the arrival of the railway turned it into a natural little metropolis of the valley, although motor traffic has now lessened much of its importance. But Tisbury can still be proud of its plethora of old stone buildings, especially the rather splendid Church of St. John the Baptist. Outside in the churchyard, where the parents of Rudyard Kipling lie buried, there is one of the largest yew trees in existence, which is split with age but still carrying on majestically, as it may well have done ever since Magna Carta.

A mile or so north of Tisbury lie the two villages of Fonthill Gifford and Bishop's Fonthill, near which, ever since Domesday, there has been a succession of magnificent houses; but the one that achieved most notoriety was an extravaganza of a building erected at the end of the eighteenth century. It was enclosed by a huge wall, 12 feet high and 7 miles in circumference, and the whole extraordinary creation came into being at the whim of a rich son and heir of another man who had already built one mansion near by.

William Beckford II, however, was not only more ambitious than his father; he was also over-imaginative and impatient. He originally intended to build a ruined 'abbey' as a feature for his garden, but having become carried away by the idea, he went on adding excrescence after excrescence like a house of cards, finally pulling down his old home and going to live in his 'abbey'. Had he not been so spoilt by wealth, it is possible that he might have been acclaimed a genius for, apparently without effort, he wrote *Vathek*, considered to be the finest oriental story in European literature.

But William Beckford is mostly remembered for his capricious egoism. He seemed to think nothing of working 500 men day and night in his efforts to have the place ready to entertain Lord Nelson for Christmas; neither did he think anything of planting a million trees in a year for which, at least, posterity must thank him. Nor was Beckford daunted by the fact that his 'abbey' tower, which he proposed should be as high as St. Paul's Cathedral and a landmark for miles around, was for ever crashing to the ground during construction. In later years, as his fortune dwindled when the abolition of slavery depreciated the value of his West Indian estates, he removed himself to Bath, from whence, so it is said, he could still see his precious tower until it fell down for the last time, taking most of the 'abbey' with it.

Little now remains of what I was brought up to think of as 'Beckford's Folly'. The site is extremely remote and difficult of access, but anyone who does discover a strange little lake hidden among dense woodland near Fonthill Gifford might well think he had stumbled on a scene from one of the more fantastic fairy tales. As a child, it always gave me a slightly eerie feeling to be anywhere near the place, which was a frequent occurrence because my father rented the coarse fishing on a larger lake close to the comparatively new Fonthill House, now owned by Lord Margadale (then Major Morrison, Conservative M.P. for Salisbury).

This lake, which was artificially produced by damming up the southern end of one of the Nadder's tributaries but which has recently sadly diminished in size, was one of our favourite haunts on Sunday afternoons. It too was surrounded by giant trees, and I remember thinking that it sometimes took on quite a sinister tone also. This may have been due to the proximity of mad Mr. Beckford's 'Folly', which had fired my own imagination, or simply the peculiarly dank pungent smell in the boat-house from which we paddled away in an old punt with more than a little trepidation, weighed down as we inevitably were by children, picnic baskets, fishing-rods, and jam-jars full of wriggling worms specially dug from the garden that morning.

The water was deep, weedy, and hazardous, but it was also full of perch. On one occasion when my cousin and I were rowing and had marooned us all on top of a submerged tree-trunk, my father's remarks were short and to the point. "This is not a dew-pond.* It is a fair-sized lake for this part of the world. How you

---

* Dew-ponds are something of a miracle on Wiltshire downs and the making of them a jealously guarded secret in the days when farmers lacked a piped water-supply. The late Tom Smith from Market Lavington was the greatest of Wiltshire dew-pond makers and, as recently as 1938, made one for a progressive chalkland farmer on top of a high bleak down. First of all a big hollow was dug, then packed with puddled clay followed by a layer of slaked lime, then straw, after which the whole lot was topped with rubble and stones before being rammed down hard. The first rainfall 'started' the pond off, after

two children have managed to hit just the right spot to sink the ship, the Lord only knows." He would then reel in his line, take over the oars, and manoeuvre us all safely into less dangerous waters.

The Nadder Valley seems to be full of these unexpected watery surprises. Strong springs gush up to make crystal-clear little contributions to swell the main river. From just above the villages of Teffont Magna and Teffont Evias one such rivulet tumbles along between the road and the old stone houses, so that each is reached by its own private little bridge.

In the nearby village of Dinton are several pleasing houses belonging to the National Trust. Hyde House, the birthplace of the influential first Earl of Clarendon, can be seen over the churchyard wall; Philipps House, with its imposing Ionic portico, stands secluded in lovely Dinton Park; while at the opposite end of the village is a cottage of great age. It was here in 1596 that Henry Lawes, composer and friend of John Milton, was born, a man who became a national figure and whose music still continues to be heard in Westminster Abbey where he himself lies buried.

To the north of Dinton there is a very steep wooded hill, vaguely reminiscent of Alice in Wonderland country, because the branches of the trees which meet above the narrow lanes cause local inhabitants to talk about going up or down the 'rabbit warren'. On the farther side of this hill from the village stands a lonely but beautiful late-Georgian house called Marshwood, which used to appeal greatly to my father. When I was young 'going for a drive' was still one of those gentler innocuous forms of pleasure undertaken by the family at regular intervals. Almost invariably, we ended up at Marshwood. "Lovely place," my father would say, stopping the car. Gently, but firmly, my mother would remind him of the domestic difficulties of living without neighbours, shops, or buses for miles around. "But that's the beauty of it," my father would remark, shaking his head and starting up the car again, gazing regretfully at the isolated grey stone farmhouse as we drove slowly by until such time as the urge to see Marshwood overtook him once more.

---

which nightly condensation exceeded daily evaporation because the non-conductive materials used always kept the pond cool. Some of the finest dew-ponds are of great antiquity, dating from Anglo-Saxon times.

Sometimes on the way home we called in to see a friend of my parents who lived at Compton Chamberlayne in an enchanting house dating from Tudor times, now lying like a small jewel in a perfect setting of parkland, complete with a church and lake. It was from here in 1655 that the hapless royalist, Colonel John Penruddock, attempted his unsuccessful rising and was shortly afterwards beheaded in Exeter gaol, leaving his wife and seven children sorrowing in their Wiltshire home. The devotion of Arundel and John Penruddock is one of the greatest love stories, and the letter Arundel wrote to her husband while he was awaiting execution is an outstanding example of wifely fidelity:

My dear heart,

My sad parting was so far from making me to forget you, that I have scarce thought upon myself since, but wholly upon you. Those dear embraces which I yet feel, and shall never lose (being the faithful testimonies of an indulgent husband) have charmed my soul to such reverence of your remembrances, that were it possible, I would with my own blood cement your dead limbs to life again, and with reverence think it no sin to rob heaven a little longer of a martyr. Oh my dear! You must now pardon my passion, tho' being the last (oh fatal word!) that ever you will receive from me; and know that until the last minute I can imagine you shall live, I will sacrifice the prayers of a Christian, and the groans of an affected wife; and when you are not, which sure by sympathy I shall know, I shall wish my own dissolution with you, that so we may go hand in hand to heaven. It is too late to tell you what I have done, or rather have not, done for you. How turned out of doors, because I came to beg for mercy! The Lord lay not your blood to their charge. I would fain discourse longer with you, but dare not, my passion begins to drown my reason, and will rob me of my devoir, which is all I have left to serve you.

Adieu therefore ten thousand times my dearest dear, and since I must never see you more, take this prayer 'May your faith be so strengthened, that constancy may continue, and then I hope heaven will receive you, where grief and love will in short time after, I hope, translate, my dear, your sad but constant wife, even to love your ashes when dead'.

A. Penruddock.

Your children beg your blessing,
and present their duties to you.
May the 3rd 1655 11 o'clock at night.

Nowadays, when the inhabitants (and especially the army contingent) in one valley visit their rivals in another, they talk about 'going over the top', as if it were still in the middle of a battle. The downland ridges dividing the different encampments seem to act as some kind of barrier to friendly communication as they did in days gone by. When the army 'opens fire' at the outbreak of cocktail warfare which takes place in the height of summer, the verbal barrage, usually over bigger and better blooms, is deafening. The Greensanders of the Nadder boast about being able to grow azaleas to the wily Wylye folk, who, in turn, jealously guard their secret weapon which enables them to raise spectacular lupins on chalk. Although not quite so bloodthirsty and a little more civilized than the days when King Alfred or Colonel Penruddock battled in these parts, pride of possession (or what some people refer to as the 'territorial imperative') is but thinly veiled on these occasions. Invariably, as the last guests tactfully but insincerely admire their hosts' roses growing by the gate, the parting shot, "Ah, but you should have been here last week," sends them happily back 'over the top' secure in the knowledge that 'their' valley grows so very much better specimens.

Because the Wylye Valley is also 'my' valley and therefore, however deplorable, I share this deadly sin of personal pride in it, perhaps I should begin its description by saying that it has at least two bad faults. One is that no one, except the chosen few, seems able to spell it, let alone pronounce it. The second is that the main road running through it is the worst in Europe.

If one gives the name 'Wylye' or even spells it out to a London shop assistant, he or she will have two or three abortive attempts at writing it down, then give up completely, and pass over the pencil. As for people trying to pronounce it who have never heard the word spoken, they often arrive at some curious interpretations. Continental telephone operators insist it is "Wee lee" or "We lie" which seems to sound worse. Some people say "While" or "Why lie?" which is slightly better, but no stranger ever seems able to come straight out with "Wily" (as applied to fox), which is the correct method of articulation.

As for the main or 'front' road, it is the constant source of driving hazards, endless arguments, and despair. For as long as I can remember something has been going to be done about it, but improvements are slow to take place. It is the sort of narrow, main, tortuous road described by an aged moonraker as where the cars go "a sight too fast to be able to draw up quick".

The dual carriage-way, threatened decades ago, rears its ugly head from time to time like some sort of Loch Ness Monster and then disappears into the sea of Ministry of Transport files again. When, quite recently, it made a more prolonged appearance, the local inhabitants got together and formed a Wylye Valley Protection Society. They want something done about the road and the increasing number of lorries on it (due to the opening of the Severn Bridge) but they would prefer the new road to go 'along the top'. Property-owners in the Wylye Valley, threatened with annihilation, have become desperate; maiden ladies living alone have been reduced to tears at the thought of their one source of security being swept from under them; the more militant residents make fierce speeches and write to the papers. During the time when Barbara Castle was Minister of Transport, one retired Colonel said he was going to ask her to lunch to see what could be done about it all; so, the controversy goes on like the lorries themselves, sometimes at high speed, sometimes at a frustrated low one, vaguely threatening, occasionally subversive, and often with bad clashes of will resulting in blockages all along the way.

But apart from these somewhat unfortunate elements, the Wylye Valley is really beautiful. It could be called the original mainspring of the county because it gave its name to Wilton, which, in turn, gave its own to 'Wileshire'; in fact, had this book been written in olden times, almost certainly Wilton would have been the core around which the life of the county revolved. From Wilton, where it joins the Nadder, the Wylye Valley stretches upstream due north at first and then west-north-west for nearly 15 miles. It is at this particular bend of the river that the valley seems at its best, and tempted the late Ford Madox Hueffer (F. M. Ford) into writing his imaginative novel, *Ladies Whose Bright Eyes*. Not long ago there used to be an old man who came every day to stand by the roadside just looking at it all spreading into the blue-green horizon. Some people said he was an evacuee who had arrived in Wiltshire during the war and stuck there. But, whoever he was, he knew a good thing when he saw it and found time to "stand and stare" which so few of us possess nowadays; or maybe we have become "too full of care" to think about arranging our lives sensibly like this elderly gentleman, who lived until he was over 90.

Close to this old man's vantage point is the village of Wishford, where, on 29th May each year, Oak Apple Day is still observed. This custom originated shortly after Henry VIII had given the estates belonging to Wilton Abbey to the first Earl of Pembroke. At that time the inhabitants of the little villages of Barford St. Martin in the Nadder Valley and Wishford in the Wylye one, were given the right to gather snapping wood in Grovely Forest on the high ridge of downs between them. They were also privileged to bring away annually a load of young oak trees with which they decorated themselves, their respective churches and houses, before processing to Salisbury Cathedral where they would dance and lay claim to their ancient rights in front of the high altar chanting "Grovely! Grovely! Grovely! and all Grovely!"

Today, Oak Apple Day is mostly confined to Wishford village where a large marquee is erected and everyone enjoys a jamboree, although the ritual ceremony still takes place in the Cathedral and an old-fashioned foursome dances in the Close. Many villagers also get up early, arousing the rest by banging on dustbin lids, before setting off to Grovely to maintain their wood-gathering rights. So determined are the local moonrakers to protect these that when one of the Earls of Pembroke endeavoured to suppress the custom following the Enclosure Acts during the last century, a courageous woman called Grace Reed from Barford, together with three others, defied him by gathering wood as usual. When summoned before the magistrates they refused to pay a fine and were imprisoned, only to be released the following day because the Earl, although within *his* rights, decided to give way to popular feeling, to say nothing of a little obstinacy. So thanks to those nineteenth-century suffragettes, my own daughter and I, at the appropriate times of our lives, have been able to join in the Wishford jollifications and, in the words of Edward Slow who wrote verse in Wiltshire dialect:

> Ta keep thic hankshent custom up
> On girt Oak Apple Day.

To do my valley real justice and continue upstream taking in all the little villages and hamlets which even W. H. Hudson, who loved them so much, said he found too numerous to count, would be a book in itself. In its entirety, William Cobbett wrote: "it is impossible for the eyes of man to be fixed on a finer country", and it seems to me that he was not very far wrong. I have spent almost half a century in the Wylye Valley, and it has never failed me at any season of the year. In the spring, when the downland clumps of trees on its northern side and the woods of Grovely and Great Ridge on the southern slopes start turning a lighter green, a whole army of little red tractors appear, working down the land preparatory to spring sowing.

Later on, when the mayfly is about, the members of the Wylye Valley Fishing Clubs★ are to be seen in the water-meadows, lazily ignored by the grazing cattle, and getting as close to a fisherman's dream as may be possible this side of paradise. The scent of hay is in the air, the sun is shining, and it really does seem as if the Wylye is singing.

As the days get warmer, along comes the visitor and fête season, the latter being one of the finest examples of voluntary corporate effort on behalf of the church to be found these days. In the parish of Steeple Langford with its little church of Norman origin, it has never rained on fête day in the history of the village, a sure sign, perhaps, that the Lord looks after His own; and when the last old petticoat has disappeared from the jumble-stall, the last tea been served, the last bowl for the pig sent flying into someone's herbaceous border, and £300 are being counted and re-counted like election results, the previous months of hard work are forgotten and it all seems so very worth while.

The visitor season also means hard work for the private host and hostess, depending on how socially inclined they feel. South Wilts is very much 'on the way' between London and Land's End. "May we really call in for a meal on our way back from Cornwall?" "Johnny gets in to Heathrow at six a.m. and says he can be with you in time for breakfast." "Do you really think you could put us all up for the night? I'd adore to see the gardens at Stourhead and I think our au pair girl ought to 'do' Stonehenge and the Cathedral before she goes home." "Is it true what they say in the *Sunday Express* about you having flying saucers at

★ The Wiltshire Chalk Streams Protection Committee is at present fighting an application by the West Wilts Water Board to abstract 2 million gallons of water per day from the Upper Wylye Valley. Ecologists fear such an operation could ruin this beautiful chalk stream, as has happened elsewhere in England.

The Double Cube Room at Wilton House

Warminster?" And finally, the *pièce de résistance*, "the children can't wait to see the Longleat Lions. Shall we meet there on Sunday?"

Longleat is, of course, a great attraction for the young. To be able to go on safari in the wilds of West Wilts near the far end of the Wylye Valley with lions strolling nonchalantly past the bumpers of the car, and pseudo big-game hunters shouting warnings through microphones to keep the windows tightly closed, does tend to wake up the Sabbath Day in Wiltshire, especially when Lord Bath himself happens to be about. Moreover, there are not only lions to be seen but other animals, including monkeys, hippos, giraffes, and zebras as well. Visitors are allowed to get out of their cars and stroll about among the last two kinds, and when one of the little striped beasts trots over the road leading through the park, a child from South Kensington may be heard to yell, "Look, Mum, there's a zebra crossing!"

After the excitement of the game reserve the house, although providing a splendid Elizabethan finale to the entertainment for grown-ups, might come as a slight anti-climax to the younger generation. For myself, I should simply like to be left alone to enjoy its undoubted beauty without the necessary concomitants, as it were. I appreciate that nowadays these are inevitable, but somehow I have never quite been able to get the 'stately home' industry reconciled in my mind.

That it is something which has mushroomed since the last war and evidently fills a need both for owners and sight-seers alike, seems obvious; although the feelings of the former must surely be ambivalent. From the point of view of the country as a whole, it must certainly have a considerably favourable effect on the invisible trade columns of our balance of payments. Yet I try to imagine what it would be like having a large notice saying: "TEAS & TOILETS" permanently at the side of my own house, and the thought makes me shudder. I realize it is no good having desperate ladies looking for bushes, especially when lions are about, but it does tend to take away the romantic aspect of the place. I cannot help but wish that the whole curious band-wagon had never been forced to start up and that there were some other more dignified use for these historic places.

There is something un-English to me about the set-up, and something infinitely sad and not quite right about seeing tables

E

The ruins of St. Mary's Church in the market-square at Wilton

laid with all the best silver for a dinner-party that will never take place. Perhaps it is better not to think about it all too much and drive away from Longleat and down the Wylye Valley, with its fields of barley showing green and full of promise on either side, feeling thankful that one's own home and farmland need not suffer such indignities.

As soon as any field of corn starts turning faintly yellow the locals say that it is "going off", meaning harvest will soon begin. At the end of July or early August huge red predatory monsters appear, often on the south-facing slopes first. The farming community eye the yearly emergence of these combine-harvesters with avidity. The farmer's wife, returning home from a morning's shopping along the hazardous A36, remarks at lunch, "I see they're on at Little Wishford." Her husband bolts his meal, rushes up the farm road in his Land-Rover, and against his better judgment and the advice of his moisture-meter, tells his foreman to "have a go" at Picket's Piece. The frustration of waiting for a certain field to be fit to combine, while all around the infuriating 'they' are getting on with the job, is often too much, even for the most placid of men.

When harvest is over many farmers start 'lighting pipes'. This does not mean they are going to sit back and 'take it easy'; it is merely the local expression for burning straw. On many fields it is not worth baling, and the quickest and often the best way of cleaning a field is to set a match to the straw when the wind is in the right direction. This causes great consternation to town dwellers who start talking about pyromaniacs and dial 999. The nearer one gets to habitation, the more often this happens and, even to countryfolk, to see a huge field, close to a housing estate, enveloped in smoke and flames is quite a terrifying sight. Occasionally mistakes do occur. Text-book young men straight from agricultural colleges, whose weather eyes have not been opened, may be a little too free and easy with the matches. Operation Burning Straw, if not carried out by a sensible moonraker, has been known to fire a neighbour's standing corn.

Soon autumn comes to my valley. The leaves turn golden; the scorched remains of Picket's Piece become chocolate-brown under the plough; members of the Royal Artillery, the Wilton and the South and West Wilts Hunt start thinking about their opening meets; the Wylye Horse Trials (an increasingly popular event recently inaugurated by Lord and Lady Hugh Russell) take place; village whist-drives get into full swing again, and the farmers ask the retired army contingent to go shooting with them. Until Christmas a lot seems to be going on, but afterwards a great change comes over my valley. In the bleak midwinter there is a certain exodus of the sun-loving more affluent members of the community; but the hard core, perhaps the really wily Wylye folk remain to do battle with January, February, and March. Sometimes it is very cold; the north wind sweeps down from the Plain; the artificial lake caused by excavating gravel at Steeple Langford freezes over and the valley waits in silent grandeur for the coming of spring. I like it best in its solitude. It seems perhaps selfish, but it is like having it all to oneself. Bare and stripped of all its trimmings one really gets to know it.

Doubtless there are people on either side of me who feel the same way about their own particular valleys. The Avon brigade, for instance, must surely consider theirs not only the most beautiful but the most important, for after all, the Salisbury Avon is the river into which all the others pour and which continues, like the broad arm of this outstretched hand, as it journeys to the sea.

It is best to think of this river as being in two parts. First of all there is the Upper Avon, which rises above Pewsey and plunges southward through the heart of the Plain to Amesbury and then winds slowly past the little Woodford villages to Stratford-sub-Castle and Salisbury; then there is the larger bolder Lower Avon, complete with all its tributaries flowing triumphantly over the Hampshire border just south of Downton.

When Cobbett rode down through the Upper Avon Valley in 1826 towards that "accursed hill" of Old Sarum, he expressed his "deep shame, as an Englishman, at beholding the general extreme poverty of those who cause this vale to produce such quantities of food and raiment. I verily believe it," he went on, "to have the worst-used labouring people on the face of the earth." Although the agricultural worker is still so lowly paid in comparison with his town brother, one hopes that Cobbett would not feel such righteous anger if he were to retrace the same path today.

South of Amesbury, a town that seems to belong more to the Plain than the valley, the Upper Avon runs through exceptionally lovely surroundings. The downs on either side of the river rise steeply and are densely wooded, hence the names of some of the villages, Upper, Middle, and Lower Woodford. There are several outstanding houses in this part of the valley; one is the much-restored Lake House of chequered flint and stone, situated near the old home of that pioneer of the wireless age, the late Sir Oliver Lodge; another is Heale House, where Charles II hid after his flight from the battle of Worcester; and in a particularly attractive setting facing the road from Wilton as it goes 'over the top' and down Camp Hill, there stands Little Durnford Manor, a house once belonging to the Devenish family and the subject of a delightful book entitled *A Wiltshire Home*, written by a daughter who grew up there at the beginning of the century.

It is not until after the Avon leaves Salisbury, however, that it really seems to get under way and the atmosphere around undergoes a subtle change. Suddenly the valley broadens; everything appears more diffuse; there is not so much of that tight little community feeling to be found near the smaller narrower streams. The countryside becomes flatter, less interesting perhaps, because the river has now become purposeful and knows that the sea will be waiting; although well-hidden from view at the southern side of the attractive village of Britford with its moated house and historic church, lies Longford Castle, the home of the Earl of Radnor and one which possesses a most unusual history.

Longford was built at the end of the sixteenth century by Sir Thomas Gorges, the second husband of Helena Snachenberg, a Swedish lady with extravagant continental tastes and the wit to see that these were fulfilled, despite the fact that her desire for a triangular-shaped castle on the banks of the Avon almost brought the couple to ruin. When faced with financial disaster she is said to have begged the hull of a wrecked Spanish galleon from Queen Elizabeth, and with the treasure found therein her husband was able to complete the building. Longford has been much altered since those early days when Sir Philip Sidney introduced it into his *Arcadia* as the Castle of Amphialus, but it was not until the beginning of the eighteenth century that it was bought by the Bouverie family, in whose possession this fairy-tale mansion with its superb collection of pictures has remained to this day.

Not far from Longford but less well known and completely hidden from view are the ruins of what was once an even more historic place, a royal palace in the old Forest of Clarendon. Although there is a comparatively new Clarendon House, at one time there was a building in these woods that started its life as a hunting-box for Norman kings and was greatly enlarged to become a palace that played a considerable part in the political history of England.

Clarendon was the first royal residence that was never fortified, and when a monarch took his pleasures here it was an outward declaration that his kingdom was at peace. This was where the famous Constitutions of Clarendon (an attempt to limit the secular powers of the Pope) were framed by Henry II and Thomas à Becket, who may well have come riding towards their appointed meeting-place along the ancient trackway that led past the Priory of Ivychurch, an Augustinian House founded by King Stephen. Today, this is nothing more than a few fragments of stone standing beside a small farmhouse, and it is now over 400 years since the ivy started gaining control over both priory and palace. Despite certain excavations to the latter in the 1930s, both have almost passed into oblivion, their secrets remaining buried in what John Aubrey was apt to refer to fondly as "a romancy sort of place".

There is only one little valley now left to be described at the eastern side of this outstretched hand, perhaps a weaker and more insignificant one than any of the others, as befits a 'little finger' or a 'winter' Bourne. Although this river rises near Burbage at the furthermost north-eastern point of the Plain, in the course of about 24 miles the river-bed is often dry for at least half the year, and only 6 miles can be thought of as permanent stream.

But if the Bourne lacks a certain aggressiveness, the hills on either side of it are strongholds of the most up-to-date kind. On Porton Down there are the Chemical Defence and Microbiological Research Establishments, while on top of Boscombe Down there is the Aircraft and Armament Experimental Station, where the jets take off and land along one of the longest runways in the country. Altogether, these form quite a formidable scientific enclave in the south-eastern corner of the county.

Porton often seems to be the butt of attacks quickly taken up by newspaper reporters, which makes it difficult for the public to understand that much of the work carried on there is of vital necessity, not only for the country's defence but also as a contribution to the improvement of world health. Despite the fact that there are 'open days' when the locals are allowed a good look round, many of them still seem to regard Porton suspiciously as a place where there are queer 'goings-on', almost on a par with those of their forefathers during the Iron Age as they went about their strange antics at the earthwork called Figsbury Rings close by.

But oblivious of the speculation surrounding both the old and new encampments, the Bourne trickles calmly on towards Salisbury and links up with the Avon on the city's southern outskirts. Already the mother river has gathered up the twin forces of the Nadder and the Wylye, so that when the westerly and slightly wayward Ebble falls in line 2 miles farther downstream, the picture of the outstretched hand is complete. It is a simple picture, but it would be hard to overestimate its geological importance in the lives of all the southern moonrakers who live with it. They make their homes along the valleys; they cultivate the downs; for recreation, they go 'over the top'; and for a variety of reasons they go "a sight too fast to be able to draw up quick", as they speed towards Salisbury and that glorious spire.

On its coat of arms the city displays five blue bands on a golden background; while on certain auspicious occasions a flag with like colouring flies gaily from the top of the Guildhall in its market-square. Perhaps these two symbolic examples are the best illustrations I can give to show the unique influence of these five rivers that flow, with such gentle determination, through 'General' country to Salisbury and the sea.

VI

PLAIN OR FANCY

ONE of the most striking features about Salisbury Plain is that it is
not plain but fancy, fancy in the sense that it has a capricious
chameleon-like quality and never looks quite the same from one
minute to the next. Here, I am referring to that brown, rather
blank space on the map just north of Salisbury, approximately
20 miles wide and 15 miles deep, that no railway and few roads
have ever pierced. Strictly, or geologically speaking, most of
South Wilts constitutes Salisbury Plain, into which five rivers
have cut through one huge chalky zone. But the real hub of the
formation, the higher harder core as it were, where the army
booms and bangs away like sudden summer thunderstorms disturbing the sleep of nervous inhabitants in the 'fringe' villages, is
the place that most people think of when they talk about Salisbury
Plain.

Maybe, because it originated below sea-level, it still seems to be
folded in waves, rising, swelling, retreating, and for ever altering
shape as the clouds above it paint this rolling landscape a misty
grey, then blue, then green, or perhaps back to a menacing darker
grey, as a real thunderstorm looms up from the south-west to join
forces with the gunners blasting away into the lonely horizons.

Occasionally, when travelling across this Plain proper on the
permitted roadways, that column of soldiers marching not far
away suddenly seems to vanish as if it had been drowned in this
heaving sea. The lone man walking along the sky-line suddenly is
not there any more. Has he, perhaps, fallen 200 feet down into
one of the disused wells so very much in use in days gone by? Or,
worse still, has he trespassed in an area firmly marked "KEEP OUT"
and met an untimely end with an unexploded shell? The Plain

71

seems to be for ever posing questions which no one can answer save the ghost of a Neolithic man taking a moonlit walk around his barrow. It is, in fact, something of a dark horse, as opposed to that famous white one exposed in the chalk on the side of its foothills.

Most of Wiltshire's white horses near this 'inland sea' were created in the eighteenth century, when there was a distinct movement for beautifying the countryside, except this particular horse at Bratton Down near Westbury, whose origins possibly date back to Saxon times or even earlier; it was most likely carved to commemorate King Alfred's victory over the Danes at Ethandune (or Edington as today's village is called) as if he wanted to say, "Look, my mark!" Throughout the ages men have always wanted to leave some kind of signature behind them and what better place could they have than these everlasting Wiltshire Downs, especially when kindly disposed descendants carry on their good work and from time to time give the old nags a good grooming, even altering their contours a little to be more in keeping with present-day art.

At the beginning of the Second World War a certain gay young officer in the Wiltshire Regiment was driving past this well-known landmark after a convivial gathering at his headquarters at Devizes. To his horror, he suddenly looked up and became aware that only the hindquarters of this usually reassuring animal were in evidence. He hastily stopped the car, got out, and rubbed his eyes, wondering whether his Colonel-in-Chief might have considered him as being a little the worse for drink. Luckily, an ancient moonraker of his acquaintance happened to be passing by and the younger man was greatly relieved to hear this local worthy remark, "Thee don't need to worry, zur. They be a-blackin' out thic thur 'oss so's Hitler's flying chaps won't know where the devil they be."

But the greatest question-mark on Salisbury Plain for anyone, either sober or not so sober, is, of course, Stonehenge,★ those unique mysterious stones just west of Amesbury which have been the object of curiosity, supposition, research, and excavations throughout the centuries. When Samuel Pepys first saw them he

★ The meaning of the second syllable of this word is uncertain. The most likely theory seems to be that it is derived from the Old English 'hengen' meaning 'hanging'. It is not difficult to imagine the trilithons as gallows, although 'hanging' was also used to describe any steep hill or something set upright.

considered them to be "prodigious", but went on to add, "God knows what their use was", a remark which still appears quite justifiable today.

There are now certain known facts about Stonehenge that are contrary to popular belief. Firstly, it has definitely been established that it was not all created at the same time, because modern researchers have found that its history seems to cover three distinct periods and spans about nine centuries; secondly, although Druids may have used its ruins, they certainly could have had nothing to do with its erection, because no new developments took place there after about 1300 B.C. and the Druids were a Celtic priesthood who never arrived in this country much before 250 B.C. Therefore, the high jinks of hooded folk which take place there at sunrise on 21st June each year, although fascinating to watch in themselves, have no connection with the original purpose of Stonehenge.

That remains as complete a mystery as ever. The earliest structures of the place in about 2200 B.C. were simply a circular bank and ditch, the Heel Stone and the Aubrey Holes, named after John Aubrey who discovered them in the seventeenth century and which have been found to contain cremated human bones, although they do not appear to have been intended as graves. About 500 years later, at least eighty bluestones weighing about 4 tons apiece and thought to come from the Prescelly Mountains in Pembrokeshire, were miraculously transported and set up to form a double circle in the centre of the site with an entrance on the north-east side. At the same time, a kind of avenue was dug leading to this entrance from the bank of the Salisbury Avon, the route by which the stones may have been hauled. This was thought to be the work of the Beaker people, who colonized Britain from the Continent at the end of the Neolithic period and may have introduced the idea of sun or sky worship.

Not long after 1600 B.C. the Bronze Age inhabitants of Wessex were evidently not satisfied with the site and started making radical reconstructions to it. The double circle of bluestones (still unfinished) was dismantled and eighty enormous blocks of sarsen stones, or 'Grey Wethers' as they are called, were dragged from the Marlborough Downs and set up in a lintelled circle and horseshoe of trilithons, while the entrance was marked with two other sarsens, only one of which now remains; this is called, somewhat imaginatively, the Slaughter Stone. The axis of this new monument, like that of the circle it replaced, points towards the midsummer sunrise. It is thought that the master mind behind this work must almost certainly have been a man familiar with the contemporary urban civilizations of the Mediterranean world. Soon after this tremendous accomplishment, some of the discarded bluestones were re-erected to form an inner horseshoe with the others making a smaller circle just inside the sarsen one. The largest bluestone of all, the Altar Stone, which is now fallen, was probably set up as a tall pillar in front of the central sarsen trilithon.

The operative words which keep recurring in any history of Stonehenge are "may have been". No one seems quite certain whether its builders *may have been* sun worshippers or merely wanted at *enormous* expense (at least of effort) to get their calendar straight. When one thinks of all the unsolicited little diaries and calendars that pop through twentieth-century letter-boxes just before Christmas, the idea of moving such weighty stones all those many miles just for this specific purpose would seem to be a little far-fetched in more ways than one, even in 2000 B.C. Moreover, it is commonly believed that on the 21st June the sun rises *immediately* over the Heel Stone to cast its shadow on the Altar Stone. The sun, of course, rises at an angle and when it first appears over the horizon it is appreciably to the left of the Heel Stone; when Stonehenge was built it would have risen even further to the left; it will not rise directly over the Heel Stone for more than 1,000 years by which time many moonrakers will probably be in Mars.

In any illustrated booklet on Stonehenge there are delightful imaginary drawings of hairy little men on flimsy rafts nursing one of the bluestones up the Bristol Channel or round Land's End, all set for the mouths of either the Bristol or Salisbury Avon. Sometimes there are pictures of hundreds of other skin-clad slaves propelling a sarsen stone on a kind of sledge from the Marlborough Downs. Then there are complex little strip cartoons of diminutive figures who must surely be rupturing themselves while hoisting these heavy-weights into position.

To someone like myself who thinks the telephone unbelievable, television a miracle, and going to the moon *truly* 'out of this world', Stonehenge seems a sheer physical impossibility. Driving up from the Wylye Valley in order to take visiting American firemen to look at it, I feel it deserves something more than just the exclamation "Say!" Although I know experiments have been carried out proving that it is possible to manoeuvre these stones by manpower only, no one has actually brought *so many* from *so far*. I still cannot believe that they could have come *all* that way *all* that long time ago. I am almost inclined to side with the old local stone-mason, who vows that Merlin dropped them while flying over these parts, or that perhaps through some extraordinary happening such as an earthquake, for instance, they were thrown up or thrown down at this particular point as nature's gift to Salisbury Plain. But then, I suppose, finding it heavy-going to carry my own suit-case, this is a mere flight of fancy or the lazy way out.

I find it much easier to comprehend Stonehenge's poor relation, Woodhenge, kept in the background until 1925 when Squadron Leader Insall, V.C., noticed a circle with some white chalk marks in the centre as he was flying over a ploughed field 2½ miles north-east of Stonehenge, near Durrington. Having been told that it was only a "mutilated disc barrow" he waited to see what the summer crops would reveal. By then there was no further doubt. Although nothing could be noticed from the ground, yet from up above, several concentric rings of darker patches appeared in the wheat that were later excavated. These turned out to be the traces of wooden posts which had long since disappeared, but the original creation must have been very similar in design to that of its grand neighbour and possibly acted as its prototype. In the centre of the rings in a place corresponding to the Altar Stone at Stonehenge, there was found the skeleton of a small child whose skull had been split before burial, one of the very few pieces of evidence for human sacrifice in prehistoric Britain.

There is perhaps a certain uneasy preoccupation with mortality on the Plain, fostered even today by the presence of the army with its weapons of destruction or defence, call them what you will. The little village of Imber which used to proclaim its whereabouts by the proud but slightly exaggerated Wiltshire couplet:

> Little Imber on the down,
> Seven miles from any town,

ought really to have an epitaph, something such as:

> Little Imber of renown
> Till the army knocked it down.

Today Imber has been blown off the map by the gunners and is nothing more than a ghost village, to which the public is allowed access on certain high days and holidays when no firing is in progress. Shortly after the village was evacuated in 1943, there came into my father's employment a gentle little man who had lived there all his life. He seemed to bring with him a kind of quiet peace acquired by many years of living on the lonely Plain. He was, however, acquainted with motor-cars and used to drive about Salisbury with an unhurried disregard for any traffic lights whatsoever, be they red, green, or amber. He was not colour-blind but simply sailed through the lot with a sublime and touching innocence. Nor do I ever remember him falling foul of the law.

Last September a friend took me to one of the very rare church services that are still held at Imber, mostly for those who once lived there or have relatives buried in the little churchyard. There were about 200 people in this deserted village, folded in one of the dips of the Plain. They came, carrying bunches of flowers which they placed on the graves, eagerly talking to those other evacuees whom they had not seen since a previous pilgrimage perhaps a year or so ago. A local press-photographer bearing the sticker "FOREVER IMBER" on the windscreen of his car, took pictures as they stood about in little clusters of twos and threes chatting to each other. In front of a large tumbledown eyeless house known as Imber Court, there was a group of picnickers, people who looked as if once they might have been eating their meal inside the empty windowless dining-room.

A bristling sergeant-major stood in the centre of the village watching hawk-eyed to see that none of us strayed from the 'straight and narrow' overgrown pathways, his manner somehow aggressively proclaiming the army's occupation as if visitors were only being allowed in on sufferance. On the very first gravestone I came upon by the side of the church were the words:

In affectionate remembrance of
Eliza
The beloved Wife
of
Elijah Matthews
who died
August 27th, 1874 aged 48
The will of the Lord be done

and I realized that here lay the kith or kin of that gentle dignified little man who treated Salisbury streets with the same kind of trust with which he accepted the road through Imber.

After the service in the church, which being on consecrated ground had been spared damage, we took the longer route on the way back and drove towards Warminster with the Plain rolling away all around us and here and there a lone tank dotted on the horizon. About a mile from Imber we picked up a little old lady walking home, who said she always took the opportunity to revisit the place when the army flags and barriers were down because her grandparents were buried there. She was evidently prepared to walk all these miles just to keep in touch with her memories, and when she got out of the car after we finally reached civilization, she summed up the whole atmosphere of the afternoon in four simple words. "You can't buy associations," she said, and as we watched her disappearing along the Warminster streets, we realized just what the army's occupation of Imber really meant to the Wiltshire people who had known and loved it. Some say that Imber may one day be restored and rehabilitated when the army no longer needs it. Certainly many people say that it should be. But it is difficult to imagine a living Imber now. It *is* such miles from anywhere and people, especially women, have become used to shops and transport and playing Bingo. Would there be a special Bingo bus laid on from Imber? It would certainly need a master-mind to reorganize the place so that it was fit for habitation in the 1970s.

In this thickly populated island, the acres we had just driven over were some of the loneliest and loveliest it would be possible to find. It seemed small wonder that our predecessors considered them such a magnificent centre for their strange 'goings-on', when all the lower land around them was forest and swamp. This strangeness remains even today. The little rhyme by Thomas Ingoldsby ending:

> It's a very sad thing to be caught in the rain
> With night coming on upon Salisbury Plain,

still applies. The part totally occupied by the army seems as remote, perhaps, as those far-off days when the giant sarsens were dragged towards Stonehenge.

There are really four categories of land on the Plain, the first three owned by the army. There is the land we had just driven over, which it uses permanently and which is mostly composed of short springy turf abounding in stemless thistles or else former ploughland now covered with a poor sprinkling of grass or lichen. Then there is the land rented to farmers at their own risk, which is subject to sudden tank crossings and manoeuvres; thirdly, land let on the understanding that notice and compensation will be paid should the army wish to use it; and lastly, that which is owned privately by individual farmers in the valleys whose acres stretch up to touch the Plain proper. One such landowner in the Wylye Valley is Lord Hugh Russell, whose downland acres take in the old Iron Age earthwork called Yarnbury Castle. Until about fifty years ago, this was the site of the annual sheep fair which was mentioned by Thomas Hardy in *The Return of the Native* and again by W. H. Hudson in *A Shepherd's Life*.

The fields 'up on top' are often known as 'Bakes', deriving their name from the fact that a long time ago they constituted reclaimed rough land that had been chopped up with the aid of mattocks and the parings burnt. Nevertheless, nowadays modern fertilizers ensure that Bakes produce good crops of barley, and the combine-harvester crawling over the Plain during August and September is quite a usual sight where once there were only sheep to blend in with the 'Grey Wethers' of Stonehenge.

All kinds and ways of life on the Plain seem to have undergone a complete revolution since the War Department purchased its first few acres in 1897. A skylark's paradise has turned into the well-known army stronghold of Larkhill; barracks have appeared at Bulford; Tidworth, on the borders of Hampshire, has produced its famous Tattoo in its gorgeous natural amphitheatre; and now parachutists can be seen floating down near the Army Parachute Centre at Netheravon, while aeroplanes trailing strange appendages fly over all these war-conscious Wiltshire acres. As the shy bustard* disappeared, so the jaunty bus began pushing its way along the Upper Avon and the tiny River Till which joins the Wylye at Stapleford. Right in the heart of the Plain, at Orcheston, lives the son of Mr. Grant, the man who started the first bus service across the Plain. What would this inspired innovator think now if he could see the big green double-decker from Devizes pull up at the village stop with its coloured conductor on board? And

* A recent determined effort is being made to rehabilitate him.

what does the coloured conductor think of his journey through what some writers call the cradle of our civilization?

Certainly nowhere else in England bears such witness to our forefathers. Long before the Romans, Saxons, and Danes arrived in this country, the Plain was peopled by races whose credentials now lie in the museums at Salisbury and Devizes, races who buried their dead together with their weapons and personal nicknacks for use in the hereafter, which eager archaeologists refer to, somewhat indelicately, as grave-goods. Near to Stonehenge is the extraordinary earthwork known as the Cursus, the purpose of which can only be guessed at, but appears to be connected with the cult of the dead owing to the proximity of the long barrow at its eastern end.

But on the whole, the changes wrought on Salisbury Plain during this century have not been for the worse. The bustard may have departed but the stone-curlew survives on the army ranges. The greater part of W. H. Hudson's Downs may have been ploughed, but the remaining regions still support twenty species of orchid and twelve species of blue butterflies and skippers. Although the "happy flying-ground" of the Adonis and Chalk-hill Blue is now restricted, the Wiltshire Trust for Nature Conservation, knowledgeably presided over by the Dowager Countess of Radnor, is tireless in its efforts to protect such precious areas and, fortunately, most flora and fauna seem to flourish alongside the artillery, especially on land where no weed-killers or insecticides have been used. Moreover, over the whole wide undulating expanse of the Plain, a kind of working compromise has been reached between army and agriculture, whereas economically the little communities round about are far better off since the coming of the soldiers and airmen.

Amesbury, if not quite as romantic a place as when the legendary King Arthur roamed these parts, is certainly like a little miniature capital of the Plain proper. The early stories of this town are so bound up with fable that it is perhaps best to leave individuals to interpret them how they will. The place is said to have derived its name from Ambrosius Aurelianus, a Roman–British general and the so-called uncle of this gallant King Arthur who kept persistently appearing all over the countryside to win the most fantastic battles.

Sometime during the sixth century (according to the more fancifully inclined), King Arthur was slain, whereupon his alleged wife, Guinevere, who seems to have somewhat transgressed during his repeated absences, tried to expiate her sins by taking refuge in a hypothetical nunnery at Amesbury, where for the last three years of her life she became its abbess. On her death, her one-time lover, Sir Lancelot, with true knightly chivalry, arrived in time to carry her body safely away from the invading Saxons and bury it with great ceremony at Glastonbury. All mention of this convent over which Guinevere presided then ceased, and it is to be assumed that, if it existed at all, the Saxons, who were pushing their way triumphantly up through Hampshire and Wiltshire, sacked and destroyed it.

Yet its sacred significance seems to have remained. In the year 980, it asserts itself again, this time in a more factual manner, and was refounded by Queen Ethelfrida as a penance for the murder of her stepson, King Edward, to make room for his infant step-brother, known as Ethelred the Unready, whose long reign of unreadiness seems to have been a most unfortunate period for the country.

At the Dissolution of the Monasteries the convent was pulled down by the Duke of Somerset, to whom the grounds were granted, and, in due course, a new mansion designed by Inigo Jones was built, in which the handsome and hospitable Duchess of Queensberry inspired John Gay to write *The Beggar's Opera*. The present Amesbury Abbey was rebuilt in 1840, but a cave in the grounds, where Gay is said to have worked, still remains.

But if Amesbury and all its little satellite towns on the fringes of the Plain now show every outward and visible sign of military activity, the northern side of this army-occupied area is quite, quite different. It is "as different as chalk from cheese", to use that old Wiltshire expression which originated because the chalk countryside raised sheep and corn while farmers in the low northern clay regions concentrated on dairy produce. In fact, the County Council coat of arms, with a bustard proudly forming its crest, also exhibits eight alternating bars of silver (or white) and green on its shield, which is meant to represent the difference between the "chalk and the cheese".

If ever a figure of speech fitted anywhere it befits the little villages between Urchfont and Westbury, so alien from all the rest as they cower under this northern escarpment. It is as though the Plain proper had suddenly been 'brought up short'. There

My father with 'the one that didn't get away' on the River Wylye

seems to be no gradual sloping upwards or downwards. It is 'back of beyond' country with the pre-Roman Ridgeway, Golden Ham and Summer Down, standing guard nearly 800 feet above. It looks like the beginning of 'foreign parts' to southern moon-rakers and gives them a slightly uneasy feeling, as they turn their backs on their native heights and stare a little insecurely across the wide Pewsey Vale, wishing that the high chalky Marlborough Downs beyond it were not quite so far away.

The whole northern edge of the Plain seems determined to spring surprises on these poor souls. Some of them come hesitantly to the tiny village of Urchfont, where, at the Manor, the County Council runs short residential courses for adults. It hardly seems possible that from Friday until Sunday (inclusive) they can attend a course on existentialism, or discuss the historical truth of the Arthurian story.

Some of these moonrakers may be parents of children at Dauntsey's public school for boys, a few miles away at West Lavington. Yet even this stronghold of Victorianism, with its one-time farming bias, now surprises the locals with a broad-minded actor for a headmaster whose cheerful debonair figure, in gay shirt and shorts, must be "as different as chalk from cheese" compared to the orthodox gentleman who dealt so strictly with my own father.

For anyone who wants greater surprise, still farther west there is the enormous church at Edington, beautiful yet out of all proportion to the size of the village. Its original grandeur was due to William of Edington, born about 1300, who became Bishop of Winchester, Chancellor to Edward III and officiated at the marriage of the Black Prince and the Fair Maid of Kent. Despite all these achievements, however, his birthplace was never far from his thoughts, and being passionately interested in architecture he created a kind of miniature cathedral set down in the heart of the Wiltshire countryside.

William appears to have been a somewhat worldly prelate, although his Will is often quoted as being one of the finest examples of splendour, care, and good sense:

And to Robert, my body servant, I give £10, and to John Romsey, my barber, I give £5, and to the boy in the bakery £5, and to Thomas, the carter the elder £10, and Philip and Thomas, who work in the brewhouse £5 each, and to William, the boy who leads the

F

Teffont Evias. The Church and Manor with a tributary of the Nadder running through the park
Sunrise at Stonehenge

first cart £5, and to John, the boy who leads the second cart £5 . . . and if there is any residue, let it be set to the work of perfecting the nave of St. Swithin's Church at Winchester; or let it be given to my House or Chantry at Edington, if it has need, or in other pious works or uses. . . . My soul I leave to Almighty God, my creator; and my body to be buried in my Cathedral at Winchester in the nave at the point where the monks make a halt on Sundays and Feast Days, as they go past in procession or elsewhere in that church, if the prior and my executors should think that more fitting.

Edington church is full of history. The huge yew tree standing guard outside it has probably watched that history unfold since the days when William planned his church as a place of worship both for parishioners and an obscure order of monks called Bonshommes, in whom the Black Prince had become interested. The church is cruciform under a central tower in which are ten bells, a priest's bell and an additional clock bell because Edington possesses one of the oldest working clocks in the country. The whole edifice is elaborate both inside and out, as befits a little cathedral built to act out a kind of dual role. The lofty ceiling of the nave is of pink and white plaster and the comparatively new altar stands in the supposed position of the original parish one. The splendid chancel, which was served by eighteen friars, is entered through a fine double screen and the formidable rails in front of the new altar here probably survive from the reforms of Archbishop Laud in the seventeenth century, who decreed that "dogs and curs be kept from the altar".

It was here at Edington during Jack Cade's rebellion of 1450, that the Bishop of Salisbury, William Ayscough,* took refuge until the angry mob broke in, dragged him from the altar and murdered him on Golden Ham Hill just above the village. Nearly two centuries later, there was a more pleasant occurrence. The Bemerton poet and music-lover, George Herbert, married Jane Danvers in this selfsame church, so that it is perhaps fitting that today Edington has quite a celebrated annual music festival, many of the singers being members of cathedral and collegiate choirs from all over the country.

Edington is especially fortunate in its present vicar. It is he who officiates at the very rare church services at Imber, and many of

* Risings of this kind were frequent in those days, the complaint against Bishop Ayscough being that, as secretary and confessor to Henry VI, he spent too much time at Court.

the furnishings together with the altar and chalice from this deserted village church have now found a home at Edington, where the vicar has carried out a kind of personal crusade to restore the building to much of its former glory. In order to do this he has managed to raise over £35,000 during the past fifteen years and he gives the impression in his quiet way of being more than a match for the death-watch beetle. I am sure William of Edington would be grateful that his original creation is now cherished so well.

But somehow, the overall shadow of the Plain seems to haunt these little villages as they lie linked together by a very minor road. Watchful and sphinx-like, it even begins to look slightly sinister in the twilight as it hugs its secrets to itself. Maybe it is the thought of Bishop Ayscough's ghost way up on Golden Ham; or perhaps it is simply the more friendly one of David Saunders, that humble 'Shepherd of Salisbury Plain', who was buried in West Lavington churchyard at the end of the eighteenth century after years of tending his sheep, fathering sixteen children, and telling everyone that "a laborious life was a happy one, because it exposed a man to fewer sins"; or it could be just the local stories of all the blood which turned the grass red as it ran down the hillside near Edington after King Alfred finally defeated the Danes. But whatever the reason, it is a fanciful time as night comes down on the northern side of the Plain, a time when past history seems to project itself into the twentieth century and makes southern moon-rakers like myself glad to head for home and away from 'foreign parts'.

There is another Wiltshire expression I was brought up with which my father used when anyone had taken the longer and more devious route to get anywhere. "God bless my soul," he would say, "you've been all the way round the world to Warminster." I never understood just why Warminster was singled out for this honour, for its only claim to fame of which I was aware was the fact that its grammar school had once educated the future Dr. Arnold of Rugby. But it struck me while returning from Edington one night that Salisbury Plain could well have seemed like the world to our predecessors, and as I thankfully reached 'my' valley I could not help feeling that although my point of departure and return had not been Warminster, I had, at least, done the 'round trip' that day and "been all the way round the world to Wylye".

VII

THE WOOLLY WILDS OF WESTERN WILTS

HALF-WAY up and just inside Wiltshire's western boundary lies Trowbridge, the present administrative capital of the county. It could be that in years to come this authoritative little place may lose its pre-eminence, if the structure of local government becomes drastically altered. Even today, there always seems to be slight uncertainty as to the county's capital town and when inquirers are told Trowbridge has achieved such an honour, they often say "Why?" and well they might. After all, Salisbury with its unique cathedral is such a splendid focal point; moreover, Swindon is actually the largest town; even Devizes would, at least, be more central; so what exactly is Trowbridge doing with its magnificent County Hall way out in the woolly wilds of Western Wilts?

The County Council, evidently fed up with so much confusion about the matter, has issued special printed details for all interested parties which can be had free for the asking, and perhaps I can do no better than quote from its leaflet verbatim as follows:

> According to the Shorter Oxford English Dictionary a 'county town' is the chief town of a county, formerly called the 'shire town', and a 'shire town' is 'a town which is the capital of a shire or a county', i.e. that place from which the administration of a county is directed. In early times the chief official of a county was a sheriff. In Wiltshire the sheriff's county court (not to be confused with the modern county court) sat at Wilton throughout the Middle Ages until at least as late as the mid-15th century, and the sheriff was custodian of the castle at Old Sarum during the same period. From the 14th century the sheriff's powers declined, and those of the justices of the peace increased, until by the early 19th century the justices were indeed the rulers of the county. It is thus inevitable that

84

Wilton, the Saxon capital of the county, should lose its position. But in Wiltshire the justices had no single meeting place; instead they held their sessions in rotation at Salisbury, Devizes, Warminster and Marlborough. Of these, Salisbury was until the 19th century, the largest and most fashionable town in the county, and in addition, the ecclesiastical centre. After 1834 the Summer Assizes were removed from Salisbury to Devizes, which was already not far behind Salisbury as a place of fashionable resort. By this time it could thus be said that Wiltshire had no single county town and that Salisbury and Devizes were its equal 'capitals'. However, the justices relinquished almost all their administrative powers to the newly-formed County Councils after 1888, and now, since it became the principal seat of county government in the 1890s, Trowbridge can reasonably claim to be the county town of Wiltshire today.

So there it is, all in black and white, straight from the mouth of County Hall itself. Yet there is more to it than just that. For one thing, this still does not explain why Trowbridge became the principal seat of county government in the 1890s, and for this answer we must look for wheels within wheels. The human element seems to have crept in in more ways than one, and the details would perhaps have been too complex for such a flat and factual statement as put out by the County Council.

To understand the situation more fully it is best to look at a map of Wiltshire depicting the railways at that time and to remember that at the end of the nineteenth century most County Councillors would have travelled by train. Owing to that great chalky barrier of the Plain proper, no railway has ever gone up and down the county from north to south. Therefore some top-hatted councillors from Swindon or Salisbury would have found it easier to make the diagonal rail trip to Trowbridge near the western boundary, rather than be horse-drawn to Devizes, although the latter is shorter as the crow flies. It is easy to imagine them, taking out their gold watches from their waistcoat pockets, "tut-tutting" to their wives in some northern, eastern, or southern Wiltshire town, then puffing to the station and twiddling their whiskers with relief as they settled into a first-class carriage all set to arrange the fate of the county.

Before the Second World War, when the motor-car had gained supremacy over the railways, there was more than one heated discussion as to whether Devizes might not come into its own and be a more convenient central capital of Wilts. But perhaps, by then, bureaucracy had dug itself in along with its papers and files and it seemed too much of an undertaking to remove it. Trowbridge, the town which bred the inventor of shorthand, Isaac Pitman, still continued to provide employment for hundreds of secretaries from the surrounding countryside who converged upon it daily, ready to 'take a letter' on moonrakers' sewerage schemes or the shocking state of the road through the Wylye Valley.

In 1937, a brand new County Hall was erected at Trowbridge. It houses, among other things, a very helpful custodian, an array of gorgeous gaily coloured maps of Wiltshire, all the county records, and some extremely knowledgeable archivists. On stepping inside the entrance hall the custodian seems to appear from nowhere and asks you where you want to go. Now I find this encouraging. He does not just sit at his desk and wait for you to come to him. I feel this gives the county a good image for a start. It distresses me to think that the administration of Wiltshire may one day be carried on from an alien and far more remote region. Bureaucratic or not, the official form-devouring place where today's driving licences are sent to be renewed, suddenly comes to life and seems quite human after all. Its custodian will tell you that if you want to look at the county archives you must go down a long passage and climb to the top of the building where, sure enough, the archivists are waiting to welcome you with Wiltshire at their finger-tips.

I have never come across many archivists before, let alone a young female one who seems to be able to answer any question without looking up the book. If you ask her, "Why did those Grey Friars at Salisbury call their Priory by such an extraordinary name as 'Bugmore'?" she will come straight back at you without batting an eyelid and say, "It was derived from 'bugge' which meant 'hobgoblin', and 'mor' meaning 'marsh', which, when you come to think of it, was just what that area used to be." If you say, "Can you please tell me anything about the woollen cloth trade at Trowbridge when my great great grandmother used to live here?" she will take you gently to the window and say, "You see that house over there, the one with the larger windows on the top floor? That was a weaver's house because the upstair windows were always bigger in order to let in the maximum light for the loom."

It feels a little lonely going out into Trowbridge after the friendliness of County Hall. It is necessary to take a deep breath before plunging into the town proper, but this is because Trowbridge is a town of smells, not by any means bad ones, but smells nevertheless.

First of all there are two quite unmistakable ones depending on where anyone happens to be; one comes from live pig and the other from processed pig, when the latter has been converted into the mouth-watering form of hot sausage-rolls and meat pies sold in local delicatessens. Under methods of strictest hygiene, the famous firm of Bowyers turn their fat pink inputs into fine fresh outputs, to be whisked away by trunker vehicles rumbling through the Wiltshire countryside at night, in order that their precious contents are available in tip-top condition for some distant housewife to buy in the shops the following morning.

Then in certain Trowbridge streets there is that curious smell which is hard to describe but takes me back about forty years to the Felt Mills at Wilton. It is a kind of 'wet-woollen-clothes-hanging-up-indoors-to-dry' smell, but this time it comes from Salters' Cloth Factory. Inside this building Mr. Ponting, who has written a charming little book on the history of the West of England cloth trade, will tell you just why Trowbridge and Bradford-on-Avon in Wiltshire lost the race to that other Bradford in Yorkshire in the middle of the last century. Contrary to popular belief, it seems to have had little to do with lack of capital, new machinery, coal, or sheep. It had much more to do with the indefinable human element resulting in those curious unstable factors, one called 'snobbery' and the other called 'demand'.

It seems to me that the West of England clothiers must have been snobs. Yorkshire ones did not mind going in for a cheaper type of cloth required by the increasing growth of the so-called working classes. But the idea of making cheaper cloth seemed abhorrent to the West Country mill owners. They clung to their long tradition of fine woollens. After 1850, they suffered another blow when the fickle well-to-do public suddenly turned to wearing rep and other fabrics instead of broadcloth. Then long merino wool arrived from Australia and helped establish botany worsteds. Here again, the long arm of tradition held out against re-equipping the West of England mills with worsted machinery.

So the South-west remained specialist country. It never went in for anything so low as shoddy.* Recently the swing of the capricious fashion pendulum has raised the demand for better-class woollens, especially in the ladies' trade, so it is possible that things are looking up for the clothiers in the West Country. Certainly, Salters', Clarks', and McCall Brothers give every appearance of booming. Salters' actually blooms as well with roses growing outside one of the entrances, which seems a nice touch and reminds me even more of my maternal grandmother and the Felt Mills at Wilton.

Another distinct smell in Trowbridge is that of malt and hops because the town is the home of Ushers Brewery, now attached to one of the largest brewing concerns in the U.K., the Watney Mann Group. This delightful aroma comes at you in whiffs as you round corners or pass dark-looking doors where the merry-making liquid is brewing up.

There are many less pungent industries in Trowbridge that go in for making valves, mattresses, egg-handling equipment, steel fittings, heating apparatus, and dairy products, but somehow the ones with a scent attached to them seem to add spice to the capital which, together with County Hall, seems such a typically Wiltshire town.

Less than 3 miles away and practically into Somerset, Bradford-on-Avon is as different from Trowbridge as the expressive "chalk from cheese". Suddenly it does not seem to be Wiltshire any more. The river which runs through the town must not be confused with the Salisbury one. This Avon rises near the north-western borders of the county and flows out into the Bristol Channel. The town of Bradford rises so steeply from its northern banks that it almost seems as if the highest houses are going to tumble down over the others into the water.

It must have been when he was standing on the top of this hill that Canon Jones, the Vicar of Bradford in 1858, meditating perhaps on such a glorious view, lingered long enough to detect in the hotch-potch of roofs below him, the outline of what seemed like a little church. Hot-foot, he must have gone hurriedly down to his own great parish church in search of records. Studying the writings of a chronicler of the twelfth century, William of Malmesbury, he found reference to a mission church at Bradford in

* Shoddy is the Yorkshire term for soft rags torn up and respun.

the name of the Blessed St. Laurence, founded by St. Aldhelm, the Abbot of Malmesbury, who died in A.D. 709.

In the twelve years that followed the Canon's discovery, the purest Saxon church in England was rescued from the misappropriation it had undergone for hundreds of years. At one time or another it had housed bones from the nearby churchyard, turned itself into a charity school, then living accommodation and almost, except for the keen eyes of Canon Jones, become lost for ever. Recent authorities have established that its original plan and ground-stage date from St. Aldhelm's time, but a building of stone probably replaced an original wooden structure sometime during the tenth century. Today it stands resurrected in all its simple beauty. It is as high as it is long and twice as high as it is wide. In the nave are fragments of stone that might have been worked on before this country was one nation. It is impossible not to go there and feel a sense of wonder and also gratitude for the perspicacity of a nineteenth-century Canon.

It seems that the busier Bradford became in the Middle Ages, the less careful it was over its antiquities. The curious little stone building on the bridge over the Avon, although once a chapel, was for years used as the town lock-up. High on the hill where Canon Jones must have been standing is another little chapel of St. Mary, which also in its time was used as a cloth factory and allowed to fall into ruins until 1930 when it was carefully restored. At the end of the eighteenth century there were thirty-two of these factories in Bradford. Today there are none. Cloth manufacturing has given way to the divers creations of the Avon Rubber Company, the manufacture of tennis balls, the production of sports cars, and the curiosity of sight-seers.

Because Bradford *is* a sight worth seeing. To me, although alien and unlike a typical Wiltshire town, I have to confess that the Bath/Badminton/Cotswold infiltration into the present county boundary is attractive. Initially, this particular area was honeycombed with quarries providing honey-coloured stone for building. Bradford has one of the loveliest mellowed old tithe barns in the country, besides a magnificent hall built by the namesake of the Salisbury gentleman who haunted my childhood. 'John Hall(e)s' seemed to abound in days gone by and the Bradford one was no exception when it came to wealth. His one-time home still stands out above all others, an Elizabethan hall built by a highly prosperous clothier. This kind of factor greatly impressed Defoe when he visited the area more than 100 years later. With his keen eye for observing the ups and downs in the social hierarchy, he described such individuals as having "from ten to forty thousand pounds a man", and went on to say that "many of the great families . . . have been originally raised from and built up by this truly noble manufacture".

The affluence of these West of England specialists (firmly established in Wiltshire since the first importation of Flemish weavers by Edward III)★ is still highly apparent in this part of the county, not only in the survival of their splendid old houses, but also in the form of the many places of worship which they founded. The Church of St. Mary, at Steeple Ashton, is a particularly fine example of a "cloth" church that owes its beauty to the fifteenth- and sixteenth-century entrepreneurs of the woollen industry.

There was one such gentleman, a certain Paul Methwin (albeit a descendant of the ancient and noble family of Methven), whom John Aubrey referred to as "the greatest clothier of all time". In 1745 one of this famous cloth-maker's own descendants, another Paul Methuen (as the name was now spelt), purchased Corsham House and its estates, prompted by a desire to secure a home for a collection of pictures and *objets d'art* which he was destined to inherit on the death of his cousin and godfather, Sir Paul Methuen. Somewhat surprisingly, that great landscape gardener, Capability Brown, was entrusted not only to enlarge and beautify the grounds but also to do the same for the house itself, and the plans submitted by Henry Keene (who happened to be working on the nearby estate of Bowood at the same time) were rejected.

Since that era, a series of architects have had a hand in remodelling Corsham Court, and this has resulted today in an impressive grey stone mansion standing with great dignity, in a most unusual and picturesque setting. Among the features of the grounds there is an enormous ornamental plane tree, with a perimeter of 200 yards, planted by 'Capability' in 1760; he was also responsible for a delightful little Gothic 'Bath House', no doubt inspired by the famous Dr. Oliver who advocated the 'cold plunge'. About three years ago, this small building acquired an addition in the form of the Bradford Porch, with a fine barrel-vaulted ceiling dating from

★ The industry received fresh impetus from Paul Methwin's second importation of Flemings in the seventeenth century.

1475, which once formed part of a house known as The Priory in Bradford, belonging to one of the family's ancestors. Today, inside Corsham Court itself, the present Lord Methuen, who is an exceptionally talented artist in his own right, may be found taking an active interest in his magnificent collection of pictures, which is open to the public, while his house also provides a home for the Bath Academy of Art.

As for the village of Corsham, it would appear that the central core of the place is made of stone, stone, and all stone. It has somewhat swelled in size since I was stationed there during the last war, and the more permanent Service Establishments now in the vicinity make it a very different place from what it must have been like much longer ago, when the local inhabitants sat diligently working in their little stone cottages, helping to build up the wealth of the 'John Halls' of Bradford and Trowbridge. Even the famous 'Methuen Arms' (where Prince Philip used to play skittles when also stationed near by) seems nowadays much more 'on the map' when compared to its remote appearance in those chilly early mornings when I rode by on a bicycle, after the terrifying task of asking hundreds of breakfasting A.T.S. whether any of them had "Any complaints?" It was difficult to appreciate the beauties of Corsham when overburdened with the problems of cold porridge and stewed tea, or the prospect of chaperoning a lorry-load of girls to Trowbridge that same evening to one of the dances arranged for the purpose of keeping up the troops' morale.

It seems today as if all the towns and villages in these parts that were once woven into a common bond by 'wool', are now individuals in their own right. From as far south as Warminster, northwards through Westbury, past Trowbridge and Bradford to Melksham and Chippenham, each community has branched out on distinctly personal lines. Warminster is now the headquarters of 'Lion Country', the School of Infantry and Unidentified Flying Objects, which have been the subject of a whole book written by the features' editor of the *Warminster Journal*, Arthur Shuttlewood, and entitled *The Warminster Mystery*. A strange 'thing' is constantly being seen hovering in the vicinity of Cradle Hill, and although I, myself, am sceptical, I still keep a hopeful eye open when passing at the most propitious time of night. After all, moonraking Wilts has a definite link-up with outer space today and apparently no town in England or, for that matter, in the world has registered so many authentic reports of U.F.O.s since Christmas 1964.

Westbury was described by Cobbett as "a really rotten place" having "cloth factories in it . . . ready to tumble down". In fact, he added insult to injury by concluding it was a "miserable hole". Although the town is not particularly endeared to me, I am fond of its old white horse up on Bratton Down; and its extensive sheets of water are almost the only reminder of Wiltshire's few mineral undertakings as they cover submerged open-cast iron-ore workings; certainly the place today deserves a better description than Cobbett's derisive account. This is evident by the fact that the area round about Westbury and Warminster is becoming more and more fashionably residential. There is a large placard outside one nearby building estate announcing the erection of "Gentlemen's Residences" as if they were some kind of relish, although this would most likely have enraged the radically minded Cobbett still further and certainly hardly seems in keeping with the twentieth century.

Melksham has become, with the exception of Swindon, the most industrialized town in the county. As might be expected, it is, in consequence, not particularly attractive. Melksham seems earnest and full of factories. It is curious how the Cotswold influence seems so completely lacking here, whereas at Lacock, only a few miles away, it is present in superabundance. Melksham seems to boom without blooming. But although urban to a degree, it does have the saving grace of being the headquarters of the 'Wiltshire Farmers', a large thriving co-operative concern which gives the place a rural stamp as opposed to the Avon rubber one from the huge factory next door to it. Every month, members of Wiltshire Farmers meet at Melksham to discuss, among other things, "vertical integration", "the outlook for wool", and that curiously worded subject (especially for townsmen) called "cleaning and dressing for farmers".

Chippenham, on the other hand, is more interesting altogether because, despite the fact that modern developments have overshadowed much of its historical past, they have not been able to efface the memory of a certain philanthropic lady of the fifteenth century called Maud Heath. Maud gave Wiltshire moonrakers the best 4-mile path in the country. It is known to everyone round about as Maud Heath's Causeway and she certainly had cause to build it. She is said to have been a market woman of Langley Burrell, a little village just north-east of Chippenham, to which she walked regularly each week, getting her feet well and truly soaked in the often-flooded valley of the Bristol Avon. When she died she left property to the value of £8 per year to maintain a footpath between Wick Hill and Chippenham Clift. On a height overlooking her Causeway she herself stands immortalized in stone with her basket and staff, under which is written: "Erected at the joint expense of Henry Marquis of Lansdowne, Lord of the Manor, and Wm. L. Bowles, vicar of the parish of Bremhill, trustees 1838.

> Thou who dost pause on this aerial height
> Where Maud Heath's Pathway winds in shade or light
> Christian wayfarer in a world of strife
> Be still and ponder on the Path of Life.
>
> W.L.B."

Slightly more cryptic but equally expressive are little couplets written in stone at each end of the Causeway, one saying:

> From this Wick Hill begins the praise
> Of Maud Heath's gifts to these highways

and the other:

> Hither extendeth Maud Heath's gift
> For where I stand is Chippenham Clift.

Alfred the Great is said to have bequeathed Chippenham to his daughter Elfrida and it is mentioned in Domesday Book as one of the manors held by St. Edward. At that time the place boasted twelve mills, and later, when the Great Western Railway awakened the town, its cloth and iron foundries were famous throughout England. But as with the fate of all the many other places in the wilds of Western Wilts, the wool trade declined and nowadays the Westinghouse Brake Company is the chief contributory factor that has industrialized Chippenham.

One little place that has had a more unique experience than any of the others in these parts is the village of Castle Combe, back in the Cotswold area again. In fact, it is only just recovering from the impact of the film world and Dr. Doolittle. About three years ago this pretty miniature Bradford suffered an invasion perhaps equal to that of Saxon or Danes in intensity if not in destruction. Castle Combe made the headlines; the village was news. A little jetty was built on the banks of the By Brook, a quiet little tributary of the Avon, to make the town into a seaport. Unsightly television aerials were removed from the cottage roofs and permanently replaced by shared invisible wiring. Local inhabitants became 'extras' at 50s. per day, with meals, alcohol, and clothes all thrown in.

One old moonraker now spends his time sitting in the sun by the Market Cross in the centre of the village and reflecting on his début into such a fantastic world. He will tell you that every morning he was made up by a "gang o' them girls". He then sucks his pipe and chuckles to himself. The recollection is evidently quite a pleasant one. For forty-five years he used to be a farm bailiff but the so-called 'evening of his life' had now been spent alongside Rex Harrison, Anthony Newley, and Samantha Eggar.

If a film producer had discovered him earlier, it is likely he might have been a star himself. He is a 'natural', as they say. "Tell 'ee wot," he adds, as he gets up to toddle off to the pub, "zome o' them vilm volk, they be all right, *out*." He lays great emphasis on the last word. If pressed a little further, he shakes his head and mutters mysteriously, "I got inside information, zno." Then with a broad grin the star of Castle Combe makes a superb exit from the scene; or "Cut," as the director would have said.

VIII

THE DIVIDING LINE OR JIMMY KIRBY'S 'KLIT'

"Don't dudder me. Cassen thee see I be in Jimmy Kirby's klit?" When I was a child this was an expression sometimes used by a hard-working volatile matron who came to help out during domestic crises. I knew perfectly well what she meant, because 'dudder' was the Wiltshire word for 'confuse', and my maternal grandmother talked about a 'klit' when she wanted to describe some kind of muddle or predicament. Therefore, in effect, what our drowner's* wife was saying was, "For goodness sake, get out of my way. Can't you see I've got enough on my plate already?"

Jimmy Kirby, however, was a little more tricky. I was never quite sure exactly who he was, although it seemed almost certain that he was a Wiltonian, as I knew this venerable lady had hardly stepped outside her home town during her life. I felt Jimmy was probably one of her deceased relatives as he never seemed to appear in the flesh; but it was obvious he was a person for ever in some sort of dilemma and therefore someone with whom I shared a fellow-feeling, so that I always regretted we never actually met up. To this day, I still think of him with affection, and throughout my life whenever I have been particularly

---

* The 'drowner' was the man who looked after the water-meadows, until the cost of labour prohibited such a whole-time luxury and the coming of artificial fertilizers ensured an 'early bite' of grass for the cattle on higher ground, thereby dispensing with the need for such careful irrigation in the valleys. According to John Aubrey, the improvement of watering meadows began at Wylye in 1635, but the greatest innovator of such methods was Squire Baverstock of Stockton, around 1700.

harassed and have perhaps found myself staring at the previous evening's washing-up, with today's milk boiling over on the stove, a baby crying, and the postman knocking on the front door, I have always felt Jimmy Kirby to be right there beside me, and that we were both in the most confounded 'klit'.

He popped into my mind again as I started this chapter because I knew I was getting on for 'foreign parts' and I was not sure which to tackle first. Lacock and Lackham should really come next, as they would automatically have been included in the 'Woolly Wilds', but for the fact that they seemed to deserve a special chapter to themselves. On the other hand, in daring to trespass as far north as Castle Combe, I am well aware I have already gone a long way 'over the water', meaning that I have bridged the Kennet and Avon Canal which cuts Wiltshire roughly in half. Therefore, after much time spent cogitating in Jimmy Kirby's klit, I decided to retrace my steps and concentrate on the semi-derelict waterway that must once have been the pride of the county.

The creator of this canal was the famous John Rennie, and the Act authorizing its construction was passed in 1794. As its name implies, it links the River Kennet at Newbury in Berkshire to the Bristol Avon at Bath in Somerset. In the early nineteenth century its barges were carrying grain, timber, Bath building stone, and Somerset coal. The Kennet and Avon was a smooth and splendid going-concern or, to use another Wiltshire expression, running "suent-like".

'Railway mania', however, which swept the country and overtook 'canal mania' in the middle of the nineteenth century, soon put a stop to all this. When the powers-that-be in the Kennet and Avon Company realized their profits were going down and tried to recoup by threatening to build a railway along the canal's course, the up-and-coming Great Western simply bought them out and constructed their own railroad across the centre of Wiltshire, which is now part of the main line from Paddington to the West Country. Canal and railway still enter the county's eastern border side by side near Little Bedwyn, skirt south of Savernake Forest, then diverge in the Pewsey Vale so that the waterway is some 3 miles north of the railway as they near Devizes. At one time, both used to continue in a kind of uneasy peace as they journeyed along towards Limpley Stoke and Somerset, but only

Cold pasture for spring lambs on Pewsey Down
Mock battle at the deserted village of Imber on Salisbury Plain

the railway's southerly branch to Westbury now remains open.

Today, the canal is the problem child of the British Waterways Board but also the much-loved baby of the Kennet and Avon Trust, a voluntary non-profit-making organization whose members seem to spend all their spare time devoting themselves to its well-being. An energetic and enthusiastic Junior Division of the Trust work really hard at what appears to be the almost impossible task of repair and maintenance of this route which is now the haunt of wild-life, anglers, and people who just want to get-away-from-it-all. Canal-lovers are a race apart; they are not like car-tuners or even sailing enthusiasts. They have that creditable and exceptionally rare desire for peace and slow-motion. General Stockwell, who lives right beside the canal at Horton, is chairman of the Trust, and if unable to escort you down the canal himself, will go out of his way to put you in touch with someone who can.

It was my good fortune to be taken down the Kennet and Avon in the company of Mr. and Mrs. Bob Dunsdon from Swindon, their baby Lucy, a young journalist, and one of the Trust's public relations officers. One bright October afternoon, I arrived at the French Horn Inn by Pewsey Wharf, which is about a mile from where the statue of King Alfred guards the little town of Pewsey itself, or 'Pefesigge' as it was called in his day. On the banks of the canal were schoolmasters and boys who had just arrived in a van marked "Marlborough College Outdoor Activities" and who intended to spend a Wednesday afternoon helping to clear some of the weed from the water. They gave us a hilarious send-off as the *Charlotte Dundas* (a paddle-boat converted from a pontoon once used behind a dredger) edged slowly away into mid-stream. Mr. Dunsdon took the tiller; the public relations officer took a photograph (before nimbly taking a flying leap on board); the journalist took out his note-book; Mrs. Dunsdon turned round to take a look at the Marlborough Downs and Lucy promptly took a header into the bottom of the boat.

But it seems canal-lovers can take this sort of thing in their stride. Having comforted Lucy, we all sat down, the P.R.O. started telling me all there was to know about the Kennet and Avon, and the *Charlotte Dundas* ploughed ahead through water

G

Saxon Church at Bradford-on-Avon

that looked like pea-green soup, with a lavish sprinkling of sorrel on top, working up to the dashing speed of three knots.

As we passed under various little hump-backed bridges, small boys clambered on to parapets to cheer us on. A family of swans with mother leading and father bringing up the rear, eyed us suspiciously as we glided by; dab-chicks dived and disappeared into what looked just like a flat green pathway, so thickly covered with duck-weed was the stagnant water ahead of us; an old man with a dog stood on the towpath grinning broadly; and the wide flat Pewsey Vale, half hidden by huge elm trees, stretched away on either side of us with here and there an occasional glimpse of the Marlborough Downs to the north and the escarpment of Salisbury Plain to the south.

We tied up for a while at Lady Bridge, a superior and fanciful construction which is crossed by a farm track where the canal runs between Pickéd Hill and Swanborough Tump, the latter being, as might be expected, a hump or barrow, but having the distinctive reputation as the place where King Alfred made his Will. It appears that, in planning the canal, the engineer found it necessary to make it run through the grounds of Wilcot Manor which displeased the lady therein. Eventually she granted wayleave, but only on condition that a bridge, now known as Lady Bridge, was specially designed and the canal made wider along the edge of her park to resemble ornamental water.

I was sorry that we had to turn back here. The canal had a wonderfully soporific effect. Lucy was asleep and it would have been pleasant to sail on westwards towards Devizes, but the sun was getting low and at the speed we had been going it would obviously be quite late enough when we tied up again at Pewsey Wharf.

On the way back, I wondered what John Rennie would have thought if he could have seen us on this backwater. How could he have guessed when he planned his staircase of twenty-nine locks at Caen Hill west of Devizes, which has been called one of the seven wonders of the waterways, that in 1969 it would lie abandoned and impassable and all-but-forgotten, save for the members of the Kennet and Avon Trust? What would he feel if he knew that his canal, that was once carrying 20 barges of 60-ton capacity, was now only frequented by boats such as the *Charlotte Dundas*, or canoes paddled by enthusiasts who raced from Devizes to Westminster during the Easter holiday each year? For a man who reckoned he was helping to advance the economic life of the country in a big way, surely he could only but be saddened by the quiescence of his original creation?

His efforts must have been so fraught with difficulties, and those navigators (or navvies, as they were known) who carried out all the spade work must surely have led rather desperate lives. In his book, *The Kennet and Avon Canal*, Kenneth Clew quotes: "The life of a canal labourer was very hard, though compassion was shown to one such person who had his leg broken by a fall of earth. The committee directed that he should receive proper care and attention at their expense and that he be given the sum of five guineas 'as an act of charity', but this was not to be regarded as a precedent."

When the canal was finally opened on 31st December 1810, no great celebration took place as it was considered that too much money had been spent on it already; and now today, here it was, a lonely stagnant victim of, firstly, Brunel's straight metal tracks carrying steam-propelled trucks, and, secondly, tarmacadam roadways which later were to bear those vehicles which cause so much concern both to the present public and Minister of Transport alike. Somehow, as I waved good-bye to my kindly escorts, even though I had enjoyed my afternoon enormously, I could not help but feel sorry that in this broad Vale of Pewsey, with its great reputation for good farming and high yields, the Kennet and Avon Canal was not running just a bit more "suent-like".

Many people think that because the Vale is so named there ought to be a River Pewsey meandering along somewhere, but this is not so. The Vale is really a large hanging or downland valley which is set up about 300 feet above sea level at its lowest point. A long, long time ago it was a chalky arch or anticline linking the Marlborough Downs to Salisbury Plain; but then one day it simply started to split. Rain, frost, and the action of running streams eroded the chalk to leave this fertile bed of greensand underlaid by Gault clay. The headwaters of the Salisbury Avon which rise under the Marlborough Downs and converge just east of Rushall at Scales Bridge, managed to find a weakness in the hard core of the Plain proper through which they plunged southward in a united journey towards Salisbury and the sea.

To the uninitiated, it is perhaps surprising that the drainage of the Vale is all inward towards this unexpected breach and that no river flows westward to drop down and link up with the Bristol Avon. Except for Etchilhampton Hill, standing isolated at about 600 feet just east of Devizes, there seems little to stop the mainsprings of the Salisbury Avon making an exit in this direction as if it might have been the most natural thing to do. But nature apparently left it to John Rennie to achieve the only waterway connecting the Vale to the western part of the county. I am told by Mr. Sandell, the Honorary Librarian of the Wilts Archaeological Society—who seems to know all about Wiltshire since 140 million years ago when it was underneath the sea—that the lowlands surrounding the Bristol Avon are gradually extending eastwards towards the Pewsey Vale so that eventually some of the streams therein will actually be diverted towards them, and that the waters of the Salisbury Avon will suffer in consequence. But fortunately, perhaps, this occurrence is a long time hence and something which neither Mr. Sandell nor myself will ever witness.

The great guardians of the Pewsey Vale, those high downs that surround it on three sides and from which Cobbett first looked down on his "land of promise", seem to protect the whole area with an invincibility. From Tan Hill, which towers nearly 1,000 feet on the northern side, it is possible on a clear day to look southwards across the Vale and Salisbury Plain to that focal point of Wiltshire, the spire of the Cathedral, a slender ephemeral landmark yet somehow very definitely 'there' as it points heavenwards 25 miles away. Behind one, the strange man-made Wansdyke traverses the Marlborough Downs, its origins only to be guessed at by present-day archaeologists and historians. Wansdyke is a huge enigmatic ditch and bank constructed sometime after the Romans left this country by people who left no clue as to their actions. That it was some kind of boundary or defence, created by slave labour against early Saxon invasions, seems likely; but just exactly when and by whom and for what is still a matter of conjecture. Eleven barely interrupted miles of it lie there still, all along Morgan's Hill, Tan Hill, Milk Hill, and on towards Savernake Forest, a surviving relic of almost another world and certainly another way of life.

Tan Hill nowadays makes itself inviolate in a more simple fashion by a notice forbidding motor vehicles and allowing only the Wansdyke and sheep to share its solitude. Majestically, it thrusts out a shoulder into the Pewsey Vale rather like the promontory of a high cliff, except there is only a fertile sea of flat arable land beneath which curves inwards to make sheltered bays all along the line. Close to the western side of this lowland, where it drops down 150 feet into the valley of the Bristol Avon, stands the most central market town in the whole of Wiltshire, appropriately called Devizes. It is thought that the name stems from the Latin *ad divisas* which means 'at the boundaries' because it grew from a point where the manors of Rowde, Cannings, and Potterne once met.

Devizes is in the very heart of moonraker country. It is solid and unpretentious, somehow managing to give the impression of strength yet modesty, which might account in a small way for it having been 'pipped at the post' in the 1930s as the administrative capital of the county. It has qualities that are not apparent at first sight and certainly none which it would ever boast about, except perhaps the assertion by the locals in 'The Moonrakers' that the pond where those original moonrakers successfully foiled the excisemen is the one they call the Crammer, now well within the town's boundaries. It is only natural that people in these parts take a more than personal pride in native wits and the name 'Moonraker' has been adopted not only by inns, but also by houses and the one-time Wiltshire Regiment, which had its headquarters at Le Marchant Barracks on the outskirts of the town. This was well known as the 'Moonrakers', although sadly nowadays the title no longer applies, for the Wiltshire and Berkshire regiments have amalgamated and are known as the Duke of Edinburgh's Royal Regiment.

Devizes is one of the oldest boroughs in Wiltshire and probably owes its very existence to the wooden castle erected by Bishop Osmund about 1080, although this was destroyed by fire shortly afterwards and had to be rebuilt by Bishop Roger. When the Plantagenets succeeded the Normans it became a fashionable royal country seat; but by the sixteenth century it was again in ruins until the Civil War led to its refortification, owing to the fact that Devizes was a strategic point between the King's headquarters at Oxford and his adherents in the West Country. When the Parliamentary forces laid siege to it, the fortress was relieved by a great Royalist victory on Roundway Down just to the north

of the town, yet only two years later Cromwell successfully
bombarded the stronghold and razed it to the ground.

The present castle dates only from the last century, although
the moat, mound, and remains of the dungeons are still reminders
of former strife. Today this impressive monument has been
turned into flats and the only barricades against intruders are
'Keep Out' notices and some rather fierce-looking goats grazing
round the moat. Devizes has settled down into a most excellent
and law-abiding place; it is the headquarters of the County Police
Force with that much-respected individual, the Chief Constable,
living only a little distance away. Wiltshire has the oldest County
Police Force in the country, and sometimes there are enough
policemen in Devizes to "dudder volks". Members of the Force
may be found pacing the streets with disconcerting walkie-talkie
attachments crackling away on their persons, giving unintelligible
instructions, like the sort of voices from outer space heard in
London taxi-cabs, so that people asking the way in Devizes are
afraid they may be hindering the law from getting to the scene
of the crime. Then there are off-duty policemen leading beautiful
intelligent-looking police dogs about, and plain-clothes policemen
looking just like other moonrakers except that they have been
giving evidence at the rather splendid Assize Courts that were
built by T. H. Wyatt.

I once went to the assizes at Devizes. I know this sounds as silly
as saying I was once caught by the "rain in Spain", but it happens
to be a simple statement of fact. I sat in the public gallery and
watched justice being done. From the caustic way in which the
judge dressed down the defending counsel, I had a feeling that
the prisoner in the dock was not going to get off lightly. Eventually the words "Four years imprisonment" were rapped out, His
Honour reached for a glass of cold water, we all stood up, a
prayer was said, the convicted man together with his escort
disappeared into the bowels of the court-room, and we luckier
ones escaped into the sunshine and the encouraging smell coming
from Wadworth's of Northgate Street, yet another enormous
Wiltshire brewery.

As I walked back to the market-place I could not help thinking
about another miscreant who had been dealt with in this very
spot on 25th January 1753, one whose record is engraved on the
Market Cross for all to read. Her name was Ruth Pierce and

together with two other women she had agreed to purchase a sack of corn. When the time came for paying, Ruth was accused of not contributing her full share, but she protested vigorously saying that she "wished she might drop dead if she had not". Whereupon, at that instant, Ruth Pierce passed from this life with the money still concealed in her hand. The Coroner's jury (or Crowner's as they say in these parts) brought in a verdict that she "had been struck dead with a lie in her mouth".

Justice certainly seems to have been meted out by the hand of Fate with more than unusual frequency in or around this little town. Not far away, where the road from the Plain approaches West Lavington, there is a large stone commemorating the adventures of brave Mr. Dean, a farmer from Imber who was attacked by four highwaymen during the last century, when he was returning home from Devizes on market-day with the wages for his men. After a spirited pursuit, one of the felons fell dead on Chitterne Down and the other three were caught, later to be tried at Devizes Quarter Sessions and sentenced to transportation for a term of fifteen years. The memorial was put up "as a warning to those who presumptuously think to escape the punishment God has threatened against Thieves and Robbers".

Another singular form of retribution is recorded outside the lovely old Church of St. John at Devizes, which might well make today's young people pause for a moment and think. It is connected with the unpardonable sin committed by some of their contemporaries in former times who set out to enjoy themselves on the Sabbath. On a strange-looking edifice in the churchyard the following words have been written:

> In memory of the sudden and awful end of Robert Merrit and Susannah, his wife, Eliza Tiley her sister, Martha Carter and Josiah Dereham, who were all drowned in the flower of their youth in a Pond near this town called Drews, on Sunday evening, the 30th June, 1751, and are together, underneath entombed.

> Remember the Sabbath Day to keep it holy.

> This monument, as a solemn Monitor to young people to remember their Creator in the days of their youth, was erected by subscription.

It evidently pays to watch one's steps in Devizes.

But as long as one does, those steps must sooner or later be directed towards the Museum, because it is here where this ancient borough hoards a most splendid collection of treasures and grave-goods. On a recent occasion when I was lucky enough to be shown them by Mr. Sandell personally, they were no longer simply bits of jaw-bone or tooth-picks from another era. They became invested with personality, as it were. Suddenly, it was possible to get a glimpse of those Beaker people and Windmill Hill types going about their curious prehistoric methods of survival. The mysterious downs around Devizes and the Pewsey Vale took on a new dimension. 'They' were actually up there once upon a time, those funny little men with odd-shaped skulls, and then their descendants who scratched a living by various means of cultivation which sometimes resulted in those steplike formations on the sides of hills that we call 'lynchets', where these agrarian ancestors of ours ploughed their long and lonely furrows.

Wiltshire's past and present seemed to link up under Mr. Sandell's expert guidance, especially when he enlarged on a beautiful bumpy relief model of the whole county, all brightly coloured to show where the different deposits of soil and rock formations begin and end. I was proud to think that my native chalk took up about two-thirds of it, but those 'unknown quantities' in the north-west where upper, middle, and lower oolite form part of what is known as the Jurassic System and where local farmers talk knowledgeably about the productiveness of 'cornbrash' areas, suddenly opened up and became less strange and complicated. It was as if 'foreign parts', properly explained by Mr. Sandell, had moved a little nearer home.

I thought about this after my visit when I sat drinking my tea at an upstairs window overlooking Devizes market-square, and it gave me quite a comforting feeling. Here I was, very much a southern moonraker sitting in the middle of my county, but the northern part was now making advances in a most amicable way. Opposite me, the statue of the goddess, Ceres, stood proudly on top of the old Corn Exchange and it somehow seemed fitting that this little central town was Wiltshire's headquarters for the National Farmers' Union, as well as the Women's Institute. From where I was sitting I could see the Bear Hotel, an old coaching inn where the landlord once set up posts at half-mile intervals to guide travellers across the lonely Plain, each landmark having an

S for Salisbury on one side and a *D* for Devizes on the other. I pictured one of his sixteen children who, at the age of 5, was amusing the Lord Chief Justice and other patrons of 'The Bear' with his little sketches of them all. It must have been good practice for the man who was to become Sir Thomas Lawrence, one of England's greatest portrait painters.

Lastly, I looked down on the Market Cross and the fountain, the former a gift from a Prime Minister in Nelson's day, Henry Addington, who was also at one time the town's Recorder and Member of Parliament; the latter, an edifice erected to the memory of Mr. Sotheron Estcourt, M.P., founder of the Wiltshire Friendly Society.

It seemed to me that here in the heart of moonraking Wilts today, there was still an exceptionally friendly little place, despite its somewhat formidable reputation for law and order. There appeared to be something very pleasant and satisfactory about Devizes with its neatly named Snuff Street, Sheep Street, Wine Street, and the fifteenth-century wooden-framed houses overhanging the tiny alleyway of St. John. Even my tea tasted unusually good. I ordered an 'indigestible' and began to think I had been a little too parochial in assuming that only a Wilton baker could put enough jam in a doughnut.

IX

LACOCK EXPERTS AND
LACKHAM LEARNERS

I HAVE often wondered whether William Henry Fox Talbot, that famous English pioneer of photography, owed his inspiration to the village of Lacock and its beautiful Abbey in which he was born in 1800. Although, as a scientist, he already knew a little about the experiments carried out by De Niepce and Daguerre in France, Fox Talbot's triumph lay in his unique discovery of a method for duplicating his photographs in the form of prints. There can be few people who visit Lacock nowadays without using their cameras and therefore taking away, in some form or another, reminders of this brilliant inventor's work.

Fox Talbot was a descendant, albeit indirectly, of the remarkable Ela, Countess of Salisbury, who founded the Abbey at Lacock in the thirteenth century. Ela seems to have been what might be described as a 'steadfast visionary'. When everyone else assumed that her husband, William Longespée, the illegitimate son of Henry II, had perished while fighting in France, Ela maintained she had seen a vision of him standing at the prow of a ship coming into a South Coast harbour. Resisting the advances of many another man who wished to gain control of her large fortune, she was rewarded by the fulfilment of her expectations. William Longespée did indeed come back to find her waiting for him, but it was not long before he died and became the first man to be laid to rest in Salisbury Cathedral. Although worn out by shipwreck and privation, it was also rumoured that he had been poisoned while attempting to obtain an apology from the men who had so ungallantly pestered his wife during his absence.

After his death, Ela found consolation by the well-known

remedy of keeping busy. She set about founding two religious houses, one for men at Hinton Charterhouse in Somerset, the other for women at Lacock in Wiltshire on land that she had inherited from her grandfather. She is said to have laid the foundation stones for both these buildings on the same day which, considering they were nearly 15 miles apart and the transport of those times was not particularly easy, must have been good going even for a lady of such sterling qualities. Ela spent the rest of her life devoting herself to the good of the county, the Abbey, and the village of Lacock. For two years she became the only female sheriff Wiltshire has ever possessed, while for seventeen years she became Abbess in her own right, only relinquishing the position when she sensibly felt it to be in the interests of all if she were to serve under a younger woman.

Lacock Abbey suffered less than most at the Dissolution of the Monasteries, although at that time it passed into the hands of William Sharington, a man of dubious character but excellent artistic taste. When he was succeeded by his brother Henry, there is a delightfully romantic story, told by John Aubrey, about the youngest daughter of the family, a spirited damsel called Olive. Luckily, as it turned out, she fell desperately in love with a young man called John Talbot, himself a descendant of Countess Ela. Henry Sharington refused to give his consent to the marriage, but one night when John in the moonlit Abbey grounds was re-affirming his love to Olive who was standing on the battlements, she suddenly decided to join him. Aubrey relates that although her petticoats lifted and "did something breake the fall", even so she landed right on top of her unfortunate suitor so that he lay "as one dead". However, all ended happily. John was resuscitated and Olive's father relented saying that "since she made such leapes, she should e'en marry him". So the long line of Talbots began and although succession has frequently gone via the distaff side, the name has been adopted or added to the husband's on marriage in order for it to survive.

In 1944, Miss Matilda Theresa Talbot presented the Abbey and village together with 284 acres of land to the National Trust. She was a much-loved lady of tremendous personality, an accomplished linguist, and a great traveller. Under her care the Abbey acquired a world-wide reputation for unostentatious hospitality and she is remembered with great affection by the inhabitants of

Lacock for her kindness and generosity. In 1946 she gave one of the principal possessions of the Abbey to the British Museum. This is the final form of Magna Carta which was reissued by Henry III. The museum made two photostat copies, one of which remains at the Abbey while the other has found a home in the Congress Library at Washington.

One of the most unusual and very pleasant characteristics about this historic building is that, although open to the public, it has always been a home rather than a show-piece. It has a friendly and very definitely lived-in atmosphere and today is still occupied by Miss Matilda's niece, who is a tenant of the National Trust. Perhaps, because of this, it is easy to picture some of its former occupants, such as a governess to the Talbots who, when she died ninety years ago, requested that her money should go towards the installation of central heating for the Abbey. On seeing the oriel window where Fox Talbot took his first successful photograph in 1835, it is almost possible to share some of the excitement he must have felt as he showed it to the rest of the family. At other times when walking round the cloisters and grounds, it is not difficult to visualize him doing the same sort of thing, except that his artistic eye would have been planning just where to plant the tulip trees, the swamp cypresses, the Judas tree, nettle tree, and the American black walnuts.

One person who may often be found nowadays sweeping up some of the fallen leaves in the Abbey gardens during autumn is Mr. George Gerrish. He is an octogenarian and one of those individuals who are fast dying out, a master craftsman. George Gerrish is a stone-mason and has only ever executed what he refers to as 'class' work. There is none of the free and easy use of the lathe where George Gerrish is concerned. He prefers a mallet and chisel. Stone, to him, is a thing to be treated with reverent care. He looks upon it as if it had personality. "See here," he says, as he lovingly fingers one of the pillars by the Abbey gates, "them be layers of cockle-shells and sand when thic thur stone started its life under the sea. See?" After caressing it a little more, he adds, "They put that one in t'other way round. Them cockle-shells be standin' on their heads."

Then, quite unexpectedly, George Gerrish says, "Come and see my dolphin." It is a fascinating invitation, far more enticing than "Come up and see my etchings." He will then marshal you along past Lacock's fourteenth-century barn, past the tiny village lock-up, where he points out the work he did on its stone top-knot; past the tower of the Church of St. Cyriac, which was rebuilt for the third time in the fifteenth century, and on which George Gerrish himself has been photographed repairing the pinnacles; and on towards his little stone cottage, beautifully kept by his septuagenarian wife.

In a shed at the bottom of his back garden stands Mr. Gerrish's latest piece of 'class', his stone dolphin. He was asked to make it by a lady from London who wanted her new abode to have an edifice such as her Dolphin Square residence had once possessed. "Didn't never see a dolphin 'afore," says George, "but someone lent I a book wi' a picture of 'un. Think he'll do?" He puts a gnarled yet tender hand on his creation which makes one sad to feel that he will soon have to part with it.

Having mutually admired his dolphin for some time, he switches on to the subject of the roses growing by his workshop and begins an account of his relationship with another lady, this time an American. George Gerrish evidently has a way with him where women are concerned. "Thic rose over there," he says, pointing to a beautiful late-flowering bloom, "she be 'Sarah Arnot'. Last week I were showin' my dolphin to this American 'ooman, and blow me if 'er name weren't Sarah Nott. So I plucked 'er the best one 'an she went off down the street carryin' it 'igh up in the air, as proud as a cat wi' two tails."

This event must have been well worth seeing. The sight of the American Sarah Nott, marching away along East Street and down the High Street of Lacock carrying one of George Gerrish's finest Sarah Arnot roses like a banner in front of her must have been interesting, to say the least, even if those streets were not as lovely as they actually are; because there is no doubt that the village of Lacock is quite unique. It is perfectly easy to understand why a present-day historian once came out of 'The Angel' in Church Street on a moonlit night and said, "I seem to be stepping into the fifteenth century." He could almost have stretched his imagination a little farther into the past, if he had happened to be looking back towards the church where King John's hunting lodge stands.

Although the old road from Melksham to Chippenham runs

through Lacock, a new by-pass now allows the village to retain far more of its medieval characteristics. The wide peaceful High Street seems to be waiting for the fairs, dancing, and cattle-market that once took place there. It is a perfect setting for that local doctor, who, on fine evenings nearly 100 years ago, would come out of doors to play his fiddle so that the young might enjoy themselves while the old looked on. It is sad to think that a present-day National Health medico would be far too busy to be able to give an hour or so to such a pleasant and salutary pastime especially as, judging by the longevity of its inhabitants, Lacock still seems to be an exceptionally healthy place.

Perhaps this has something to do with the air or the water because Melksham, which is only a few miles away, once had aspirations of becoming a spa owing to its chalybeate and saline springs; on the other hand, maybe Lacock's salubrity is owing to the fact that it is so quiet and no one seems in a hurry. There are few people about and the High Street, flanked by its crooked stone houses, looks a bit like something out of Grimms' Fairy Tales, so much so that if a hobgoblin were suddenly to appear out of one of the front doors he would not seem all that out of place. On thinking about it, George Gerrish looks uncommonly like a genial little one himself.

Another person who seems to thrive in Lacock and can rarely have needed the services of any doctor with or without his fiddle, is Mr. William Charles Minty. 'Bill' Minty has spent most of his life on the land and is now one of the most active and independent nonagenarians it would be possible to find. Although he shares a large house with his sister, he is quite capable of looking after himself during her absence on holiday because, as he says, "There bain't nowt I can't cook." Pancakes are his speciality and he has his own particular formula for successfully tossing them. His married daughter in New Zealand wants him to go out there to live, but he explains that he does not want to leave Lacock because "here I knows everyone and everyone do know me". Every evening he toddles next door into 'The George', where he is described as a "tonic", and not one that comes out of a bottle either.

His knowledge of what is going on in the world is astonishing and he has a flair for summing up people that would put most

modern students of society to shame. He has a rhyme which he
applies to the female sex in general that goes:

> Where there's a woman, if she will she will,
> You may depend on it.
> If she won't she won't
> And there's an end of it.

He refers to a certain lucky man as being the sort who "if he fell
from the top of the Co-op building he would land in the divi".
As for the threatened changes in the administration of local
government which, if they went through, would make Lacock
subject to control by 'foreigners' in Bath he says quite simply,
"Thee tell Maud to keep away. I got a gun."

But on the whole, Bill Minty's wit is not quite so caustic. He
is grateful to all those people round about who help him to
pursue his life-long interest in hunting, by driving him in their
cars whenever the Avon Vale Foxhounds are meeting. He is
generous in his praise of most local inhabitants, referring to him
or her as "one o' the best", and especially does this apply to Mr.
J. O. Thomas, Principal of the nearby Agricultural College.
Lackham House and about 600 acres of land were bought by the
Wiltshire County Council in 1945 for £42,500, since when it has
provided instruction for young men who wish to obtain posts of
responsibility on farms or with organizations connected with
farming. There are now about eighty male students and for the
past five years Lackham has gone co-educational, accommodating
twenty girls who take a one-year course in Rural Home Economics.

Lackham lies in a crook of the River Avon between Chippenham and Lacock, and this particular piece of land has been the
centre of a manor since before the Norman Conquest. In the
Domesday survey it is recorded as one of the manors granted to
the stormy Count of Eu which, with its "two mills and two
miles of wood"* was then as comparable an estate as that of
neighbouring Lacock.

From about 1200 until the early nineteenth century, Lackham
changed hands only twice and even then, as the dowry of its
heiress. A very old English family, the Montagus, held the manor
until 1815, when the economic crisis of that time forced George

* One square mile.

Montagu, who was badly in debt, to sell off parts of the estate to the trustees of the young Fox Talbot at Lacock. Memories of the old feudal system of landowning are strong in this part of the county and, not far away, there is an enchanting and historic cluster of buildings (now belonging to the National Trust) known as Great Chalfield Manor. A massive archway guards the forecourt and the way to the little parish church; whereas heavy oak doors and spy-holes in the great hall and dining-room (together with water protecting two sides of the whole establishment) no doubt gave an added sense of security to Mr. Thomas Tropenell, the fifteenth-century landlord who created this near-perfect example of domestic medieval architecture. Great Chalfield has a close rival in South Wraxall Manor, a few miles westwards, but nearer at hand, Neston Park, Corsham Court, Bowden Hill, Spye Park, and the Marquis of Lansdowne's Bowood seem to make up quite a formidable nucleus of 'country seats' still to be reckoned with today.

At the beginning of this century the owner of Lackham was that famous Wiltshire soldier, General Llewellyn-Palmer, whose son was, during the 1930s, the very popular Master of the Wilton Hounds and lived at Rushmore Park just inside the county's southern border. The family must always have been keen horsemen because General Palmer added the large yard and stabling at Lackham which has now been successfully turned into a teaching block for agricultural students.

These young people need to be keen and workmanlike but not necessarily to have high scholastic qualifications. Preferably, the boys should have gained one year's practical experience on a mechanized farm and be 17 years of age before starting at Lackham. Some pay the full fees; many have grants from the local authorities. They may stay one, two, or three years at the college depending on what kind of certificate they require on leaving, such as the National Certificate of Agriculture or an Ordinary Diploma in Farm Mechanization. The girls aim at an N.C.A. with Home Economics, or they make take a one-year farm secretaries' course. An interview with Mr. Thomas is the final hurdle to be overcome in order to gain a place at Lackham, and the lucky ones (because most students rightly consider themselves fortunate to be there) then begin their further education under the surveillance of their strict but benevolent Principal.

The semi-derelict Kennet and Avon Canal, near Devizes

Mr. Thomas is friendly, downright, but gives the impression that he misses nothing. He has been at Lackham twenty-two years and it is obvious that he has got the whole set-up running "su-ently". He manages the difficult task of making the farm profitable and educational at the same time. Besides teachers and students, he has under his care a permanent farm staff, two herds of dairy cows, a small herd of Aberdeen Angus and Friesian cows, a few Hereford cattle for beef, forty sows, 200 fattening pigs, 2,000 laying hens, a flock of 100 pedigree Clun Forest ewes, three different types of soil ranging from heavy clay to light cornbrash, an apple orchard and a demonstration garden, an apiary, a miscellany of modern machinery, a museum, a meteorological station, 40 acres of woodland, and some 'corn dollies'. The last item I feel bound to include, although such frivolity comes more under the direct supervision of Miss Dunn, the Senior Lecturer in charge of the Rural Home Economics Department.

I am sure Miss Dunn and her three assistant experts, who also go round the county advising and lecturing at other Colleges of Further Education, provide instruction quite equal to or above Constance Spry standards. In one room she has students arranging the most exotic decorations with variegated kale leaves; in another there are young women studying joints of meat, with the aid of a model cow which comes to bits in all the right places; while others are learning how to pickle onions without tears. In the centre of the R.H.E. Block there is a large larder with shelves packed with preserves and home-made wine, an example of perfect domesticity as illustrated in glossy magazines; and then there is the room where the 'corn dollies' are being made.

There are, I suppose, some people who might consider this old-fashioned craft, which originated in pagan times as a harvest symbol, simply not worth bothering about nowadays. Certainly, if these girls are one day going to be the wives of young farmers with two or three children at foot, the telephone ringing, the eggs to be collected, the garden to be tended, and a cooked meal ready on the dot of twelve noon, it is difficult to imagine just where corn dollies are going to fit into the picture. Sitting down and plaiting straw in order to make decoration (especially now that long straw is scarce to come by since the advent of the combine-harvester) does not seem quite right for a young woman in 'Jimmy Kirby's klit'. But maybe a course in Rural Home

H

The White Horse on Bratton Down, near Westbury
The Principal of the Lackham College of Agriculture talking
to some of the students

Economics prevents anyone from ever becoming so disorganized and it should also be remembered that our grandmothers, who most likely had seven children, an open-fire range, and no inside sanitation, still found time to make the most beautiful corn dollies as and when required. I also understand these ornamental works of art are becoming quite a commercial proposition today and there happens to be a most shapely one in a handicraft shop in Salisbury at this very moment.

Perhaps one of the many good things about Lackham is that it does not scorn the past and for all its accent on the latest up-to-date methods, it still finds time to think about just why and how these have come into being. There is a fascinating museum full of old agricultural machinery so that students may find it easier to understand the evolution of the complicated monsters which appear in today's fields. There are two granaries re-erected near the museum, the 400-year-old one having been carefully transported brick by brick from the Marquess of Bath's estate at Longleat, and the 200-year-old wooden one having been transported with equal care from Great Chalfield Manor. Both are raised off the ground by the old-fashioned staddle stones that townsmen sometimes regard as simply decorative mushrooms with no utilitarian purpose, but which actually used to allow for the dual advantage of keeping the grain dry and the rats out.

Lackham is recognized as the home of Agricultural Education in Wiltshire and sometimes takes students from farther afield. Although other counties have similar establishments, this is the largest in the south-west of England. It provides a rather unique service to this predominantly agricultural county and much of its credit must go to Mr. Thomas and not a little to the present Chairman of the Governors, Mr. Michael Stratton.

Mr. Stratton is a very well-known and well-liked Wiltshireman who farms in the Wylye Valley. He is the sort of efficient person who gets things done in the nicest possible way. If anyone is able to persuade the County Council that Lackham needs some new building or other, it is Mr. Stratton. He tells me that Mr. Thomas is soon to retire and I feel sorry about this for he will be a difficult man to replace. On the other hand, I have every confidence that Mr. Stratton will discover the most suitable man for the job or, as Bill Minty might say, "another o' the best".

X

'MR. BACON'

DOVER has soles, Aylesbury has ducks, the Scotch have whisky, and Wiltshire has ham. In fact, Wiltshire has ham in a big way, not only as traditional county fare but also in the guise of a delightful village by that name, situated near the eastern border just south of the Kennet and Avon Canal. In order to avoid confusion, perhaps it would be better to refer to the edible variant as bacon; bacon which comes in all forms, shapes, and sizes: 'Sweetcure', 'Wiltshire Cure', sides, middle, and back. You name it and the firm of C. & T. Harris Ltd., of Calne, produce it.

There is usually a reason for most things, and just why this splendid pig-processing concern started as long ago as 1770 in this particular spot is quite a little saga in itself. In the Middle Ages the prosperity of Calne depended, as so many other places in this part of Wiltshire, on the woollen industry. Water power was available from the River Marden and at one time there were twenty spinning and fulling mills in the town.

But as that industry declined, fortunately for Calne, two up and coming brothers from Devizes, named John and Henry Harris, took the bold steps of migrating some 7 miles northwards to this little town where they set up two separate butchers' establishments. John, who appears to have done better than Henry in every way, was also fortunate enough to have married a splendid wife who carried on his business after his death, having borne him three even more splendid and up and coming sons, namely Thomas, George, and Charles.

Before the arrival of the Great Western Railway, Irish pigs were shipped to Bristol, after which they were driven in herds towards London. Calne happened to be one of the most convenient resting-places for these poor animals. Evidently the Harris brothers took advantage of the availability of good porkers on their doorstep, before the flesh and staying-powers of these beasts had had time to diminish as they trotted along on their marathon march towards the metropolis.

During the potato famine of 1847, by which time John, Henry, and their wives had long since been dead and buried, the supply of Irish pigs was severely reduced. However, upholding the family tradition of enterprise, George Harris set sail for America where he intended to kill and cure pigs which he then proposed to ship back to his brothers in England, but unfortunately at that time this proved to be an unsatisfactory solution. A ready supply of good porkers has always been of concern to the bacon-manufacturing industry in this country and local pig-rearing used to be greatly encouraged. Until about thirty years ago, it was common practice for Harris's employees to have a pig-sty at the bottom of their gardens or an allotment on which they kept half a dozen beasts. Pig clubs were very popular in this part of the countryside as they assisted pig-owners in buying feeding stuffs and gave insurance against loss and disease.

While in America, George Harris became most impressed with the idea of ice for preserving purposes and when he returned he developed this technique to prolong bacon-curing during the summer season. 'Wiltshire Cure', which can be said to have originated in Calne, was a long process that could only be carried out during the colder months as it required a low temperature. Even when conducted in cellars underneath the ground, those sunny summers of long ago appear to have called a halt to proceedings.

After George returned from his travels, the firm of Harris began to provide curing cellars with very strong false ceilings, in which tons of ice could be stored and the melting water was measured daily to give an indication of how long the supply would last. Perhaps, in those days, the summers really were hotter and the winters colder, such as those depicted on Christmas cards where fascinating ladies, wearing muffs and long skirts, glide gracefully over the glassy surface of ponds. Certainly, there were more ponds about at that time from which ice could be collected, and it must be remembered that when non-existent it could be brought from as far afield as Norway and delivered via the Kennet and Avon Canal. The price apparently varied from 15s. to 2s. 6d. per hundredweight according to supply and demand.

Although the firm of C. & T. Harris dates from 1770 and a patent was taken out in 1864 for the curing of bacon with the aid of refrigeration, the methods used were, of course, primitive in those days compared with today. The sides of bacon were manually handled after each process, and offal was washed in the River Marden. The density of curing-brine was assessed by simply throwing a trotter into the tanks and observing the rate of sinking. Men worked long hours and their arrival on time each morning was ensured by the old-fashioned 'knocking-up' process.

Until 1880 the family business was run as two separate entities. Trade was brisk and there was competition, albeit of a friendly kind, in the labour market. The Harris family was greatly respected in Calne and typified all the virtues of a Victorian age. Its members converted the Peach Tree Tavern into a coffee house where any travelling pig-drover was supplied with free vouchers for refreshment, the main object being that it was not alcoholic. They also built the Free Church, ran soup kitchens, and gave a fine recreation ground to the town.

By 1900 an average of 2,000 pigs were slaughtered each week and sausage-making became definitely established. During and after the First World War, great extensions and improvements were made to the factory. Mechanized refrigeration and a power house were introduced, the latter lighting the whole of Calne and district until the coming of the National Grid. Besides the production of bacon and sausages, other commodities came into being such as pies, lard, and cooked meats, which in turn created ancillary industries connected with wood- and cardboard-box-making, printing, and coopering. The firm survived the post-war depression, although at that time it was greatly assisted by the Marsh family from Brierley Hill near Birmingham, famous for its York hams.

There is little doubt that C. & T. Harris Ltd. have dominated Calne in ever-increasing manner since the day when John and Henry took those adventurous steps in the last half of the eighteenth century. At the Paris International Exhibition of 1889, the firm won the first prize for Wiltshire bacon; in 1929 it was granted a royal warrant as bacon-curers to the monarchy, an honour it has held ever since. During the last war the factory geared itself in a big way to the national effort, producing thousands of tons of food to feed both the armed forces and the civil population. Although in 1965 Harris's were taken over by the Fatstock Marketing Corporation, one of the largest meat-handling combines in the country, the firm still seems to have a very definite family atmosphere about it and the bold white letters, "C. & T. Harris Ltd", on top of the huge red buildings which overshadow Calne, still proudly proclaim its exceptionally fine and long-standing tradition.

Being taken round the factory today is a kind of revelation. Although I have been shown the whole set-up from pigs trotting in to pork pies 'trunkering'* out, it has not daunted my desire to buy my customary 4 pounds of 'Wiltshire Cure' with the same regularity. Hot boiled ham is a favourite in our household, and, served with a sauce made out of the juice the meat has been cooked in to which red currant jelly and a liberal quantity of port or sherry has been added, it is something which has never failed when dished up for any visitor of any age. A small American girl who came to stay with us for the second time not long ago, said to me confidentially soon after arrival, "Is it pink meat and sauce night?"

Those in charge of C. & T. Harris in 1969 seem to be as justly proud of their firm as they show people round it as those pioneer brothers must have been so many long years ago. In order to see what went on I was given a dazzling white overall to wear before I was allowed as much as to sniff a pig. Then a rather saucy little white hat with 'Harris' written on it was also produced. I was a little dubious about this one as hats have never sat easily on my head, especially white pork pie ones. However, the factory manager seemed to think it important that I should wear one, and who was I to argue with the rules of such an obviously well-run organization that was going so "suently"?

Feeling highly conspicuous, I followed him along numerous passages, but soon forgot my embarrassment when I found that hats were the 'in' thing at Harris's. Everyone wears hats. Besides being hygienic, they also act as a kind of status symbol. My hat was a visitor's hat, presumably denoting that I was not suddenly going to go berserk with a carving knife. My kind factory manager wore a superb white panama hat like the sort of thing

* Local jargon for goods being carried by trunker vehicles.

holiday-makers wear in the South of France. The importance of other supervisors is symbolized by hats with red bands, green bands, red peaks, and blue peaks. The ladies wear turbans, while the more important ones have hats with dark blue or yellow bands and the Lady Chief wears a special garden-party hat unlike any other in the entire building.

We started off in the slaughter-house and I was more than a little relieved to find that when we arrived, slaughtering happened to be over for the day. Certain mopping-up operations were going on around the gas-chamber, but there is no doubt that this daily necessary evil is done under the most humane and well-regulated conditions. Everything is subject to the continual stringent scrutiny of outside personnel such as Public Health Inspectors and Veterinary Surgeons, so that the methods used for finally producing those succulent slices of bacon that are fried for today's breakfasts, seem very far removed from those which must have been undertaken by the original brother Charles and brother Thomas.

We passed along between row upon row of various parts of the pig, the factory manager waving his hand to right and left and using mysterious words such as gambrels, chitterlings, rames, chines, plucks, and fleck. For the sake of the squeamish, I shall not dwell on them except to say that there they were, all hygienically separated into their respective categories, and that they constitute the necessary ingredients of those appetizing end-products that emerge from the farther end of the factory.

I wondered a little about father John Harris and his three sons, as I was escorted through this huge establishment employing 1,500 people in an area covering one and a half acres and which is capable of a 'throughput' of 1,000 pigs per day. What would they say if they could see the huge ovens where thousands of hams are smoked (by heating sawdust), the vast brine tubs, the rows of 'sides' hanging in well-refrigerated rooms, the method of 'Sweetcuring' heavy hogs that was introduced when F.M.C. took over in 1965, so that together with 'Wiltshire Cure' all tastes might be satisfied? What would they think about the enormous boiling stoves which the factory manager referred to as 'missionary pots', because they reminded him of darkest Africa? Would they approve of the canning machine and the Harris labels being automatically stuck on the tinned tongues?

Could they possibly understand the testing laboratory and the up-to-date medical unit for the staff? And those pastry-mixers that never make a mistake? How I should like a small replica of one of them myself so that none of my home-made offerings went soggy or down in the middle.

Lastly, would not their ghosts gaze in utter bewilderment, if they were to watch the fleet of huge trunker vehicles moving out at all hours of the day and night from this round-the-clock concern, carrying ton after ton of bacon, ham, meat pies, big sausages, little sausages, liver sausages, cold meats, canned goods, black puddings, faggots, hamburgers, and polony?

There is a little window let into the side of Harris's factory wall, showing a model of the original father John Harris in his butcher's shop looking keen and ready to serve all comers with a smile. It is perhaps one of the many examples of the human touch to be found in the firm of today. Harris's have not forgotten the people to whom they owe their success. Although taken over by F.M.C., a natural pride in a family firm is still self-evident throughout. Its chief industrial engineer, who has the same name as the nearby village of Bromham where Thomas Moore, the Irish poet, lies buried, has compiled his own little history of C. & T. Harris Ltd.; while a commissionaire to the firm has just published a most charming little article entitled "Sweet Calne in Wiltshire". Charles Lamb referred to the town as such long before the name 'Sweetcure' was conferred on the heavy hogs of today. I cannot help being rather fascinated by this method, as it is only used on the joints of large porkers that are capable of being 'tailored' to a standard size. There is something so tragicomic about the idea of 'tailoring' a pig.

C. & T. Harris, of course, are not the only bacon curers in Wiltshire. The firm of Bowyers at Trowbridge, which I have already mentioned elsewhere, is another of the county's major meat-processing establishments, which is run on the same efficient lines with as fine and almost as old a tradition. But there seems little doubt that the John Harris from Devizes was the father of the Wiltshire bacon-curing industry. It must also be remembered, however, that not all ham comes from Wiltshire, or ducks come from Aylesbury, or soles from Dover, or whisky from Scotland, even if described as such. The prefix 'Wiltshire' before the word 'ham', which is so often seen on menus everywhere, may not necessarily refer to those splendid ten score porkers that Mr. Thomas showed me at Lackham.

On the other hand, I still feel more than content that what seems to be the produce of 'my' county should figure in this kind of way and, as I give my order to some waiter or waitress in 'really foreign parts', I like to think I am supporting home industry in much the same way as the loyal gentleman who was once talking to my father about an actress who lived in his native village of Teffont Magna. Apparently, her husband had presented this aged cattle-dealer with a free ticket for a show in which his wife was appearing in Bournemouth, and had offered to drive him down there on the appointed day in order to see it. My father felt that possibly this kind of jaunt might have been a little out of keeping with this natural countryman's way of life, so he asked him whether or not he had accepted the invitation. "Aw, yes," came the reply. "Thee's know. Volk in the same village. I couldn' do no less than to goo down an' gi'e 'em a start." There is a lot to be said for local pride. Father Harris, wherever you are, please take a bow.

Another of Calne's one-time residents who might also take a bow is Dr. Joseph Priestley, because it was here at the end of the eighteenth century at a certain spot by the side of the River Marden (which is now known as Doctor's Pond), that he is said to have collected gases from water-bubbles which led to his discovery of mankind's greatest life-saver, oxygen. It has always seemed ironical to me that Calne seems to have gone in for quite a bit of killing and/or curing, one way and another.

Priestley was the literary companion of the first Marquis of Lansdowne, who lived at Bowood, only 2 miles away, and for eight years he worked in the library there while cataloguing and indexing the Marquis's collection of books and manuscripts. Bowood, in its magnificent park and woodlands spreading over 1,000 acres (expertly laid out by Capability Brown) is one of Wiltshire's most famous stately homes.

Since the first Earl of Shelburne took it over in 1754, it has always attracted men of letters, and its doors were once thrown open to Jeremy Bentham, Benjamin Franklin, Dr. Johnson, Macaulay, Mirabeau, and Thomas Moore. Much of the original building designed by a series of architects, including Robert Adam, has now been greatly altered or pulled down altogether, although

Bowood still remains, as portrayed by John Britton in *The Beauties of England and Wales*, an epitome of "the sublime, the picturesque and the beautiful". The grounds, including their renowned rhododendron walks which are open to the public at certain times during the year, also possess a large lake with a rippling cascade at its outlet, as well as the celebrated Mausoleum, built by Adam for "the man of worth and Christian sincerity who founded this great estate".

Bowood formerly lay within the ancient Forest of Chippenham, the demesne forming the legal entity known as the Liberty of Bowood, which is included in the parish of Calne Without. It is a large parish and a particularly lovely one, although Calne Within is today an attractive place that bears no resemblance to the "villainous hole", as it was once described by the irascible Cobbett. The two great calamities that once befell the town are rarely spoken of and mostly forgotten. Just a few people such as Mr. Bromham will tell you that one of Harris's new factories stands on the reputed site of a building where, in 987, all members of the Witenagemot* (except Archbishop Dunstan who clung to a beam) were either killed or injured as they crashed through an upper floor, after hotly debating the vexed question of priestly celibacy. Dunstan, who naturally was upholding the cause of the monks against advocates of secular procedure, was accused of having staged the disaster; although it was generally conceded afterwards that he was far too saintly an individual to be capable of such underground tactics and, in any case, was always more of a moderator than a partisan. Nevertheless, it is quite interesting to speculate on how many people throughout the centuries might have wanted to emulate Guy Fawkes.

The other calamity about which the local historian, Mr. Bromham, appears to be very well-informed is the day when the church tower crashed to the ground in 1638 and made at least one poor soul die of fright. Fortunately, this second architectural disaster

---

* The Witenagemot was the greatest national council of England in Anglo-Saxon times. The king was supposed to be guided by it in all his main acts of government. It was, however, highly undemocratic, being composed of bishops, eldermen of shires, a number of the king's friends, dependants, and thanes. The last category was a class below nobility but above landowners. It is misleading to identify any functions of the Witenagemot with its present-day successor, the representative House of Commons.

was remedied by Inigo Jones, and the Church of St. Mary is now in an excellent state of repair. When a strong east wind blows from the Marlborough Downs it has little effect on the solidity and cheerfulness of the Calne of today. The girls from the well-known St. Mary's School go about their work on the top of the hill and the rest of the town goes about its business at the bottom. That it is brisk business and mostly Harris's business, there seems no doubt.

'Mr. Bacon', a final curtain, please.

XI

'THEY'

NOT very much was known about prehistoric Avebury and the area round about it until that splendid character, John Aubrey, came across it in 1646 and reported that "it did as much excel Stonehenge as a cathedral does a parish church". I have never been quite sure, myself, just why Stonehenge has been able to keep in the limelight while the larger and older monumental Avebury, together with its various satellites, has remained modestly in the background.

The village stands in the valley of the River Kennet about 8 miles north-east of Devizes, and it seems that our ancient forefathers must have taken a great fancy to this part of the country. In an area of only a few square miles there is enough evidence of former 'goings-on' to keep any modern professor of archaeology happily burrowing for the rest of his life. There is Windmill Hill which has given its name to the strange folk who constructed the camp on top of it a long time before the Avebury architects got to work. Then there is the gloomy West Kennett Long Barrow, the ritual centre called the Sanctuary on Overton Hill, the Kennett Avenue that connected this with Avebury itself, and lastly the man-made mound named Silbury Hill where recent excavations have been covered by television cameras on a kind of scoop by scoop basis.

For most of my life the only 'digs' that really interested me were the ones in which I, or later on my daughter, might have to live; and the only proper 'dig' I ever went to see was at the little village of Marden, near Devizes, when everyone happened to be packing up to go home and a huge mechanical digger was shovelling all the mess made by the human ones back into place. There was nothing to my untutored eye that resembled the remains of a temple which I had been hoping to find, and when I asked one young girl if she could tell me exactly what she had been looking for she said she was not quite sure. Then I saw a very handsome young male digger in the distance and put two and two together.

But sometimes, when visiting Avebury, I feel it might be possible to get bitten by the digging bug, especially if there happened to be a kind, good-looking professor in charge of operations. I can quite sympathize with the American lady who once rushed up to me in the village street and said, "Gee, these stones kinda get you, don't they? I simply gotta have a little book about them so I can give the folks the gen back in Massachusetts. I've only got ten minutes." And off she went, panting along past the church and the Elizabethan manor to the tiny museum, where she could buy a guide-book in order that she might be clued up for Hank and Bud back home.

The unusual feature about this huge circular bank and ditch with all the great sarsen stones inside it, is that they all seem to be muddled up with the village of Avebury itself. Looking out of the windows at the Red Lion Hotel people are apt to remark, "Good heavens, there's another one." Sarsen stones appear to be everywhere, but this is because originally there were several smaller settings inside the outer circle.* Where the originals are missing, the places have been thoughtfully marked by little concrete miniatures, thanks to that great archaeologist and lover of Avebury, the late Alexander Keiller and the devoted assistance of Mr. W. E. V. Young, who was a permanent member of the excavating staff from 1925 onwards and later the expert curator of the local museum.

The best way to get a proper impression of Avebury today is to be in a low-flying aeroplane. Failing that, it is necessary to do the round trip along the top of the circular bank, which is interrupted by the four entrances (two of them main roads) that converge on the village. There is perhaps a certain toothy appearance about the place, the big stones and little markers giving an irregular effect as if in need of dental care; or perhaps a kinder way to describe Avebury would be to say that it resembles a green flan where the cook has stuck different-sized almonds vertically all over the top of it. Some of the largest boulders weigh over 40

* These once amounted to about 100.

tons. They have not been 'dressed' like those at Stonehenge and there appear to be two distinct forms, a tall pillar with vertical sides and a broad diamond next to it, which makes some people go as far as to say they are connected with 'fertility rites', as they represent the male and female form. Although I realize that the fortunes of the builders of Avebury largely depended on the increase of their flocks and herds, I find it difficult to accept this theory as, to me, the stones seem singularly unrepresentative of any animate object.

Since the time when the huge surrounding ditch was dug out with the aid of tools made from antlers to enclose an area of about 28 acres, the bottom has silted up to at least half its former depth. It has been said that because the ditch is inside the bank, the site must have been used for some kind of ritual purposes rather than a dwelling-place, as the latter would have required a ditch outside for defence tactics. Certainly within the site there has been found little evidence of domestic occupation to do with the first group of Beaker people who constructed it around 2000 B.C., and the later ones who reconstructed it to form the great circle of stones on the inner edge of a bank and ditch.

It is known that sometime after A.D. 634 a small Saxon church was built outside the bank yet right up against it, somehow implying an attempt to challenge a pagan cult by a new faith. Yet heathen practices must have continued well into the thirteenth or fourteenth century, for there is evidence to suggest that at that period the Christian authorities found it necessary to take drastic action by making a breach into the bank nearest the church and overthrowing some of the stones. A skeleton has been found crushed underneath one of them and is thought to be that of the village barber–surgeon, complete with his scissors and some coins dated 1307. In the guide-books there is a photograph of this poor gentleman which is apt to cast an extra shadow on a sunny afternoon in Avebury. Was he induced, as has been suggested, to take part in some kind of religious quarrel? Or was he simply joining in a looting escapade in order to obtain a little sarsen stone for building a house? Or was there some even more sinister reason for his remains being found beneath a heavy horizontal Grey Wether, to leave yet another question-mark for his present-day descendants? Once again, as at Stonehenge, it is the repetition of those operative words, 'may have been'.

There is little doubt that the stones were subjected to a great deal of demolition work, especially in the eighteenth century. The antiquary, William Stukeley, has left a lively sketch of how they were tipped over a pit filled with burning straw and smashed to pieces with sledge-hammers to provide building material and clear the land for cultivation or, in his own more cryptic words, to produce "a little dirty profit".

Fortunately today Avebury seems extraordinarily peaceful and a place where the profit-motive does not operate. Inside the charmed circle, guarded by the Department of the Environment, sheep graze round the bank, residents mow their lawns, sight-seers wander about, and it seems difficult to realize that an average of 45,000 of them visit the tiny museum in a year, while treble or quadruple that number go round the stones themselves. The fortunately situated Red Lion does a splendid trade with snacks and excellent meals in a little dining-room, where it is possible to look down into an 80-foot well which has been lit up to show the natural ferns growing therein.

Leading away to the south-west from Avebury is the Kennett Avenue of stones which originally ran for about a mile, passing the village of West Kennett and ending in what is called the Sanctuary on Overton Hill. The northern end of this was excavated just before the war and the missing sarsens marked with concrete, but all that remains of the rest of the course is now just one or two odd stones sticking up in a kind of abandoned fashion, as if waiting hopefully to act as a resting-place for some tramp (or 'milestone inspector' as these gentlemen are called in Wiltshire).

The Sanctuary itself is another ritual centre belonging to the late Neolithic and Early Bronze Age. Excavations have revealed that there were wooden structures earlier than any of the stone circles at Avebury, but that the final erection on this site was of sarsen stone and probably built at the same time as the Kennett Avenue and Avebury itself, somewhere between 1600 and 2000 B.C.

Not far from here on the way to Beckhampton lie Silbury Hill and the West Kennett Long Barrow. The latter is reached by climbing a footpath from the road and is the largest chambered tomb in England and one in which visitors who are not squeamish can take a good look round. Personally, I think it is helpful to have a torch and some moral support. It is quite a walk from the A4 and definitely lonely. 'They' seem very much with you up on these Wiltshire Downs with the nearby mysterious Silbury Hill defiantly interrupting the landscape for miles around.

West Kennett Long Barrow is said to have been constructed about 2700 B.C. and used, although perhaps not built, by the people who occupied Windmill Hill a little farther away. The tomb itself consists of a long passage with two pairs of burial chambers opening off its sides and a larger area at the far end which I imagine to have been for the 'big shots'. The barrow seems to have been in continual use over a number of centuries, the earlier occupants being unceremoniously swept aside to make room for the new-comers along with all their necessary grave-goods.*

On the other hand, perhaps 'they' might consider it even more unceremonious for a party of university students to be sprawling on top of the West Kennett Long Barrow on a sunny October day in the twentieth century, nonchalantly making surmises as to what their ancestors could have been up to. If Neolithic men really came there to make offerings to the dead in front of the tomb, like the drawings in books suggest, I cannot help feeling 'they' might be appalled to find such unisexed young people making merry on such a sacred site with the aid of "Beat me Daddy, eight to a bar" coming from a transistor in the background. But it is all this inconclusiveness about archaeology that really bothers me. I do so wish one of those ancient savants had got busy with a stick and some non-fading dye in order to portray *something* he could have placed in safe keeping for Professor Atkinson to find in the centre of Silbury Hill in the summer of 1969.

Silbury is a maddening mound. It is the largest man-made one in Europe and stands teasingly by the side of the main road 6 miles west of Marlborough. The one thing that seems to be certain about it is that it is pre-Roman in origin, as one of those straight Roman roads has been forced to diverge in order to get round it. It has been built on top of a natural small knoll and Professor Atkinson estimates that the volume of solid chalk which its builders dug out and piled up (by basket) could have taken 500 people at least ten years to complete. It covers $5\frac{1}{4}$ acres at its base and reaches a height of 130 feet. Originally, it was even larger,

* It is now thought that owing to lack of space the dead were exposed for some months on wooden frames outside the long barrows, where their bodies were devoured by birds until the bones fell through to the ground. These were then collected into little heaps for interment.

Lacock Abbey
Great Chalfield Manor

because the surrounding ditch is mostly filled with silt eroded from the mound by frost and rain. The building of Silbury Hill has been compared as the equivalent in its own time of the whole of the American or Russian space programmes today.

Both Aubrey and Stukeley, those two indefatigable recorders of times long past, made sketches of the hill and Aubrey gives an interesting account of one of his visits to the site when he had the honour to wait upon King Charles II and the Duke of York. Apparently the Duke was most taken with some small snails on the turf of the hill and commanded Aubrey to collect some. He reports that "the next morning when he (the duke) was abed with his Duchess at Bath, he told her of it and sent Dr. Charleton to me for them, to shew her as a rarity". Aubrey also refers to a mythical king called Sil (or Zel, as countryfolk would have pronounced), who was "buried here on horseback and the hill raised while a posset of milk was seething". Either our forefathers had methods of which we know nothing or a very good non-stick saucepan.

Many attempts have been made to probe the secrets of Silbury. In 1776 the Duke of Northumberland aided by his friend, Colonel Drax, imported a party of tin-miners from Cornwall to dig a shaft from the centre of the top to the ground surface beneath, to be rewarded with nothing save a fragment of oak timber. In 1849, the Archaeological Institute undertook a more elaborate operation under the supervision of Dean Merewether. A tunnel was dug, but once again all that was found were some disappointing "fragments of a sort of string made of what appeared to be grass". In 1867 the Wiltshire Archaeological Society excavated the east side of the hill to ascertain whether or not the Roman road from Marlborough to Bath was buried beneath the mound, but this was subsequently discovered in the fields to the south where its pronounced swerve established for all time that Silbury was pre-Roman. In 1886 pits were dug into the ditch to find out their original depths; in 1922 Sir Flinders Petrie excavated the causeway in search of an entrance to a burial chamber; while in 1959 Dr. McKim of Marlborough College made a series of electrical tests, once more with dishearteningly negative results.

Now, during the past three years, Silbury has been under the latest methods of attack by modern researchers, backed by a whole battery of television cameras which culminated in a final Saturday evening programme in the summer of 1969. There was great

I

Stone circle at Avebury
Silbury Hill

speculation as to what Professor Atkinson might find on the last lap of his marathon dig. Would it be the remains of King Zel and his horse? Would it be the great architect of Stonehenge? Or would it be, as some ribald people suggested, the veteran correspondent of a daily newspaper? Off-screen music played "Til Eulenspiegel" while Magnus Magnusson admitted that "We are not quite clear that the burial, if any, was at the centre."

The archaeological party, however, did discover Dean Merewether's urn which he had been thoughtful enough to leave in 1849 for future generations to discover. The twentieth-century treasure-hunters, astonishingly reminiscent of some of my daughter's birthday parties, found inside the jackpot a Victorian halfpenny, a farthing, a letter, a newspaper, and a set of verses written by Emmeline Fisher, the daughter of a Salisbury cleric. But I still think our hairier ancestors might have been kind enough to leave some kind of memento, even it if were just one of those mugs the Beaker people used on feast days, such as the sort of thing children received at the jollifications to commemorate the coronation of Queen Elizabeth II.

The last member of this strange archaic cluster of curiosities lies about $1\frac{1}{2}$ miles north-west of Avebury on a dome-shaped down rising between the headwaters of the River Kennet. As the first of its type to be extensively excavated, it has conferred its name on the material culture of those people who immigrated to this country from France somewhere around 3000 B.C. The Windmill Hill folk could really be called England's pioneer agriculturalists, as they went about the deliberate production of food as opposed to a hand-to-mouth existence. They therefore raised the prehistoric standard of living from mere dependence on nature to the first rung, albeit a very low one, of some kind of planned economy. It was only after this had been established for some time that man suddenly began to look around him and find energy for more complicated achievements such as Avebury and Stonehenge.

Neolithic earthworks of the Windmill Hill type are called causeway camps because their circular banks and ditches are interrupted by bridges of untouched chalk, which curiously enough were not merely entrances but often the result of the work being carried out at different times by different gangs of labour. This particular one is ringed by three concentric lines of earthworks and dotted about it are round barrows which were built at a later date.

It is thought to have been a tribal meeting-place or cattle corral used chiefly in the autumn for a round-up of beasts, when they would have been ear-marked (nicked with flints) and slaughtered because there was no winter feed. The remains of pottery found in the ditches are said to have belonged to the temporary dwellers who used them as shelter at these times.

There is no doubt they would have needed that shelter, judging by the kind of permanent gale that sweeps over Windmill Hill today. In fact, the one great certainty about the place seems to be that it was well-named in the Middle Ages and a splendid site for the purpose for which it was then needed. When I was last there, it was on one of those days when the sun was shining down on the Marlborough Downs, making the dark green clumps of trees on top of them look like well-plumped-up cushions; while over to the north-west a thundercloud was looming up and beginning to send thin cold needles of rain slantways across the site. To add to the rather startling effect, there was a rainbow curving down over that well-known landmark above the village of Cherhill, the tall Lansdowne Column, erected by the third Marquis to commemorate one of his ancestors, Sir William Petty, the seventeenth-century economist. As I struggled into a mackintosh I wondered whether my own long-forgotten forbears kept an extra skin or two handy for the same protective purposes. It seemed more than likely that they did, if the ingenuity of their exhibits in the little museum in the village below me was anything to go by.

Thanks to the careful excavating carried on under the personal supervision of Alexander Keiller in the 1920s, we know a few fascinating details about them. They appear to have grown wheat, barley, and flax, because stray grains, seeds, and chaff were sometimes accidentally mixed with the wet clay during pot-making and their impressions preserved in the surfaces after firing. I hope the up-to-date Wiltshire farmers are not too upset by the fact that the size of these grains compares well with that which is grown today. The Windmill Hill farmers and their womenfolk ground their cereals by placing them in a hollowed stone saucer and rubbing a smaller round stone on top of it. It has also been discovered that besides keeping long-horned cattle, sheep, and pigs, they also kept dogs of an unspecified breed but mostly resembling a chow, of which a skeleton can be seen in the Avebury museum. Experiments have also proved that one of their polished flint axes can fell a pine tree, 7 inches in diameter, in five minutes *flat*. The most numerous of their surviving tools are flint scrapers which they used for cleaning fragments of flesh and fat from animal hides when preparing bedding or clothing.

But possibly the most interesting thing, from the point of view of someone of my own sex, is that even in those far-off days when it is doubtful whether they ever got around to anything as sophisticated as the crudest form of textile-making, they appear to have found time to carve little ornamental chalk pendants. Perhaps, all those thousands of years ago, adornment of the female form was still riding high way up on windy Windmill Hill.

XII

NO ONE-HORSE TOWN

MARLBOROUGH, especially in the minds of those not really acquainted with it, is sometimes brushed aside as being just another small and rather insignificant Wiltshire town. Unfortunately, a recent television programme did little to dispel this illusion. In "What the Hell ever Happens in Marlborough?" this ancient borough was portrayed as a place where little went on except for various activities undertaken by the Kennet and Avon Silver Band and the local amateur dramatic society. Although both these formidable institutions appeared to be flourishing, many moonrakers (including myself) felt that there was much more to Marlborough than actually met the eye on the evening when this particular programme was shown.

Therefore, in all fairness to Marlburians, I have decided to call this chapter "No One-horse Town", because I do not consider it is. That it happens to have a white horse carved on the side of the downs by the road leading to Avebury, is totally irrelevant. Neither am I thinking of some of the calamities connected with horse-drawn vehicles for which the neighbourhood became notorious, such as the fatal accident which befell the architect, James Wyatt, in 1813, and a somewhat less serious incident that took place in the 1920s. This latter eventuality concerned the horses assigned to the local fire-engine which, on an occasion when they were otherwise engaged in pulling a brake full of Marlburian matrons up Granham Hill to a grand function in Pewsey, were halted in their tracks and hastily transferred to fire duty, leaving the unfortunate socialites stranded for the afternoon.

Nor am I referring to those spirited animals belonging to the five establishments near Marlborough, which may be seen every day careering over the gallops way up on top of the downs; although this sight in itself is enough to put Marlborough completely 'on the map'. Watching these race-horses in training, ridden by tiny young lads whose hearts are all set on becoming Lester Piggotts, is almost better than a day at the actual races; and being 'put in the picture' by Mr. Robbins, who looks after Mr. Marshall's* stables at Ogbourne Maizey, is even better still.

Mr. Robbins never goes racing, never bets (because he sees no point in keeping the bookmakers), and never stops working on something he loves, 'his' horses. He seems to be almost as much a part of the Marlborough Downs as the springy turf which, since the importation of thousands of tons of peaty soil many years ago, has now become a permanent fixture on the training courses. "Look," he says, as half a dozen of his long-legged hopefuls, with manes and tails flying, come suddenly into view. "Keep quite still now. These young 'uns get easily scared. That's a little beauty out in front. Good bunch we got this year." His knowledgeable eyes miss nothing as they stream past. Then, as he gets into his car again in order to be back at the stables in time for their return and to organize the next sortie, he adds, "I once went into a factory. Half the hours and double the pay. But I didn't stay long. I reckon once you've been up on these downs all seasons of the year, you don't want nowt else."

It is true that owing to the huge high expanse of these downland acres surrounding Marlborough, the extent to which the town itself can grow is limited. This, however, I take to be one of its greatest assets. It is protected by these sentinels, except for the narrow breach created by the Kennet Valley which runs through the town from east to west, and Savernake Forest which graciously guards any approach from a south-easterly direction.

Marlborough therefore does not attract industry and has no natural products other than chalk, of which there is, of course, plenty. The noisy A4 unfortunately accompanies the Kennet through the town and somewhat spoils the broad High Street, which is one of the loveliest in the whole of England. (Marlburians cannot help hoping that when the M4 is in operation just south of Swindon, much of the heavy traffic now rumbling to and fro will be diverted in that direction.) Before the great fire that swept the town in the seventeenth century, this unique street had the

* Mr. Marshall has recently taken over from Sir Gordon Richards.

charming characteristic of having penthouses, supported by pillars, extending the whole length of either side, although sadly there is little of this kind of architecture now still apparent.

Dropping down into Marlborough (because that is the only way to describe arriving in the town from the north or south), is a singularly pleasant experience. I think possibly coming from Pewsey on a fine autumn morning is the best means of approach. The Wiltshire Downs are exceptionally high here. Half-way between Pewsey and Marlborough there lies a curiously shaped one called Martinsell which, when viewed from a certain vantage point, looks rather like a natural green pyramid or a gigantic Silbury. A little farther along, the road crosses the route of the mysterious Wansdyke, the remains of which appear to pop up so inconsequently and can be traced at intervals right across southern England for as much as 40 miles.

Soon after this point, the descent from Granham Hill begins and, quite suddenly, there is Marlborough lying gracefully in the Kennet Valley, half secluded by green and golden trees from which the College buildings slowly emerge to dominate the scene and give the impression that this is by no means a one-horse place.

The feature I find quite fascinating about Marlborough College is that in the grounds there is a man-made mound half the height of Silbury, which few people notice and yet which appears to have the same kind of mysterious origins. It has been suggested that Marlborough derives its name from this structure, 'Marl' being a kind of soil and 'borough' being a mound or barrow. There have, however, been so many theories put forward about the name of this Wiltshire town that it seems to be another of those delicate decisions best left to personal choice. The Marlborough College mound is covered by trees (which happily hide a water-tank once placed at the top) and the whole edifice is not really apparent, unless pointed out by kind schoolmasters who are only too willing to take you to see it. Were it not for the mound, it is unlikely that they would be doing any such thing and therefore some account of its history seems to be necessary.

People have said that it is possible that both the Silbury and Marlborough mounds were raised for worshipping a river god or perhaps a kind of local Pan in the Kennet meadows. At one time, the river would have been a broad ill-defined stream sometimes filling the whole width of the valley, and therefore both mounds would have been surrounded by water. Not very many years ago, the people of Avebury still used to gather on Silbury Hill in the spring and feast on cakes and drink water fetched from the swallowhead of springs that are close by. Likewise, until about seventy years ago, a fair was still held in Marlborough during May, when the inhabitants joined hands and danced through the town, ending up by throwing various articles into the river and chanting, "The tailor's blind and he can't see so we will thread the needle." The exact meaning of these words is obscure, although obviously both observances had something to do with water and could well have been connected with reliance on some river deity.

Although the first mention of Marlborough is in Domesday Book, it is reasonable to assume that it was a busy little trading centre in Saxon days and had some kind of defence. Because it occupied such a strategic position during the Conqueror's advance, the mound must have been considered an excellent site for a royal castle. The initial one would probably have been of wood, and then replaced shortly afterwards by a flint and stone building. The first evidence that any castle was habitable comes from a report which says that Henry I spent Easter there in 1110, while later on Becket arrived to join Henry II for Christmas.

King John appears to have been very fond of Marlborough. He granted the town a charter, and tradition says that some of his children were baptized in the font that is now in Preshute Parish Church. He is also said to have granted a certain lady called Eva, who was a resident in this same parish, the free gift of a penny a day. Unfortunately, however, history is guarded as to the reasons for such a magnanimous royal gesture.

Later still, Marlborough Castle was the place where the hapless William Longespée came in anger for an audience with Henry III in an attempt to seek vengeance for the way his wife, Ela, had been so shamefully treated during his absence abroad. It was the King's Justiciar, Hubert de Burgh, then the most powerful man in the land, who had gained the young monarch's support for a marriage he had hoped to arrange between his nephew and Ela, whom he conveniently assumed to be widowed. Hubert was now afraid that the King, on hearing the other side of the story, might side with Longespée against himself. He therefore tried to placate the returned warrior with the offer of a team of horses and a ceremonial feast in his honour. This is the fatal meal at which

Longespée is said to have been poisoned by the Machiavellian de Burgh.

Fortunately there is a happier report of feasting at Marlborough during the year when Henry married Eleanor of Provence, and the order for the bulk of goods to be despatched to the castle at that time reads as follows: "24 gallons of wax, 5 measures of almonds, 50 small baskets of figs or a like quantity [about 16 hundredweight] in larger ones, 12 gallons of dates, 25 cases of raisins, 4 dozen napkins, and 5 or 6 small jars of good ginger." Except for the wax, it would not appear to be so very far removed from the Christmas order of some large establishment of today.

But by far the most important date in the history of this castle on the mound occurred in 1267, during the reign of the same but ageing Henry, when a parliament was called at which representatives from the boroughs and the knights of the shires attended, and where the Statutes of Marlborough were drawn up for the betterment of common justice throughout the realm. The leading spirit behind this great event was Henry's son, Edward, soon to become one of England's greatest monarchs. Although the Statutes of Marlborough and Edward's so-called 'Model Parliament', which he summoned thirty years later, were far removed from the kind of free-for-all proceedings now indulged in by the present House of Commons, yet in a tentative way, they might be thought of as the birth-pangs of democracy and the beginning of the end of those autocratic powers wielded by such a select blue-blooded company as the ancient Witenagemot, who fell through that upstairs floor at Calne 300 years before.

The Statutes of Marlborough proved to be the greatest but also the last noteworthy episode in the life of the castle. By the end of the fourteenth century it was beginning to fall into ruins, and by the time Queen Elizabeth visited the town in 1592, she was unable to be accommodated either in a castle or its successor constructed on higher ground in the outer bailey by the Seymour family, to whom the whole property now belonged. At the end of the seventeenth century yet another mansion was built by the sixth Duke of Somerset and this, fifty years later, was turned into an inn. A cordial announcement advertising the great change appeared in the *Salisbury Journal and Devizes Mercury* on 17th August 1752 and reads as follows: "I beg leave to inform the Publick that I have fitted up the Castle at Marlborough in the most genteel and commodious manner, and opened it as an Inn, where the Nobility, Gentry, etc., may depend on the best accommodation and treatment; the favour of whose company will always be gratefully acknowledged by their most obedient Servant, George Smith, late of the Artillery Ground, London. Neat Post Chaises."

There is also a rather charming letter written by a certain Lady Vere in which she describes her feelings of nostalgia shortly after the castle had been taken over as an inn. She says, "we lay at the Castle Inn and could not help moaning over it, as it was an ancient habitation of the Seymours ... would the grandfather Duke of Somerset have liked to have been told that his grand-daughter would have put his family house to this use? Lady Betty does not dare to write to the Duke of Dorset on account of this house, for fear it should put him in mind that some time or other it may be thought that Knowl may make as convenient an Inn for Tunbridge, as this does for Bath."

Despite Lady Vere's regrets, however, the Castle Inn soon became a noted and very welcome refuge for travellers who had braved the bleak route from the west past Silbury Hill. Events of the road, not perhaps as numerous or so instantly reported as the pile-ups on today's A4, must yet have been even more sensational once they had percolated through to Marlborough to be discussed in the ancient bar parlour. After all, the fighting which the town had witnessed during the Civil Wars was now long forgotten, and perhaps this was a time when an entertainment called "What the Hell ever Happens in Marlborough?" might reasonably have had more justification for its existence.

It must have caused untold drama when, during the great snowstorm of Christmas 1836, His Grace, the Duke of Wellington, while journeying to the mansion of the late Duke of Beaufort in order to give away the latter's daughter in marriage, was forced to stop for the night at the Castle Inn. The following morning his carriage became fixed in a wheatfield somewhere between Marlborough and Badminton, but, fortunately, one of his outriders discovered a small gang of workmen who hastily came to the Duke's assistance and their surveyor was able to pilot him across country until they came to a 'sound-bottomed' road. This must have happened only a little time before the Harris brothers of Calne were installing those ice-filled ceilings in their bacon factory, and, I imagine, if that kind of weather was then not an uncommon occurrence they hardly needed to import so much foreign ice as might have been expected.

The Duke of Wellington had seen the inn almost at the end of its career because soon the railways began driving the coaches from the roads. By the middle of the nineteenth century no one wanted to take on the lease of a place that was losing custom, and when the Reverend Charles Plater and his inspired committee, including Mr. Sotheron Estcourt from Devizes, began looking around for a suitable establishment in which to start a school, primarily in order to give a first-class education at a low price for the sons of clergymen, the Castle Inn appeared to be more than suitable. In 1843 200 boys between the ages of 8 and 16 gathered in the old halls of the Seymours, and the birthday of what is now known as Marlborough College took place. I trust not too many of the younger ones were scared by the rumours, rarely heard of late, that occasionally they might see a phantom coach and horses driving round the courtyard at night; possibly the same Duke of Wellington returning from Badminton?

Today the old Castle Inn is a kind of nucleus around which Marlborough College has spread itself in a very pleasing fashion and which looks like what it says it is, a college and not a school. Although, naturally, a great many additions have been made in order to accommodate the 800 boys who now reside there, the overall impression is one of mellowness, as if, perhaps, it were a younger relative of one of the more ancient Oxford colleges.

The atmosphere is strangely peaceful. The masters and boys seem to stroll and not to rush; Marlborough College appears to have progressed in the best kind of way. It has taken boys from Swindon Grammar School for an A-level course, and would do so again if educational grants permitted. It has also adapted to a co-educational experiment, and female A-level students can be seen walking in the town escorted by young male ones. The way in which Marlborough has accepted this revolutionary idea may be summed up in the words of one of its housemasters, "We have really forgotten the girls are there." Initially, most of them came because they had brothers at the college; nowadays this is not a necessary qualification. The forty young ladies now present at Marlborough are all fashionably dressed; the boys all look reasonably tidy and their hair is of a reasonable length. When spoken to they are friendly and anxious to please.

I once asked a younger boy the exact whereabouts of the White Horse on the hill near the school; his reply was encouraging and made me wonder whether the wheel had come full circle since the days when I myself was struggling with mathematics. I watched his brow crinkle up like a worried bloodhound puppy as he debated with himself whether to explain the distance in yards or miles. Eventually he plumped for a quarter of the latter, saying apologetically, "I think that's right, but I'm all squiffed up on my English distances." I sympathized with him having felt permanently that way myself, and 'squiffed' was a word strangely reminiscent of my own schooldays.

I watched him as he pedalled off on his bicycle to take part in a Wednesday afternoon's outdoor activities. These seem to be a great feature at Marlborough. Boys either belong to a Cadet Force or become members of some works group. There is a tremendous accent on social services at the College, and many boys can be found spending this 'half-day' weeding or digging old folks' gardens. Others may be seen trimming hedges in the school grounds under the supervision of one of the gardeners. A small contingent is responsible for the upkeep of St. Peter's church-yard, where they cut round the gravestones and generally tidy up. The eldest boy in this group today told me that he had been working there every Wednesday afternoon in term time for the past three years, and I found the way in which he made this simple statement, as if it were the most natural thing in the world for him to have done, somehow extraordinarily impressive.

In fact, to me, the whole of Marlborough is rather impressive. I am not quite sure how much this has to do with the College, the High Street, the trees, or the Downs. Perhaps it is an admixture of all four. There is certainly a majesty about the Marlborough Downs that is unlike the gentler atmosphere of the rolling type I was brought up with in the south of the county. I am just a little overawed by the steep heights around Marlborough and am glad that my particular focal point of Wiltshire can still be seen from some of them. There is an altogether different feel about Hackpen Hill to the north and Martinsell to the south of the town. Going to Marlborough from Wylye is not just a question of going 'over the top', as the southern moonrakers do when they happen to visit neighbours in those five lovely valleys that converge on Salisbury. On reaching Marlborough, one has also put the vast lonely stretch of the Plain proper between 'foreign parts' and home. Obviously, the Marlburians' link with the south is not so strong although, owing to the College's great connection with the church, many a present-day schoolmaster has, or has had, a father who was a cleric in the Close. Likewise, many an old boy is a southern moonraker, including that very able Chairman of the Governors at Lackham, Mr. Michael Stratton.

Somehow, the changing times have dealt kindly with Marlborough. They have taken place gradually and many of the old customs remain. One of them, for instance, is the annual Mop Fair held around Michaelmas each year, when the High Street is closed and the twentieth century has to play second fiddle. This used to be an occasion when employees changed their jobs, and their various trades were symbolized by the tools they used. A mop was representative of a housemaid; she flourished it in order to attract the attention of a new employer.

Although those days seem very remote, I still know at least two moonrakers of my own age and sex who remember what it was like to have their precious half-day stopped because they had forgotten to dust along the top of a picture-frame, or were perhaps one minute late in getting down to work at seven o'clock each morning. Twenty years ago, one of these heroines rashly offered to come and take the rough with the smooth in our household, for which blessing I have been ever grateful but also not a little worried, because Mrs. Down seems to have had so much more of the former than the latter. But this never seems to worry her. She rises to every occasion and is always cheerful, besides being the best cook in Wiltshire.

Mrs. Down is also a constant mainspring of information on the county, the country, and the world in general. She keeps abreast of the times, as it were, and always tells me when there is a television programme which she feels it would be good for me to see, because she knows that my viewing habits are erratic and often non-existent. In fact, it was Mrs. Down who told me to watch "What the Hell ever Happens in Marlborough?" and the following morning we discussed the programme. I think it now seems wisest to put a full-stop to this chapter and our conversation.

XIII

THE VERT AND THE VENISON

It has often been said that William the Conqueror "loved the tall deer as though he were their father". This expression somehow seems to me to be a little far-fetched. Fathers do not usually love hunting or eating their children, which, as far as these beautiful animals were concerned, happened to be what the monarchs in those days mostly did with them. It would, perhaps, be fairer to suggest that William 'loved' his forests (and all that lay therein, including the fact that they were places over which he could exercise absolute power). There was, therefore, good reason for both him and his descendants to make continual and solicitous inquiries as to "the state of the forests, alike in vert and venison".

The Marquess of Ailesbury, the twenty-ninth hereditary Warden of Savernake, in his delightful book *A History of Savernake Forest*, has offered the following definition of what this sort of countryside is, or in former times, was. He describes a forest as "an area of land which has been requisitioned by the Crown and which is administered under the Sovereign's direct authority; used for the purposes of a game reserve". It was not, as is commonly supposed, an entirely wooded place; in fact, it might consist mainly of rough grass interspersed with heath and scrub. The grazing was good and those who lived around the forest (the borderers) had traditional claims as to pasturage.

The rights of these poor countryfolk, however, were infinitesimal when compared to the fines, fees, and dues that might be levied by the monarch and which all helped to fill the royal exchequer. In the case of Savernake, it was common practice for the king to apply these revenues to swell the jointure of his consort or to provide an income for royal princes. It is therefore hardly surprising that during the Middle Ages there were nine royal forests in Wiltshire alone, namely: Braydon, Chippenham, Chute, Clarendon, Grovely, Melchet, Melksham, Selwood, and lastly, but by no means least, Savernake.

It has been established without doubt that this forest near Marlborough was in existence in 1066 and that it probably existed some time before that. When the man who so 'loved' the deer decided to create yet another forest in Hampshire, it became known as New Forest, thereby implying that the others in the south of England were already old.

William had not been on the throne long before he put Savernake in the charge of Richard Esturmy,* a man who had fought with him at Hastings and who now became the very first of a long line of hereditary wardens. The post stayed in the Esturmy family until the middle of the fifteenth century, when it passed via the female line to the Seymours; after which, in 1676, once again through the distaff side, the wardenship devolved on the husband of the late William Seymour's grand-daughter, Thomas Bruce, the eldest son of the Earl of Ailesbury.

Owing to its particular geographical position, Savernake was one of the most useful of southern forests. It was conveniently 'on the way' from London to the West Country, during those days when a king was wont to travel around his kingdom 'putting up' at one or another of his royal castles. It seems obvious that the one at Marlborough must have been highly popular because not only was it *en route*, but also had on its doorstep a well-stocked forest where as many as thirty bucks or does could be requisitioned at a time. In the Middle Ages fresh meat was hard to come by all the year round, as farmers were unable to keep large herds and flocks in the colder months, owing to lack of fodder. Beasts not required for breeding were therefore slaughtered in the autumn and their flesh preserved by salting. Meat of any kind was often non-existent for the poor, unless game was poached at the risk of losing life or limb. Any forest warden who could supply the royal party not only with fine sport but a 'good table' during winter, was a most valuable kind of employee.

Some of them were naturally better at the job than others; the

---

* The local historian, the late Mr. H. C. Brentnall of Marlborough, put forward the interesting theory that the name is derived from 'l'estormi' and could be translated as 'the alert one', or 'the wary'.

history of Savernake and those who looked after it is certainly a stormy one. Wardens, Foresters of Fee,* Lieutenants, Rangers, Verderers, Woodwards, Regarders, and Under-foresters, together with their royal employer and his Justices in Westminster, all came in for trials and tribulations at one period or another. Forest Law was a thing apart; the protection of the "vert and the venison" (not a thing that combined easily owing to the latter's predilection for the former) literally a matter of life and death.

It is hardly surprising that for 150 years after the Conqueror's claim to Savernake, the forest gradually spread itself and absorbed much of the surrounding countryside. Yet neither is it surprising that this infringement greatly angered the landowning knights and squires, who were insistent that the absolute powers which the monarch enjoyed over these ever-increasing acres must somehow be stopped.

Likewise, the lowly borderers who lived around these areas resented the fact that they were not protected by Common Law but were subject to this curious and totally undemocratic Forest Law. Great was the indignation felt because of the numerous petty restrictions whereby anyone going about the forests was liable to be stopped and questioned, while during the Fence Month in midsummer when the forests were *'défendu'* (in order for does and new-born fawns to be free from disturbance) no one could really move freely at all. A forest dweller was not permitted to keep a dog unless he allowed its paws to be maimed to prevent it chasing deer. Moreover, if he had a piece of land and wished to cultivate it, he could not fence it against the king's deer, who had first priority on whatever he attempted to produce.

Therefore there was more than justification for the two clauses (seldom remembered) in Magna Carta, one which stated that "all forests which have been afforested in our time shall be forthwith disafforested"; the second which purported that "justice should likewise be done in respect of those areas which Henry our father or Richard our brother afforested". The barons, influenced by the political views of the knights and squires, forced the unwilling

---

* Foresters of Fee presided over outlying bailiwicks; Lieutenants were directly under Wardens and were, in turn, served by Rangers. The position of patrolling Verderers was honorific and the humbler ones known as Woodwards. The status of Regarders is a little doubtful but Under-foresters were simply deer-keepers.

Marlborough High Street
The Grand Avenue, Savernake

King John to set his seal to a charter which attempted to control the misuse of that indefinable Royal Prerogative, the convention in the British Constitution which nowadays is only exercised in mercy but which was then used against the freedom of the individual. There seems no doubt that behind the Forest Law in medieval times, there stood nothing but the 'Divine Right of Kings'.

Gradually, there came to be no shame in flouting that right, even by people of so-called higher social standing, especially after 1224 when the death penalty for slaying one of the king's deer was removed. There are records of Marlburian vicars "taking a doe with a bow and arrow on the Tuesday of Pentecost week", or being engaged in the same sort of crime "on the third Sunday in Lent". The way the dates are related to such devout gentlemen somehow makes their offences appear to be a great deal worse than if the offenders had been merely John Baynton and others who "kylled a ffawne without licence or warrant", or simply poor Thomas Hyde who "overlayed the said fforest with more cattell than he should kepe".

Bad King John, of course, had no intention of honouring his promises made in 1215, although the boy-king Henry III issued a Charter of the Forests reiterating that which his father had pledged. The disafforestation of Savernake was really left to the conscientious monarch, Edward I, who did his best to implement the Charter by sending one John de Berewyke to conduct a kind of perambulation and realignment of the boundaries. Unfortunately, the subsequent ruthless slashing away of four-fifths of Savernake resulted in untold repercussions. Even Edward himself appears to have been rather shaken by de Berewyke's zeal. Finally he allowed his conscience to let him ask Pope Clement V to absolve him from his promise which he felt to have been too rashly undertaken. This procedure seems to have been a customary 'get-out' for medieval monarchs and, although this time undertaken by a far better one than most, was a repetition of King John's policy after Magna Carta.

Savernake, reprieved, continued to be a splendid royal recreation ground. Its tentacles stretched out again and even began creeping over the borders of Hampshire and Berkshire, despite disappointment and simmering discontent from most sections of the community. It was not until 1330, when England was governed

K

Racehorses training on the Marlborough Downs

by a Council of Regency on behalf of the young King Edward III, that full opportunity was taken by this powerful body to curb the sprawling forest and bring it back within well-defined limits. Yet, although this was hailed with great satisfaction by the majority of people, within Savernake itself bitter feuds took place. Something akin to present-day 'redundancy' arose; claims and counter-claims for possession of dwindling bailiwicks went winging to and fro between Savernake and Westminster, resulting in a most unhappy period in the forest's history.

Moreover, not always were the monarch's subjects alone upset. Sometimes the monarch himself would give vent to his displeasure as when, nearly 200 years later, Henry VII, evidently dissatisfied with the state of the "vert and the venison", reaffirmed his inten-tion to "have our game within our said fforest to bee reserved, cherisshed and kept for our disport and plaisir". Later on, Henry VIII became a frequent visitor to Wolfhall, near Burbage, the home of the hereditary warden, who by that time was Sir John Seymour (the fourth generation and third warden of that name).

One of this monarch's visits occurred in 1535 and the twenty-ninth Warden of Savernake suggests that "it is reasonable to sup-pose that Jane Seymour would have assisted her mother in playing hostess to the royal guest; young ladies are seen to advantage in a domestic role of this sort, and it may well be that, enjoying the hospitality of this home of the wardens of his Forest of Savernake, the susceptible monarch began to take something more than a friendly interest in Jane". It seems more than likely this was the case, because when the unfortunate Anne Boleyn was beheaded in the spring of 1536, the King took Jane Seymour for his wife the following day.

The marriage also appeared to open the way for Jane's ambitious brother, Sir Edward Seymour, to begin his astonishing rise towards that unique post of power, Protector of the Realm. To so in-fluential a person, it was then evidently quite an easy matter to arrange for the ownership of Savernake to be transferred to him. After the death of Henry VIII, in Letters Patent issued in 1548 by the tender young Edward VI, the forest (together with the castle at Marlborough) passed from the Crown into this "well-beloved" uncle's hand. When the Protector overplayed this eager hand and fell from grace, all honours and land acquired by him after 1540 were meant to be forfeited. But the undaunted Seymours, aided by the length and confusion surrounding the Letters Patent, somehow managed to retain possession of Savernake, and were able to bestow the property and the wardenship on their more conscientious descendants, most of whom have admirably lived up to their responsibilities for the "vert and the venison".

There was, however, a serious attempt to curb the ambitions of the Seymour family soon after the Protector's head had been chopped off. The land and foundations of a huge palace he had planned to build in part of the forest known as Brail Woods which, had it been completed, would have been similar to Sir John Thynne's stately home at Longleat, were now granted to the Earl of Pembroke, who was directed to remove the vast stock of building materials. It was not until the Protector's heir, Lord Hertford,* had been released from the Tower and forgiven by Queen Elizabeth for marrying without her consent, that the problem of a suitable house for the new owner of Savernake arose once more. The old home of the wardens, at Wolfhall, was now too far gone in ruins for repair. It was therefore decided to enlarge a small house called Tottenham Lodge to the south of the forest, which was soon to become the forerunner of several great mansions that have since occupied the same site.

The Protector's heir happened to be a good warden. He lived well into the seventeenth century and accomplished the almost impossible task of procuring peace for Savernake Forest. He created two immense deer parks and was so successful in management that instead of disorder and defiance, there was cheerful cooperation, perhaps best illustrated by the fact that the borderers of that time assisted in a "Vewe of the Deere". This was a kind of annual census to see how many of these animals there were, and seems strangely akin to the present-day 'partridge counts' which take place on land owned by keen shooting Wiltshire moonrakers.

Hertford often played host to James I, these occasions being the first of their kind to be recorded after the forest had passed into private ownership. A ceremonial blast on the great medieval hunting horn of the Esturmys would then have been blown in honour of the sovereign's arrival, a tradition that was last carried out in 1940, on the occasion of a wartime visit to Savernake by the late King George VI.

* This Earl of Hertford married Lady Catherine Grey (sister of Lady Jane), who bore him two sons, but died while she was still imprisoned.

Unfortunately, Hertford's descendants began running short of both money and male heirs. In 1676 the wardenship once again passed via a female heiress to Lord Bruce, eldest son of the Earl of Ailesbury. The mansion which Elizabeth Seymour should have inherited and which was set in what John Aubrey fondly referred to as a "romancy" sort of park, then no longer existed having been burnt to the ground. By the end of the century Wolfhall itself was nothing but a crumbling ruin; Lord Bruce, a staunch Jacobite, was in exile; his wife was dead; the remains of Tottenham House were haunted by an aged employee living in a few rooms, while much of the forest had been turned into agricultural land.

But with a tenacity of purpose which appears to have been bestowed on many hereditary wardens who have been able to save Savernake 'in the nick of time', it was now given to Lord Bruce's son to restore his mother's property. With his exiled father's blessing and the help of a kindly practical uncle, the young man methodically began building up both the fortunes of the forest and also a new Tottenham House, designed for him by his brother-in-law, Lord Burlington. Moreover, he made the happy choice of selecting for an heir the youngest of his sisters' sons, who not only carried on his good work but extended the Grand Avenue and recreated Tottenham Park.

The celebrated Mr. Lancelot ('Capability') Brown, who during his life kept 'progressing' from one country seat to another, used his famous expression liberally (from whence came his nickname) with regards to the new lay-out of this park. There was some interesting correspondence between the new warden and his agent in which the latter wrote to his employer, who was away in London, saying that Mr. Brown: "advised the trees to be thin'd thro-out the whole open Grove about the Loggia, but not too much, as he proposed a shady ride through those plantations with little opens judiciously cut to catch the view of Proper Objects, such as Martinsell Hill, Wolfhall House, Brimslade Wood etc. . . . Mr. Brown thinks there is great *Capability* about the Loggia and Octagon Buildings. . . . He seems very fond of having large Clumps made upon the Downs at a Distance, which he has hinted at more than once before." I am sure many a moonraker, as he gazes at Mr. Brown's 'Clumps' today, must feel that gentleman was, indeed, more than capable.

In *A History of Savernake Forest*, the Marquess of Ailesbury has given a fascinating description of how Mr. Brown seemed to think everything at Savernake possessed 'capability', and that one day while "riding or driving through the forest with Ailesbury's father-in-law, old Mr. Hoare of Stourhead, he let fall what may have been his most pregnant suggestion. It inspired Mr. Hoare to make a very rough sketch, and to send it to his son-in-law. The latter preserved it, adding a memorandum as follows: 'Sketch by Mr. Hoare of what He understood to be Mr. Brown's Idea for Improvements in the Forest so as to make it one great Whole'."

It was indeed through Capability Brown's plans that the Lord Ailesbury of that time was inspired to plant trees on an ever-increasing scale, and turn Savernake from a hotch-potch of small coppices, rough grazing, scrub, and waste ground, into a visibly well-arranged unit. It must have been a difficult task to accomplish when confronted by the numerous claims of the 'borderers' round about; but it must be remembered that this beautifying period in the history of the English countryside also coincided with the Enclosure Acts, so that doubtless some form of compensation was given to those with former grazing rights.

Today this 'One Great Whole' covers about 4,500 acres of Wiltshire and is unique in the fact that at no time has it ceased to be called a forest, a name usually reserved for Crown Property. Since the end of the last war, Tottenham House, an enlarged and more imposing mansion than that created by Lord Bruce in the eighteenth century, has been leased to the well-known Hawtrey's Preparatory School. It must, I feel, have a good effect on little boys to be educated in the peace and seclusion of a forest, and John Aubrey could not possibly have found a better adjective with which to describe the surroundings of today's school. They are still completely "romancy", and even if the children now occupying Tottenham House are not acquainted with this word, I am sure they must sense some of the mystery and wonder of Savernake as they walk down the Grand Avenue, or simply gaze from their windows along Capability Brown's magnificent vista at the end of which is a highly "Proper Object", a most imposing column erected in the name of George III.

Earlier this century it became evident to the sixth Marquess of Ailesbury that he was living in times which made it impossible for him to maintain the forest as his forebears had done. In 1930, with many misgivings, he opened negotiations with the Forestry

Commission for leasing the sylvicultural rights of Savernake. There appeared to be many obstacles in the way of a final settlement. Perhaps, like those monarchs of olden days the twenty-eighth hereditary warden was justly concerned about what might now happen to "the state of his forest, alike in vert and venison", but in a far more aesthetic sense than its original owners. Would all the deer have to be slaughtered? Would Savernake, hitherto a hardwood forest largely consisting of natural oak and Capability Brown's beeches, now suffer the humiliation of being planted up with military-looking rows of little conifers?

In 1939 an agreement was at last signed, fortunately with an accommodating spirit on both sides. The lease was for the usual 999 years and the hereditary wardenship was retained by the Marquess and his heirs. There was a clause (not absolutely binding on the Commission) restricting the use of soft-woods, and a committee was set up to deal with the amenity aspect of the forest. It was agreed that within an area comprising the old deer park, the only conifers to be planted should be larch and these for the sole purpose of nursing the young hardwoods. Certain glades remained unplanted and here charcoal burning was a major feature during the last war, the product being used for gas masks, which practice still survives.

The lessors undertook to remove the deer from their old enclosure and confine them in Tottenham Park. This was an extremely tricky operation. Aided by Marlborough schoolboys, the first manoeuvre failed, but a second Operation Deer Round Up was successfully carried out with the help of the army. When Tottenham Park came under the plough during wartime, many of the deer had to be killed, but fortunately today there still exists a smaller deer park to the south of Tottenham House, where both fallow and red deer* flourish. In the forest itself, there are also a few roe and fallow deer which happily are no longer hunted, the size of the herd being kept in check by judicious culling on the part of the Forestry Commission. The twenty-ninth warden no longer lives at Savernake, but his son still occupies Sturmy House in the little forest village of Durley.

Although the network of roads now running through Savernake is private, all may be used for legitimate recreation and, to me, at any time of the year, there are few more beautiful places in the

* Usually red deer have not done well at Savernake unless carefully 'nursed'.

whole of Wiltshire. John Aubrey offered one of his lively and original suppositions as to the meaning of this forest's name. He suggested it was a mixture of 'sweet' (sa or sav), 'fern' (vern) and 'oak' (ake), and this seems a most agreeable theory, even if arbitrary. Certainly there is now a generous planting of what I hope will one day become stout-hearted oak trees and the "sweet cis" fern (to which he was referring) is still to be found at Savernake. I never go there without experiencing the same kind of fairy-tale feeling that woods have always given me, and without half-expecting to hear the sound of the Esturmy's hunting horn echoing down some glade.

Savernake also makes me feel small and rather selfish because I have never personally planted a tree, at least, not the kind of gorgeous oak and beech to be found in this Wiltshire forest. I feel tree-planters are very special people, good philanthropic types who rarely live long enough to be completely rewarded for their initial actions. I can well understand why Disraeli once wrote, "I like very much the society of woodmen," because these people plan and plant not for themselves, but for posterity. I know that I must have the wrong spirit, as the thought of planting any tender young sapling always makes me feel sad.

I think maybe this is because I once gave my father a small walnut tree for his birthday which he planted with great ceremony and aplomb; but I remember a remark made by one of the birthday guests as we all trooped back into the house after the last shovel of earth had been carefully trodden down. "By the time that tree's bearing nuts, Arthur," said this moonraking friend, "you won't have any teeth to eat 'em with." I could not help thinking he was right, but also that it made an unfortunate anticlimax to an occasion which, until then, had been quite a merry one.

Therefore, whenever I drive through Savernake, I cannot help silently saluting those twenty-nine gentlemen who, be they good, bad, or indifferent, have somehow managed to preserve such a long line of hereditary Forest Wardens in the same way that they have preserved, and are still preserving, the "vert and the venison".

XIV

JEFFERIES' COUNTRY

IT is morning on the hills, when hope is as wide as the world. . . . Let us get out of these indoor narrow modern days." Yes, Richard Jefferies, let us indeed.

Let us, perhaps, go up to Barbury or Liddington Hill when the sun is in the east and the great mushroom town of Swindon seems dwarfed by the Wiltshire, Berkshire, and Gloucestershire landscape stretching away into infinity, and remember that just over 100 years ago a boy grew up in these parts who came to be known as the finest writer on the English countryside since White of Selborne.

The farmhouse where Jefferies was born is down there somewhere below us, tucked away behind those elm trees near Coate Water, from where he said:

> There was a hill* to which I used to resort . . . the labour of walking three miles to it, all the while gradually ascending, seemed to clear my blood of heaviness accumulated at home. . . . I began to breathe a new air and to have a fresher aspiration . . . at every step my heart seemed to obtain a wider horizon of feeling. By the time I had reached the summit I had entirely forgotten the petty circumstances and annoyances of existence. I felt myself. I was utterly alone with the sun and the earth.

It must have been difficult for a small farmer and his wife to understand this son of theirs who kept tramping up to the hills south of Swindon and spending his adolescence lying on the grass and thinking. It must have been a relief when a chance meeting with young Mr. Frampton, a new reporter on the *North Wilts*

* Generally thought to be Liddington.

152

Herald, resulted in long lanky Richard Jefferies getting a job at last. For the time being, the worrying question "What was he going to do?" which his parents kept asking each other, was shelved. The unsuspected genius of Richard Jefferies was now brought under the discipline of a newspaper office. He was taught to get down to the actual job of putting his thoughts on paper, which, as one of his great admirers and biographers, Reginald Arkell, said, "is a beastly and laborious business—unless you happen to be in the mood, when it is as satisfying as any other natural function".

Considering that Richard Jefferies died at the early age of 38 (the last five years of his life having been spent fighting a losing battle against tuberculosis), and had by then published some twenty books and countless articles, it would appear that he must have got down to the job of putting his thoughts on paper more often than not. His apprenticeship with the *North Wilts Herald* was an invaluable experience, although, for his particular personality, the enforced spells of proof-reading must have come unusually hard. Yet his colleagues appear to have borne no antagonism towards him, even though his inability to get down to routine jobs threw more work on their own shoulders.

One day when Richard Jefferies was 24 and Mr. Joseph Arch from Warwickshire happened to be trying to form his Agricultural Labourers' Union, readers of *The Times* were rather startled when, on a certain November morning in 1872, they were confronted by an unusually well-written letter from an unknown Wiltshire moonraker. In retrospect, perhaps some of its contents might seem a little out-of-keeping coming from a man with such strong altruistic tendencies and who, at a later date, appeared to be an ideal communistic philosopher. It began: "Sir—The Wiltshire agricultural labourer is not so highly paid as those of Northumberland, nor so low as those of Dorset; but in the amount of his wages, as in intelligence and general position, he may fairly be taken as an average specimen of his class throughout a large portion of the kingdom. . . ."

Readers of *The Times* then went on to learn that the lumbering gait of the Wiltshire labourer around Swindon was the result of walking behind the plough in early childhood, when weak limbs found it hard labour to pull heavy nailed boots from the thick clay soil; furthermore, the writer suggested that their diet had something to do with this seeming lack of vitality, as it consisted of bread and cheese, soft oily bacon twice or thrice a week (occasionally enhanced by onions) while, if a man happened to be a milker, he enjoyed a good tuck in at his employer's expense on Sundays.

Although long, however, the letter was not long-winded. Neither was it impassioned nor prejudiced. It was more of a plain statement of fact written by an observant man on the conditions in an area about which he seemed extremely knowledgeable. He considered that the Wiltshire farmworker was better clothed and better housed than formerly, except for those who erected their own cottages on waste plots. There was a detailed account of a scheme organized by a certain clergyman of the writer's acquaintance, who had turned his glebe land into allotments. Interested readers of rural politics then learned that wages were 10s., 11s., or 12s. per week according to supply and demand, while milkers received a shilling extra. A farmer on the Marlborough Downs appears to have paid the phenomenal amount of 18s. per week during harvest, his reapers sometimes earning 10s. per day, enough to pay their year's rent in a week. These men also received from 6 to 8 quarts of beer per man every day during this period, and many farmers paid £50 or £60 a year on this cheering beverage in order to see that all was "safely gathered in".

The letter was received with mixed feelings. Landowning readers of *The Times* felt Mr. Richard Jefferies, whoever he might be, was on their side; even that great philanthropist, Lord Shaftesbury, wrote agreeing with Mr. Jefferies that there were many instances of a rise in the farm labourers' standard of living; Wiltshire so it seemed, had somewhat settled down since the terrible riots of 1830 when there was a pitched battle between the farmworkers and the yeomanry at Tisbury, and a certain Mr. Rider from Westbury was forced to give up making his portable threshing-machines, because of the labourers' antagonism to such innovations. Although Mr. Joseph Arch was now rekindling the flame which had been extinguished so brutally when the Tolpuddle Martyrs attempted to stand up for their rights some forty years previously, his disciples were unable to get a hold on a county where, as a mass, the agricultural workers were comparatively well paid. Only a reply from someone who signed himself "the son of a Wiltshire Labourer" suggested that Mr. Jefferies was "talking through his hat" on the subject of working-men's cottages but, according to Reginald Arkell, this was apparently "easily disposed of in a third epistle from Coate Farm".

The correspondence eventually closed with a leading article in *The Times*, but it was far from closing Richard Jefferies' career. The editor of *Fraser's Magazine* had been looking for just such a *rara avis*, a man who could write factually and forcefully on country matters. He invited Jefferies to send him regular articles and thus threw open the way for a young man's genius to expand "as wide as the world".

In Salisbury Cathedral there is a marble bust of this prose poet of the English fields and woodland, sculptured by the late Margaret Thomas. It is a very fine piece of work of a very fine man. It has been placed facing eastwards, which seems appropriate for such a visionary who once wrote, "The dawn at my window ever causes a desire for larger thought . . . as infinite as the sky are the possibilities of the morning."

Under this monument is written:

To the Memory of
Richard Jefferies
Born at Coate in the parish of Chiseldon and County
of Wilts, 6th November, 1848
Died at Goring, in the County of Sussex
14th August, 1887
Who observing the works of Almighty God
with a poet's eye
has
enriched the literature of his country
and
won for himself a place amongst
those
who have made men happier
and wiser.

I feel Jefferies would surely approve this memorial, because he gave a most beautiful appreciation of his love of good statuary in his essay "Nature in the Louvre", which was published a month after his death. Surprisingly, this was declined for publication in *Longman's Magazine* in 1884 with a letter from Mr. C. J. Longman in which he writes: "I am sorry to say that I do not find the enclosed quite suited to my magazine. I don't think the general public care much about statues—have a vague impression that they are improper."

In *The Story of my Heart*, Jefferies' strange and moving auto-biography, he regretted how little good statuary he had ever seen, but added: "Still, that I have is beyond all other art. Fragments here, a bust yonder . . . the broken pieces brought from Greece, copies, plaster casts, a memory of Aphrodite, of an Apollo, that is all; but even drawings of statuary will raise a prayer. . . ."

Richard Jefferies often prayed, although not perhaps in the accepted sense of the word. He was one of those exceptional beings who possess a kind of cosmic consciousness. It is difficult for us lesser mortals to follow his mind completely. He is ahead of us, up there on a higher plane, far, far higher than those green downland rings called Liddington and Barbury Castle, where he used to build his own castles in the air and write such words as, "The heart looks into space to be away from earth."

Only quite recently I read an article about man reaching for the moon, in which Dr. George Mueller pleaded for him to "continue and expand his space adventures or else 'fall back from his destiny'. The mighty surge of his achievement will be lost and the confines of this planet will destroy it." I feel Jefferies' aspirations, however, had nothing to do with mechanical space-craft probing other planets; he was attempting to show men the way towards a better life on this one.

Not long ago I went up to Liddington and Barbury on a day that was so clear and bright that even infinity seemed to draw just that much nearer. I looked at the view of three counties at which Richard Jefferies must so often have looked. In the wide blue sky above me lay the long white curving trail of a jet aircraft; below, near Wroughton, there was an aerodrome and a large hospital; here and there, I became aware of the Ridgeway rolling along on its old cross-country run; and just south-east of Swindon, I could pick out new earthworks where modern man was busy continuing the M4 across North Wilts. But none of this really intruded on the scene before me. Just for a moment, I hope I understood what Jefferies meant when he wrote, "The day . . . was as marvellous, as grand, as all that had gone before."

For this was an especially good day. I had started it by going to Coate Farmhouse and up into the high attic rooms that are now given over to a museum, in which are recorded all the interesting documents connected with both Richard Jefferies and Alfred Williams, the local hammerman poet who was born just ten years before the former died. It is the house about which Jefferies said, "I chose the highest room, bare and gaunt, because as I sat at work I could look out and see more of the wide earth, more of the dome of the sky."

It is not now, of course, as he described it in *Meadow Thoughts*; neither is it the same as when Reginald Arkell set off on his bicycle as a young man intent on looking for the "old house by the silent country road, secluded by many a long, long mile and yet again secluded within the great walls of a garden . . . lime tree branches overhung the corner. . . ." The road by Jefferies' house is now a dual-carriageway; the wall has been pushed back, although the lime trees (albeit pollarded) have been spared. But the town of Swindon has crept up on the half-hidden "milestone with its chipped inscription 'To London, 79 miles'". Instead, there is a very large road sign telling everyone how to speed everywhere by all possible methods of direction.

Coate Water, where Jefferies used to sail a home-made boat and which inspired his *Bevis, the Story of a Boy*, has now been taken over by Swindon Corporation. The place is open all the year round, Christmas Day included, and the charges for entry are extremely low, although a little higher for fishermen. Eager young boys may still be found enjoying themselves there and, who knows, one of them may be blessed with an imagination that can superimpose itself on the well-laid concrete path that now confines Coate Water. In his inventive mind, this small lake and haunt of wild fowl that started its life as a reservoir for the old Wilts and Berks Canal, might still be thought of as Bevis's "New Sea"; the streams running in and out could quite conceivably be the Nile and the Mississippi; and if the advent of the M4 does rather spoil the surrounding "swamps and jungle", yet all the cars in the world cannot detract from the thrill of a perch on the end of some small boy's fishing-line. With a final stretch of imagination, the voice of mother saying that it is time to go home, could be simply that of Polly, the dairymaid, who stood at the door of Coate Farmhouse over a century ago, calling Richard (Bevis) Jefferies back to his supper.

I could not help wondering what it had been like being brought up in this house at that time with a London-born mother, a down-to-earth countryman for a father, two brothers, and two sisters, one of whom was killed at the early age of 6 by a runaway horse on the Coate road. The old part of the house (which is now occupied by the head librarian of Swindon's reference library), is early eighteenth century; but the newer part with those attic rooms in which Jefferies used to work, was added more than 100 years later. At face value, this addition is not particularly attractive. The rooms inside seem depressingly small and square. Having visited them and then re-read the first draft of *The Story of my Heart* (which was not published until many years after the revised one), I have even more sympathy for this unusual and imaginative youth who said: "Immediately after getting up I used to go out to the outside of the garden and rickyard to a spot whence, under an elm, I could see clear across the fields eastwards to the hill. . . . I forgot everything . . . the house, the people about, the sounds; even the grass wet with dew, in front where the fields stretched away to the Down, just for the moment was quite gone."

The two attic rooms which now house Jefferies' possessions, manuscripts, first editions, and paintings of the district by an American lady, Mrs Kate Tryon, together with memorabilia connected with Alfred Williams, have a certain sadness about them; yet I was cheered by the very human letter written by Jefferies to his publishers, Messrs. Smith, Elder and Co., on 9th November 1878, regarding *The Gamekeeper at Home—Sketches of Natural History and Rural Life*, which must be the same kind of letter as authors have written to their publishers since William Caxton first began to print. This particular one reads: "Gentlemen, I have just received your note and am very glad that the *Gamekeeper* is going into a third edition. I have no corrections to make to the text. But on page 41 of the second edition, the last line at the bottom of the page, the letter 'l' has dropped out of the word 'leaves'. It there reads 'decaying *eaves*'—it should be 'decaying leaves'. Such mere literals however. . . ."

Although Jefferies moved to London in 1877, he was Wiltshire born and bred and his memory is kept very much alive in the county, especially in this part of it. There is an active Richard Jefferies Society, and its able Chairman, Mrs. Frances Gay (who can remember Swindon at the end of the last century and is also an ex-mayoress of the town), knows so much about Richard

Jefferies and his works that her knowledge makes me diffident in writing my own small appreciation, but perhaps I may be forgiven because I sincerely believe Jefferies to have been an exceptional man, and I was more or less brought up on *Bevis*. Moreover, I can well remember Reginald Arkell and my father discussing all his books during my youth.

In his biography, Reginald Arkell described the young author's move from his native countryside as a mistake, although Jefferies was not entirely unhappy in London. He had by now married the daughter of a neighbouring farmer and although he still delighted in nature and the country, he was fond of what he called "a thickness of people", and wanted to "feel the indefinable life which animates the mass". He longed occasionally to mingle with the crowd although not to be forced to meet the individual, a sentiment with which perhaps many would sympathize.

It was in his first little house at Surbiton that, while wondering what to send to the many editors with whom he was now acquainted, he began remembering his Wiltshire upbringing more and more. It has been suggested that there was possibly an element of "distance making the heart grow fonder" about this. The time he had spent in the company of Keeper Haylock of Burderop now resulted in the articles in the *Pall Mall Gazette*, which later became the well-known *Gamekeeper at Home*. The following year saw the publication of *The Amateur Poacher* together with *Wild Life in a Southern County*. Soon after this came *Round about a Great Estate*, *Green Ferne Farm*, and *Hodge and His Masters*. As soon as Jefferies forgot about aspiring to be a writer of novels and stuck to his fantastic store of knowledge on country matters, he was, as they say, 'away', even though in body he was far away from his native Wilts.

In the early eighties Jefferies went to live in Sussex, the ostensible reason being the poor condition of his health. But there is little doubt that his overriding passion for the downs and the sea had a great deal to do with the choice. He was always referring to the sea, even when in Wiltshire, and there is a heart-breaking account of how one day, when living in London, he was overcome with desire to get to it, so that without any premeditation on the mechanics of such an undertaking, he simply set off on a frustrating haphazard journey, finally reaching his goal late in the afternoon. Both ocean and rolling downs seemed to give him the same kind of thrill. Having been brought up in an inland county where the hills often seemed like an immobilized heaving swell, Jefferies decided to spend the rest of his life within sight of the active and passive forms of his great loves.

He never came back to Wiltshire, at least not in person; although in mind, he most certainly returned to his native boundaries again and again, and the house which he once occupied in West Brighton was appropriately named 'Savernake', one of his favourite destinations on his marathon walks from Coate. In *My Old Village*, he wrote that he had never put himself in the charge of many-wheeled creatures that move on rails and go back: ". . . lest I might find the trees look small and the elms mere switches and the fields shrunken and the brooks dry, and no voice anywhere—nothing but my own ghost to meet me by every hedge".

Sometimes, when Jefferies became too weak to hold a pen himself, he dictated his writing to his wife. During the last year of his life, *Amaryllis at the Fair* was published, a book which many consider to have been his masterpiece.

Others, perhaps, now took up the cudgels where Jefferies left off, such as his contemporary W. H. Hudson, who lived to be twice his age, and Alfred Williams, whose writings entitled him to a share in the Jefferies' Museum.

Alfred Williams was born in the little village of South Marston, a few miles north-east of Swindon. He was brought up by a very poor but industrious mother whose husband had deserted her and the family of eight children. When he was 12 years old, Williams went to work on a farm, but three years later followed his other brothers into the Swindon Railway Works. This big change in his way of life had a tremendous impact on such a sensitive youth, and his outstanding social document, *Life in a Railway Factory*, gives this vivid picture: "There is the striker's hammer whirling round, this one pulling and heaving, the forgeman running out with his staff, the stamper twisting his bar over, the furnace man charging in his fuel, the white slag running out in streams sparkling, spluttering and crackling—the steam, the thick dust, the almost visible heat, the clouds of smoke, the ring of metal under the blows of the stampers, the horrible prolonged screeching of the steam saw, the roaring blast."

Not surprisingly, Williams' health suffered, although not sufficiently to prevent him embarking on a mammoth study of

Lydiard Tregoze
Queen's Park, Swindon

English, French, Latin, and Greek, despite the fact that he had to walk or cycle to work in all weathers to be at the factory each morning by six o'clock. During the years before the First World War he published numerous books and poems on the country way of life around Swindon and was much encouraged by the Poet Laureate, Robert Bridges, and Lord Edmond Fitzmaurice, a member of the Government and a leading figure in Wiltshire life.

Although still in poor health, he volunteered and was accepted for active service in 1914, embarking on a soldier's life with characteristic enthusiasm. While stationed in India he became fascinated by the people and their religions, subsequently mastering Sanscrit, the ancient language of India, from which its modern tongues are derived. He translated a number of folk stories which were published after his death under the titles *Tales from the Panchatantra* and *Tales from the East*.

After his return from India, Williams and his wife, Mary, personally built their own cottage to live in which they named 'Ranikhet', after his hill station in India. In 1930, when his wife was desperately ill in the Victoria Hospital at Swindon, Williams himself collapsed and died. Mary, at her own request, was taken back to 'Ranikhet' to spend the last few weeks of her life putting her husband's literary affairs in order. It is sad to reflect that the Civil List Pension granted Williams by the Prime Minister, Ramsay MacDonald, came too late to be of any assistance to him. Yet Alfred Williams appears to have been the last person to worry about that sort of thing, for he once wrote, "All life has its recompenses. I am not unrewarded."

The riches of Alfred Williams and Richard Jefferies were not of this world. The railwayman and the farmer's son both died comparatively poor men. They set their sights on something higher than material rewards, perhaps best illustrated by this particularly revealing quotation from Jefferies: "The pageantry of power, the still more foolish pageantry of wealth, the senseless precedence of place; I fail words to express my utter contempt for such pleasure or such ambition."

As the M4 bulldozes its muddy way by Coate Water, as the stray visitor climbs the narrow staircase to the museum at the top of the farmhouse, as a small twentieth-century schoolboy, armed with his fishing-rod, pays to go into Bevis's "jungle", let us remember that high on the Wiltshire Downs above, stand two

L

Malmesbury Abbey
The Market Cross, Malmesbury

memorials. On Liddington Hill is a plain Ordnance Survey Post on which is written:

The hill beloved of
Richard Jefferies
and
Alfred Williams

On Barbury there is a 3-ton sarsen stone, on which, facing east, is written:

Alfred Williams
1877–1930

Still to find and still to follow
Joy in every hill and hollow
Company in solitude.

And on the side of this stone that faces towards his birthplace and far, far beyond that, is the simple but moving inscription:

Richard Jefferies
1848–1887

It is Eternity now.
I am in the midst
of it. It is about
me in the sunshine.

XV

ALL CHANGE HERE

If an artist suddenly decided to paint a large jumbo jet in the top right-hand corner of a picture that otherwise chiefly consisted of clear skies and green rolling downs, the result might be somewhat representative of Swindon's position in the Wiltshire of today.

Swindon is a big up-and-coming industrial town of 100,000 people; by the end of the century it may well have reached the 250,000 mark. It is no longer a 'railway' town—the embryo M4 has now come to Swindon; so have divers industrialists, to say nothing of a large proportion of London's overspill population. True, the town may seem alien to the Wiltshire that I have always known and loved, yet at the same time 'Swindon, Wilts' is a force to be reckoned with and I cannot help but be very impressed by it.

There is an old Wiltshire word which I feel to be highly applicable to Swindon and that is "jonnick". It means 'straightforward' or 'fair'. Even if Swindon seems a little out-of-keeping with the county as a whole, I trust the town and the people who run it may appreciate this compliment. Because those in charge of Swindon today are some of the most efficient and easiest people to get on with that it would be possible to find. If they say they are going to telephone at a certain time, they telephone on the dot; if they say they are going to put something in the post on a certain date, then they do so; or (and this is the great criterion), if they are unable to do so for some unforseen reason, they telephone to say why. For this, I could forgive Swindon anything. Not that I have anything to forgive. It may be rather like a big brother who has grown a long way from the family nest, yet I feel him to be a kind and generous brother who, although he has done remarkably well for himself, has indirectly spread a great deal of security over a large part of his native county.

A long time ago Swindon was just another little market town like its neighbours, Wootton Bassett, Cricklade, and Highworth. In fact, until around 1800 the town's postal address was 'Swindon, Nr. Highworth'. It was situated on a small hilltop on the southern edge of the Thames Valley, with the Cotswolds farther to the north and west and the Marlborough and Berkshire Downs to the south and east.

Swindon was, perhaps, fortunate in possessing some quarries of Portland Stone, the exploitation of which was stimulated during the early part of the nineteenth century by the construction of the Wilts and Berks Canal; but apart from this there was no industry in the town. It appeared to be too far east to take much part in the wool trade, and was rather a sleepy little place which in all probability had derived its name from the fact that it was at one time known as 'Swine Down',* or the hill under which the pigs were kept. A very influential landowning family, the Goddards, settled there in 1560 and soon seemed to be running Swindon and much of North Wilts as well. The grounds of their ancestral home, 'The Lawn', now constitute a very pleasant kind of recreational park. Although the house itself is no longer in existence, part of the old parish church near by has been preserved, while there is also a small lake complete with swans which lends a rather stately touch to this big industrial town.

Until the coming of the railways, it would seem that few people bothered to go to Swindon, and few Swindonians bothered to leave it for the wider world outside. There was no monastery which might attract or discharge scholars, and generation after generation of Swindonians appeared just to stay at home, so that the same names kept recurring on tombstones: Goddard, Levett, Avenell, Looker, Haggard, and Fluck; the last mentioned being the real name of a certain Miss Diana Dors, one person at least who did not uphold tradition by remaining in her native town.

In 1840, however, far more surprising events than the birth of a future film star, started happening in Swindon. One fine autumn day during that year, the great builder of the iron railroads,

* Richard Jefferies preferred 'Sweyn's Dune' as the possible origin of 'Swindon', Sweyn being the name of a Danish nobleman who was overlord of the area many centuries ago.

Isambard Kingdom Brunel, came to Swindon at the invitation of another clever engineer, Daniel Gooch, and the two of them sat down to enjoy a picnic together on some poor land covered with furze, rushes, and rowen, land which was thought to be so worthless that only a fool would consider buying a strip. This little outing would never have taken place at all but for the fact that Swindon was already 'on the map' as far as a railway was concerned, because the Marquess of Ailesbury of that time had refused to allow such a monstrosity to follow the Kennet Valley through his Savernake estate. Therefore, those in charge of the Great Western Railway were forced to alter their plans and look farther north for their route from London to Bristol, and even a little farther north again, owing to the fact that the Goddard family was not exactly keen on having a line anywhere near 'The Lawn'.

It would be interesting to have a verbatim report of the conversation between Gooch and Brunel on that auspicious occasion of so long ago. But it seems that evidently the former persuaded the latter that Swindon was in too strategic a position to be 'just another station', and was an obvious choice as a place of special importance to the G.W.R. Gooch considered that it would be necessary to keep pilot engines there in order to haul trains up the steeper gradients west of the town; that Swindon, together with Reading, would nicely divide the route across the country into three equal parts; that it was, in any case, the intended junction with the Cheltenham branch line; and the Wilts and Berks Canal would allow coal and coke to be obtained at a moderate price. This canal and its reservoir at Coate could also be used in the last resort as a water supply, the possible lack of which seemed to be the only serious drawback.

Whether Gooch plied Brunel with cherry brandy or whatever people drank at these sort of picnics in the nineteenth century, it is hard to say, but there is a persistent legend attached to their meeting which is highly reminiscent of the way in which the site for Salisbury Cathedral was chosen. It appears that at any rate they had more than enough to eat because at some stage of the proceedings, Brunel threw a sandwich into the hinterland of Swindon, and the point at which it landed is said to have marked the spot for the first building put up by the Great Western Railway. Twice in the history of the county there are accounts of objects being sent through the air at random which have given rise to outstanding results. A chance arrow and, hey presto, there was Salisbury Cathedral. A little Wiltshire ham in between a couple of slices of buttered bread, and before the end of the century here was the largest establishment in the world for constructing and repairing railway engines.

A whole new 'railway town' began to grow up at the bottom of what was now referred to as Old Swindon; and for the next sixty years it was as if "never the twain shall meet". The town on the hill desired no contact with the growing menace below it either physically, socially, or administratively. The reputation of those bare-chested devil-may-care navvies, who had scared the wits out of the respectable section of the community as they thrust their steel tracks through the English countryside, still clung to the more permanent employees of the G.W.R., now successfully housed in 300 railway cottages that had been specially constructed on the flat ground near 'the works'. The Old Town gathered up its skirts and tried to ignore the noisy shuntings on its doorstep. Not that it could hold out for ever. Steam power had come to stay, at least for the next 100 years. Even the protestations of Lord Bolingbroke, who complained that the Swindon Works' hooter disturbed his early morning sleep at his country seat at nearby Lydiard Park, went unheeded. The Industrial Revolution was well away, and New Swindon was doing more than its share to help it.

By the turn of the century, however, it was obviously impossible and impractical for the two towns to remain at loggerheads any longer. They had by now at least coalesced physically, and certain enlightened Swindonians such as the great reformer and idealist, the late Reuben George, who gave his whole life to the betterment of the entire neighbourhood, made impassioned pleas to the effect that it was ridiculous for Old Swindon and New Swindon to be governed by separate local boards, and that amalgamation would make the town one of the finest in the West of England. In 1900 a merger at last took place, turning Swindon officially into one municipal borough; yet even today, although it gives every appearance of being (as Capability Brown might have said) "one great whole", there is still an indefinable 'something' about living in the part which is still proudly referred to as the Old Town. Here it is still possible to find many ancient buildings among the thriving new shops, and in Cricklade Street there is an outstanding example of early eighteenth-century architecture which Sir John Betjeman once referred to as "one of the most distinguished town houses in Wiltshire".

But the main thing to remember today is that Swindon as a 'railway' town is past history. A visit to the Railway Museum seems to confirm this more than anything else. There they are, those gigantic puffing billies such as the Lode Star, the City of Truro, and an exact replica of the broad-gauge North Star, all of them shiny, static, but still magnificent. I have never been fond of cars or aeroplanes, but boats and trains I love. Waiting to meet the down train from Waterloo as it used to puff round the bend just before Salisbury station, always gave me a kind of thrill, and reminded me of those lines of Kipling's:

> but why don't poets tell?
> I'm sick of all their quirks an' turns—the loves an'
> doves they dream—
> Lord, send a man like Robbie Burns to sing the
> Song o' Steam!

Even though the diesel engine has now taken away much of the romance, I still enjoy hearing the bell ring on my own home platform which tells me the London train is coming through the tunnel under Bishopdown, and watching its huge grey form snake in and come slowly to a halt. There is something dignified about the operation and, oddly enough, these old steam-engines at Swindon Museum seem to have retained that dignity although they are no longer in use, rather like valued old cart-horses put out to grass.

There is a room in this museum given over to records of Brunel's achievements, as well as another dedicated to Daniel Gooch. Brunel was said to be a man of great personal charm and good humour. Some say he was also the greatest engineer of all time; it is certainly strangely moving to see his very own drawing-board and the fascinating pictures of Clifton Suspension Bridge and the Royal Albert Bridge at Saltash, which he designed. In the upstairs gallery where Daniel Gooch's talents are recorded, there are some show-cases with mementos of Queen Victoria's coach, including some splendid gadgets which she used in order to tell the driver of her train whether to go "Quick", "Slow" or, as the museum attendant nicely put it, "stop altogether so that she could get out and pick moon daisies". There is also a most attractive advertisement for an excursion from Exeter to Weston-super-Mare in 1869 for the princely sum of 1s. 6d.

A rather obvious but nevertheless interesting point connected with communications throughout the ages often seems to crop up in conversation in this part of Wiltshire. At one time Swindon's main contact with the outside world was the coach pulled by three piebald horses that left the 'Goddard Arms' daily; Swindonians turned out *en masse* just to watch it pass. Then the Wilts and Berks Canal was constructed and trade was considerably improved between the agricultural Vale of White Horse in Berkshire and West Wilts, where it linked up with the Kennet and Avon. It was spanned at Swindon by the Golden Lion Bridge and the locals watched fascinated as this was raised in order to allow the gaily painted barges (chiefly carrying coal and grain) to pass underneath. In less than fifty years, along came the railway and gradually the canal wasted away, its course now dried up and barely discernible. The railway, of course, is still there; Paddington is only one hour and ten minutes away by fast train. But the M4 is now pushing along past Swindon. A broad expanse of heavy, wet, newly dug clay heralds its approach, and soon it could be taking over more of the railway traffic. Therefore, it is hardly surprising that many moonrakers ask themselves how long it may be before this new wonder of a motorway is but a dying race track and hovercraft are zooming along carrying Swindon's latest products.

Because Swindon today seems all set to produce a great many things. The railway age may have departed but Swindon is still 'full steam ahead'; it has a lot on its mind, or perhaps one should say the mind of one man in particular. This is the Town Clerk, Mr. Murray John, a man who more than thirty years ago had enough vision to think about the decline of the railways and the need for diversification of industry. Swindon could well have reverted into just another Wiltshire town (and a depressed one at that), but for the genius of this quiet and unassuming person in charge of it. His task was perhaps helped by the fact that during the Second World War many industries, such as Vickers-Armstrong and the Plessey Company, moved to Swindon for security reasons, liked what they found and remained when hostilities were over. On the other hand, one feels that they would not have been so keen on staying, but for the fact that someone somewhere behind the scenes had the town's interests very much at heart, and was guiding it gently but firmly in the way he felt it ought to go.

And Swindon has certainly gone from strength to strength. It is a town with a quite remarkable record. Until 1943 the only library in the place was that belonging to the Mechanics' Institute. But during the war the Corporation took the bold step of opening its first municipal public library, which now has the distinction of lending more books in proportion to population than almost any other town in the country. Moreover, apart from the County Council itself, it is the only borough council in Wiltshire that subscribes (and subscribes generously) to the Victoria County History series. It was the first town to inaugurate an Arts Centre entirely financed and administered by a local authority, while it has a museum and an art gallery to which entry is free, the latter containing works by many contemporary artists including Henry Moore, Augustus John, Paul Nash, and Graham Sutherland. Swindon has also built more council houses since the last war than any other similarly expanding borough, as well as having successfully carried out countless housing schemes of a different nature; and quite apart from this formidable record there is another human feature about the place which I consider far too important to overlook. This is that it is actually possible to park a car in Swindon today and, what is more, park it at a very reasonable charge.

The Town Development Act of 1952 greatly aided Swindon's plans for expansion, and, by an arrangement with the London County Council, it became possible to attract more industry to the area and to house those Londoners who were badly in need of homes. Economists often talk about taking "work to the workers" or even "workers to the work"; but to accommodate both workers and work without weighting the scales too heavily on one side or the other seems to me to have been an amazing achievement.

So many industries have now taken root in Swindon. Many of them are to do with engineering or electrical work, but there are also large establishments and factories connected with clothing, tobacco, plastics, chemicals, household equipment, packaging, building, and countless others. Many more industries are on their way to Swindon, including Burmah Oil. Swindon seems highly conscious that it is a place that knows where it is going. It has a plan, a big plan, and exudes every confidence that, Government policy permitting, this will be carried out. Even the traffic warden by the Town Hall or the waiter at the 'Goddard Arms' will tell you that "Swindon will be even better in ten years' time". Some of the older folk regret that when they walk down the High Street they mostly see strangers; yet they do not seem to bear any resentment about this. It appears to be in the natural order of things. Perhaps a town which has seen the arrival of the Railway Works in the nineteenth century has now learnt to accept change in the twentieth a little more easily than, say, my own home town of Wilton.

As for the new 'immigrants' (and these include Indians, West Indians, Italians, Pakistanis, and Poles), most of them say they like Swindon because it is so easy to get out into the surrounding countryside. Swindon is certainly devoid of mile upon mile of grimy suburbs or slums. As an industrial centre it is almost unique because all at once, here is Swindon and then, quite suddenly, there is the Wiltshire countryside and this, as Edward Thomas wrote, "is beautiful". He also referred to it as "a quiet, an un-renowned, and a visibly ancient land. The core and essence of it are the downs. . . ." I could not agree with him more.

If my work took me to Swindon, I should prefer to live near the downland countryside south of the town rather than to the north, where the Thames Valley, although delightfully rural in parts and possessing those rare and lovely acres where the shy fritillary still flowers, is nevertheless too flat for my liking. This, of course, is a purely personal matter because I happen to feel like Nebuchadnezzar's wife, who missed her native hills so much that her husband built the Hanging Gardens of Babylon in order to make her feel more at home. As I feel it would be highly unlikely for any such event to take place in my own case, I should have to venture farther north to the Cotswolds or east to the Berkshire Downs, which would then take me out of my beloved Wiltshire, in which I am hope to live for the rest of my life.

But flat or otherwise, there is no doubt that the prosperity of Swindon has had a marked effect on all the countryside around it. Every small town and village is much sought-after for residential purposes; but whereas in South Wilts the villages are somewhat full of retired army personnel, in North Wilts they are full of young industrialists, and these people are, of course, raising young families. Therefore, unlike the rest of the county, where primary schools are closing or amalgamating, in North Wilts they are full and flourishing.

Swindon is within commuting distance of a great many attractive places and enjoys what I believe is otherwise termed "a pleasant employment hinterland". Although this ranges for a good 20 miles or more, in the immediate vicinity, Highworth, Cricklade, and Wootton Bassett still have the advantage of being comparatively rural but within 5 or 6 miles of the job on hand. Swindon's expansionist policy is all mostly to the west so that, if all goes well, Wootton Bassett will become considerably nearer the town, while places such as Purton, Lydiard Millicent and Lydiard Tregoze may ultimately become entirely within its benevolent embrace.

I refer to this benevolence in all sincerity because the planners of future Swindon seem to have thought of everything. Like Capability Brown, they are well aware of 'proper objects' which will have to be considered in the general urban structure. They realize, for instance, that the view of the Marlborough Downs from Swindon is enhanced by the open foreground which separates them from the town and which, at present, is only interrupted by the village of Wroughton. They, therefore mean to contain development here and preserve this precious amenity.

Moreover, Lydiard Park, which was bought by Swindon Corporation in 1943 and has been most beautifully restored to become a conference centre and a show-place well worthy of a special visit, will be maintained in its particularly graceful setting, despite all modern developments around it. For Lydiard mansion and the lovely old church beside it, which once lay within the bounds of the royal Forest of Braydon, is really rather unique, although no trace of the hamlet, which was once Lydiard Tregoze, now remains.

The Tregoze family, whose name was added to that of Lydiard to distinguish it from the adjoining parish of Lydiard Millicent, came from a village in Normandy called Troisgots and settled here in the twelfth century. Soon they began playing an important part in the government of Wiltshire. It is not known exactly when a house was first built on this site, but by the middle of the fifteenth century the estate passed via the female line to the St. Johns, who were to hold it for the next 500 years. This family certainly rebuilt a mansion, and this came to be used as a holiday home or a place to which to send their children whenever they were ill; the estate was also a source of country produce which helped to stock their larders at Battersea wherein the St. Johns' chief interests lay. A viscountcy was created in 1716 but gradually less and less attention was paid to Lydiard Tregoze, and by the middle of the last century the place was going rapidly downhill; no money was being spent on the estate or the mansion, and it is said that the last Viscountess Bolingbroke and her son moved from room to room as the ceilings fell down in each. In one small ante-chamber there is an unusually lovely window of painted seventeenth-century glass which miraculously escaped destruction owing, presumably, to some fine domed roofing above it.

As for the church, which comes within the Bristol diocese, its spectacular furnishing makes it quite unlike any other I have ever come across. The structure of the building is of thirteenth-century origin, although much enlargement and improvement has taken place at various later dates. But there are, I think, only two words to describe the interior and they are 'bizarre' and 'boxy', because it is full of effigies, while all the pews are carefully shut in by high wooden doors vaguely resembling stabling. It gives the impression of being a private chapel belonging to a patrician family rather than a parish church, and it is small wonder that John Aubrey wrote in 1670 "for modern monuments . . . it exceeds all the churches in this countrie".

The effigies are strange and wonderful, testifying to the great wealth which the family undoubtedly possessed at one time. There is a highly elaborate triptych said to be the most splendid and remarkable monument of its kind surviving in England; it was created for a certain Sir John St. John in memory of his parents. There is also an extravagantly canopied, sculptured monument for himself and his two wives, who lie on either side of him with a little host of kneeling marble children at their heads and feet. In the chancel a very individual memorial called the 'Golden Cavalier' has been erected to the memory of his son, while there are effigies of an earlier Nicholas and Elizabeth St. John kneeling with great dignity, dressed in fine Tudor clothes. A curious edifice has also been conceived for one of the daughters of the house who is seen sitting with a finger against her cheek and a skull on her knee, listening attentively as her husband, Sir Giles Mompesson, reads to her.

The *tout ensemble* is, perhaps, a little like Madame Tussaud's, and the macabre effect is heightened by the sombre light cast by the heavy stained-glass eastern window which depicts a symbolic tree. Somehow I cannot help feeling that had I been brought here as a child I should have been too distracted to pay much attention to the service, because the figures would have fascinated me as, indeed, they would today if I attended one of the regular services that are still held here.

On leaving this historic little Church of St. Mary and driving down the avenue of lovely old elm trees, it is still possible to catch a glimpse of Swindon, but only just; although considering that the Railway Works' hooter used to waken Lord Bolingbroke a century ago, the town is not really so very far away. Soon, it may start creeping nearer and nearer, and then there is bound to be a more persistent noise penetrating the peace and quiet of Lydiard Tregoze. I trust that should this happen it will not disturb the more permanent slumbers of the St. Johns too much. Somehow I like to think of them lying there protected in a little green oasis, while they sleep on into the twenty-first century unperturbed by progress and even, perhaps, a little grateful to it because, after all, it is big go-ahead Swindon that has now been able to bring back more than a touch of glory to their stately ancestral home.

XVI

FOREIGN PARTS

On 12th March 1625, in the tiny hamlet of Easton Piercy, in North-west Wilts, a boy was born who grew up to describe his native countryside as, "a dirty claye country". He also added that the people "speak drawling" and that they were "phlegmatique . . . slow and dull, and heavy of spirit". Moreover, he continued, "hereabout is but little tillage or hard labour. They only milk cowes and make cheese; they feed chiefly on milke meates, which cooles their braines too much and hurts their inventions." Not content with this dismal picture, he added insult to injury by calling the natives, "melancholy, contemplative and malicious, their persons plump and feggy* by consequence whereof come more lawsuits out of North Wilts—at least double to the southern parts".

I may be a southern moonraker but I feel Mr. John Aubrey, celebrated antiquary or no, was not being exactly fair to his home ground. It may seem rather flat in parts; it certainly is very wet and muddy in winter and, of course, three centuries ago Easton Piercy could hardly have been much fun for a boy with such a gregarious character, who later became a confirmed gossip and restless seeker after company of all kinds. Even today, Easton Piercy seems about as 'off the map' as anyone can get in Wiltshire, barring those lonely army-occupied stretches of Salisbury Plain.

Yet it has its attractions, and most certainly for the less convivial-minded. The home where Aubrey was born exists no longer, although there is another lovely old Cotswold stone house standing on the same site. Not far away, there is also the most beautiful Priory Farm, which, as might be expected from its name, was

* Thought to mean 'liverish'.

174

once the old home of nuns who, so John Aubrey wrote, "learned needlework, the art of confectionery, surgery (for gentlewomen did cure their neighbours), physics, writing, drawing and spinning". Perhaps his love of riotous living did not always include the female sex as he regarded this as "a fine way of breeding up young women". Priory Farm now breeds up the Monkswood Herd of British Friesians, but the house somehow still retains the cloistered atmosphere of a nunnery, serene, remote, and timeless.

In the church at nearby Kington St. Michael, there is a stained-glass window in memory of John Aubrey and another Wiltshire antiquary, John Britton, who was born 150 years later in this same parish. By comparison with Aubrey, Britton has not, perhaps, received the acclaim he deserved. At a very young age he went off to London, where he eventually met a publisher who had in mind a topographical book on Wiltshire. He invited Britton and another young man to help with this which resulted, first of all, in *The Beauties of Wiltshire* and later in *The Beauties of England and Wales*. The joint authors are said to have travelled thousands of miles inspecting the localities described, but unfortunately at a cost of thousands of pounds. Britton was also responsible for many other works including *The Cathedral Antiquities of England*; but although his illustrated creations have been declared the most beautiful of their kind, the elaborate methods of production could hardly have been profitable, and some of them, therefore, failed lamentably. Like Aubrey, he ended his life in comparative poverty, but was assisted by Disraeli, who gave him a Civil List pension which he enjoyed until his death in 1857.

It seems, however, surprising that this small parish between Chippenham and Malmesbury should have produced two such men who rose to fame, despite one of them considering he came from an area that made men "dull and heavy of spirit". I feel, perhaps, that Aubrey was possibly suffering from some sort of hangover when he wrote that, or was encumbered by one of the many lawsuits which seem to have bedevilled his life; for at least he should have felt grateful for his early education at the village of Yatton Keynell where, it is said, some of his school books had been salvaged from the Abbey library at Malmesbury which, until the Dissolution of the Monasteries, had been such a great seat of learning.

Moreover, Malmesbury is not flat like the rest of the district round about it. This ancient borough, which claims to be one of the oldest in England, is set up on a little rocky eminence. It is virtually embraced by the watery arms of the Avon, and one of its tributaries, which join forces on its eastern side and turn Malmesbury into a small peninsula, only approachable by land from the west. In days gone by this gave the town a natural protection and, as it was on the direct route between Oxford and Bristol, it became a place of great strategic importance. During the Civil War period of 1642-6, Malmesbury changed hands no less than five times.

The name of the town is said to be the result of mingling two words, 'Maildulf' and 'Aldhelm'. The former was the name of a Celtic monk who founded a small monastery school there about A.D. 600. The latter happened to be that of his most promising pupil, Aldhelm, a young relation of King Ina of Wessex. Aldhelm, who later became so great and wise that he was canonized, succeeded Maildulf as the first abbot of the new abbey, which was then just a small wooden structure. Gradually, Aldhelm's fame spread and he left Malmesbury to become Bishop of Sherborne, where he founded another abbey, besides being responsible for the little Saxon church at Bradford-on-Avon, which was only rediscovered in the last century.

Many strange and wonderful deeds are attributed to St. Aldhelm. He is said to have built the first organ in England for his abbey at Malmesbury which was "a mighty instrument with innumerable tones, blown with bellows and enclosed in a gilded case". He was apparently a great writer and singer of verse, a gift which he used to good account when he felt his congregations were fleeing too unceremoniously after Mass. He had all the makings of an advocate of the 'swinging service', because he would nip out of the Abbey and waylay the miscreants in St. Aldhelm's Mead (now the town's recreation ground), where he would sing a few songs in a lighter vein, gradually blending scripture with jest, thereby bringing everyone back to the fold. To this day, his name is greatly revered in Malmesbury and it is possible, with a certain kind lady's permission, to see a small grotto at the back of a house where the saint is said to have meditated. It is known as The Well of St. Aldhelm and is prettily covered with fern; neither the depth nor the temperature of the pool varies at any time of the year, and there is much speculation

The Thames at Ashton Keynes

as to exactly why and how the water arrives there, considering it is some 60 feet above the level of the Avon.

Two centuries later, another man became a great benefactor to Malmesbury; he was King Athelstan, a favourite grandchild of King Alfred. Many people consider that the reputation of Athelstan has been rather overshadowed by his cake-burning ancestor, who, although he made 'popular' history, was not nearly as 'great' as this particular grandson. Athelstan was valiant, rich, and appeared to have what the Americans refer to as plenty of 'know-how'. He had a genius for government and began to organize it on departmental lines, bringing about a kind of prototype of the Civil Service. His court was famous throughout Europe and he was highly successful in arranging 'political' marriages for his four beautiful sisters; at one time he actually sent two 'on approval' for Henry, King of the Teutons, the unsuccessful candidate presumably having to be consoled by a duke. After every marriage, Athelstan became richer and richer as his future brothers-in-law sent him fantastic gifts in return for each sister's hand. Athelstan gave these priceless treasures to his favourite Abbey of Malmesbury, notably pieces of the Cross and of the Crown of Thorns worn by Our Lord.

The King's great love for Malmesbury, which was likewise reciprocated, arose from the loyal support he received from its inhabitants at the famous but unlocated battle of Brunanburh, where he defeated the Danes. For this, he rewarded Malmesburians with what is known as 'The King's Heath', some 500 acres of land, the ownership of which has descended throughout the generations until this day. Until quite recently, a curious ceremony always took place there when a man was entitled to claim his inheritance either by descent or marriage. He was taken to his allotted portion of land where he was given a turf cut from it, while a steward tapped him on the back with a twig saying:

> Turf and twig I give to thee,
> As King Athelstan gave to me.

In olden times this kind of ritual was not unusual as it was a convenient method of transferring land ownership when illiteracy was so general. Although nowadays Malmesbury still possesses 'commoners' of a more scholarly character who let their land to a

M

Littlecote Manor
Castle Combe

local farmer, it is rather sad to think that there are movements afoot for bringing this kind of tenure to an end altogether.

The town has been fortunate in that its early and somewhat remarkable history has been better recorded than most, owing to the fact that in the twelfth century another 'expert' appeared to enact his particular role in the Malmesburian scene. This was a certain William, that famous chronicler known to posterity quite simply as 'William of Malmesbury'. He was educated at the Abbey School, but when he grew up he preferred what has been described as "the warm life of the library" to the "full rigours of monastic duties". I am not sure just how warm (in the physical sense) the library at Malmesbury may have been all those centuries ago, but certainly William made it one of the finest in Europe; it is said that the Pope himself used to borrow books from it. Here again, perhaps, imagination becomes slightly confused by a mental image of His Holiness queueing up with a little ticket in order to obtain one of the latest additions.

Although William travelled widely and procured many works from foreign historians, he also found time to do a great deal of writing himself, saying, "I proceeded during my domestic leisure to enquire whether anything concerning our own country could be found worthy of handing down to posterity. Hence I began myself to compose, not indeed to display my learning which is comparatively nothing, but to bring to light events concealed in the confused mass of antiquity." Fortunately he took great pains to check and double-check this "confused mass", in spite of having all the makings of a good gossip columnist, so that his authenticated accounts were highly readable. Some of his original MSS., written in vivid medieval Latin in his small neat script, are preserved in Oxford at the Bodleian, Magdalen, and Lincoln Colleges, and also in Lambeth Palace.

Besides writing on more profound subjects, William must have had much to say about two occurrences which took place within a century of his birth. One would have been a description of 'the daring young monk in his flying-machine' who attempted to be the first aeronaut in the world. His name was Oliver (or Elmer for those who prefer to adopt the Saxon tongue). Fastening wings to his hands and feet, he made a spectacular take-off from the top of the Abbey but, "agitated by the violence of the wind and the swirling of the air, as well as by the consciousness of his rash

attempt, he fell and broke his legs and was lame ever after".
Oliver attributed his lack of success to forgetting to provide himself with a tail, and later wished to try again, but was sensibly
restrained by the abbot of the time. He had, however, covered
over a furlong before he landed in the garden of what is now
'Oliver House', the charming home of Dr. Hodge, who is not only
a much-respected Malmesburian physician but also the town's
very able present-day historian.

Not many years after Oliver's brave attempt which had caused
such a sensation throughout the land, a second event took place at
Malmesbury for talented William to record. The town suffered a
severe fire and the wooden abbey was destroyed as well. Building
of a more permanent nature in stone was started and Hermann,
Bishop of Ramsbury, began casting envious eyes on this, proposing
to make it the centre of his bishopric. This idea greatly distressed
the monks who, in spite of the King's sanction, bitterly opposed
such a scheme and, surprisingly enough, managed to defeat it; but
had they not done so Malmesbury might well have become the
Cathedral city of Wiltshire, an honour which eventually went to
Salisbury, which became a great rival.

Another prelate who had designs on the town some fifty years
later was Bishop Roger le Poer,* an aggressive character who gave
full vent to his ambitious nature by building not only cathedrals
but also numerous castles. About the year 1100 he purposely
built one of the latter near the west end of Malmesbury Abbey to
maintain his claim on the whole borough. This was a source of
great annoyance to the monks; members of the garrison harried
them unmercifully, creating a situation comparable to that which
arose at Old Sarum, but fortunately a century later during the
reign of King John, the castle was ordered to be destroyed.

Malmesbury was really in its heyday during the fourteenth
century, when it became a centre of the wool trade. The abbey was
by now safely established with a spire higher than that of Salisbury
Cathedral. It must have been a magnificent sight, taking into
account that the whole building stood on the top of the highest
ground for miles around. But evidently a house built upon rock
does not always stand for ever; towards the close of the fifteenth
century this spire fell, taking much of the abbey with it; while the

* Not to be confused with good Bishop Richard Poore, the founder of
Salisbury Cathedral.

splendid gilt ball which adorned the top, and which must once have shone like a miniature sun over the Wiltshire landscape, rolled unceremoniously down the High Street.

Although for some time repairs to the abbey had not been carried out, this fatal event seemed to herald the tragic end of a long line of Benedictine monks in Malmesbury. When the final Dissolution of the Monasteries came, the ruined abbey was bought by a wealthy clothier called William Stumpe for £1,516 15s. 2½d., and he set up looms in all the remaining space. Stumpe was a typical forerunner of today's business tycoon. His son, who was later knighted, married the daughter of Sir Edward Baynton of Bromham (the man to whom Henry VIII had granted the ruined abbey and its lands), and Stumpe himself became grand enough to entertain the King, besides representing Malmesbury as one of its two Members of Parliament.

But perhaps Stumpe should not be too much maligned, because he later gave the nave of the abbey back to the townsfolk as their parish church. Although cynics have said this was probably due to the fact that his mills were not paying at the time, it is also asserted by the more charitably minded that he, himself, put up the money for a special licence for this purpose. After all these years, it seems kindest to give Stumpe the benefit of the doubt, because had it not been for him, it is almost certain that Malmesbury Abbey would have been a total ruin.

When Americans visit it today, they sometimes ask whether it was bombed during the last war and, for the uninitiated, this does not seem an unreasonable question. The abbey is still unmistakably a semi-ruin, although the central structure was last restored most beautifully in 1928. The interior is very simple and very light. The vaulting in the roof is quite magnificent, but the east wall, which is at present a source of constant discussion, worries me by its blankness, and I can only hope that the committee set up to deal with it will soon come to a worthwhile decision about its adornment. Although both St. Aldhelm and King Athelstan's true resting places are unknown, what purports to be that of the latter stands in the abbey with the effigy of the king recumbent on an empty stone tomb. Owing to its incredibly long and rather disastrous history, the abbey does not now possess as many treasures as might be hoped for, although it can be justly proud of the few remaining ones, such as four beautiful volumes from the Vulgate, which it has acquired since the library was broken up at the time of the Dissolution. There is also an old wooden chest which is reputed to be *the* one from which the story of "The Mistletoe Bough" originated. Since there are five 'kists' that lay claim to this, it is better left to the individual to decide whether this really is the chest in which Lord Lovell's daughter, from nearby Cole Park, hid on her fateful wedding night.

But perhaps the most striking feature about Malmesbury Abbey is its porch, which is quite unique, both for its form and its carving. As an example of twelfth- or thirteenth-century work there is hardly anything so lovely, either in this country or on the continent. The carvings of the twelve apostles in their elaborate flowing robes have sometimes been thought to be of Saxon origin, and possibly transferred from one of Aldhelm's former churches, but, whether this is the case or not, the porch of Malmesbury Abbey seems undeniably *old*, in the truest sense of that word. Although the present building has only been in existence for a mere matter of some 800 years, on passing through its porch it is impossible not to become conscious of all those men who must have tramped over this same ground for a much longer period than that: Maildulf, Aldhelm, Athelstan, daring old Oliver, William, to say nothing of the more modern Stumpe, Thomas Hobbes (the philosopher son of a Malmesburian Vicar), and Dryden, who married Lady Elizabeth Howard from Charlton Park,* and wrote his *Annus Mirabilis* while taking refuge there from plague and fire in London.

Although it seems to be 'men only' who have contributed so much towards the history of this ancient borough, I feel that during more recent years Malmesbury has come very much under the influence of the female sex. This is because in the last century it became famous for making gloves, silk, and lace. I am aware that all such apparel can be worn by men (after all, a Regency Buck loved a lace frill), but nevertheless it does appear to have a predominantly feminine flavour; and although the old silk mills down by the river have now ceased to function as such, part of them has

* Lady Elizabeth was the daughter of the Earl of Suffolk and Charlton owes its magnificent conception to the first Countess who was a descendant of Stumpe. Today, this much-altered major Jacobean building is under the care of the Protection of Ancient Buildings and recently advertised as in urgent need of an owner.

been taken over by Mr. Peter Saunders, a man who has become well-known throughout the whole country for his "made-to-measure, colour-matched, classic clothes for women".

Moreover, Malmesbury still possesses one of the real old-fashioned lace-makers left in Britain. Mrs. Annie Goodfield, aged 76, crippled by arthritis but one of the merriest old ladies it would be possible to find, has actually given me a demonstration of her art. In her little front room in her cottage in Gastons Road, surrounded by cups, trophies, photographs, and her box of 'treasures', I watched fascinated as she stretched her fingers a few times and then announced ceremoniously, "I'm starting now." On her lap she balanced an enormous round pillow (or peel, as some call it), which was stuffed as hard as a drum with straw and once belonged to her grandmother. Stretched across it was a parchment pattern pricked out with tiny holes resembling an old pianola strip in which Mrs. Goodfield had placed a number of special lace-making pins. Carefully arranged round these was some real silk thread that had once been made in the Malmesbury Silk Mills. The ends of this were tightly wound round the countless hand-cut mahogany bobbins that hung down over the side of the peel. With a deftness that was quite astonishing, Mrs. Goodfield's fingers picked up one and then another, all the while plaiting and interweaving the thread or altering the position of the pins, as in less than ten minutes she produced a quarter of an inch of real Malmesbury lace. "And if you don't think that was sweated labour at tenpence a yard," she said firmly as she passed her precious peel over to her Home Help to put safely away upstairs, "I don't know what is. Come to think of it, my grandmother only got sixpence."

She then reminisced about lace-making in what, I suppose, were the bad old days. There was hardly a cottage in Malmesbury without a wife who made lace to help buy the necessities of life. These valiant women wore bonnets, shawls, and black skirts always covered by an apron. A gentleman by the nickname of 'Seftum Pudding', clad in silk hat and morning coat, used to tour the countryside for orders from 'the gentry'. Mrs. Goodfield's grandmother was commissioned to make the lace for the christening robes of Lady Suffolk's son at Charlton Park; while Mrs. Goodfield herself helped to make the trimmings for the Princess Royal's trousseau in 1912, a piece of which is now carefully stored in her treasure box. It was this same Lady Suffolk who started a weekly lace-making class at the King's Arms Hotel which Mrs. Goodfield attended as a young girl, dressed in a lace-embroidered smock and black lace-up boots.

When not making lace, Grandmother supplemented the family income still further by going out to do a little upholstery. A groom driving a small trap would be sent from the elegant Easton Grey mansion (now the home and boutique of Mr. Peter Saunders) in order to collect her. She would then be whisked 4 miles westwards to Easton Grey, which in those days was owned by a relation of Prime Minister Asquith, who could often be found there pacing the gardens in the summer months and discussing burning political issues with some of his colleagues.

While all these activities were going on, Grandmother's husband was down on the King's Heath, possibly cutting corn with a scythe on his little plot of land, a plot which Mrs. Goodfield eventually inherited and which entitles her to say proudly, "I'm a 'Commoner'." When Grandfather finished harvest he would go to a shed by Daniel's Well where, to quote Mrs. Goodfield verbatim, "he used the threshel, or dreshel. Now there's a Wiltshire word for you. An' my, didn't Grandmother bake some good bread from it later on when 'twere ground."

Mrs. Goodfield's own mother used to work in the silk mills as a girl, under conditions that must have been very different from those which govern the three separate establishments * which have taken it over today. The bell rang for work at 5 a.m., again for breakfast at eight, dinner at one, and then again at 6 p.m. when employees were allowed to 'call it a day'. The very young workers often spent half a day at school and the remaining half making ribbons. At some time during her employment, Mrs Goodfield's mother helped to make the actual silk for the balloon used by a certain Mr. Powell in a dramatic ascent from Malmesbury marketplace in 1880. Unhappily, during a subsequent attempt from Bath a year later, this same gentleman sailed out of sight over the South Coast and was never heard of again.

In Mrs. Goodfield's own youth, as one of a family of ten, she can remember the marriages that used to take place in her parents' kitchen, which also happened to be the local registry office of which her mother was caretaker. Many of the poorer people

* Keyford Antique Gallery, Ranalagh Wrought Iron Works, and Peter Saunders Ltd.

dispensed with a ceremony in church and simply came to her family home (known as the Round House) for a cheap, quick wedding. The bride and bridegroom must have had an unusual 'congregation' with such a large family milling about, for there was little space either here or in the small cottage to which they eventually moved and in which Mrs. Goodfield lives today. "The Lord knows where we all slept," she said. "Heads to tail and all in the same bed, I suppose."

But she was happy, and still is. Her grandmother once besought her not to let the art of lace-making die in Malmesbury and, despite early widowhood, a long period in domestic service, and increasing arthritis, she has honoured that request nobly. At the Malmesbury Flower Festival a short time ago, she sat in the abbey demonstrating her skill. "I thought I might 'ave forgotten," she said, "but bless 'ee, it come as natural as if 'twere yesterday. I mayn't be able to use my legs but I've still got my hands, thank the Lord." And these are never idle. Besides lace-making she sews, crochets, and makes beautiful tapestry; and in between times, she goes through her 'treasures'.

"Look at this," she said, lifting a lace-trimmed handerkerchife out of her box. "Someone sent it to me from . . ." and here with great tact, she paused and added simply, "another county. Best not say which. But it ain't a patch on Malmesbury lace, is it? Rough stuff, if you ask me." It was rough, indeed. Although I cannot make lace like Mrs. Goodfield, I know a good bit of stuff when I see it, and felt happy that I was able to share with her a proper feeling of pride in Malmesbury, Wilts.

XVII

MARCHING WITH THE BOUNDARY

North-west and North

"OLD GEORGE bought that piece of land because it *marched with his boundary.*" This kind of remark was one that I occasionally overheard as a child, if I happened to be in the room when my father was talking with some of his farming friends; and how puzzling it was. To me, land never marched. *I* might march; my father certainly marched about at times; but land stayed put.

It was not until I was almost grown-up that one day, quite by chance, I happened to come across all the other sorts of 'marches' there were in the dictionary. Besides the more ordinary meanings of the word, I learned that a march (noun) could also mean "the border of a country" or "a tract of land on the border of a country", or even "a tract of *debatable* land on the border of a country". On the other hand a certain kind of march (verb) simply meant "having a common frontier with". Immediately my mind flitted back to old George (or Henry or Joe, as the case may have been), who had evidently got fed up and simply wanted to acquire an awkward bit of land that boundered (or marched) with his existing farm, so that he could turn it all nicely into "one great whole". The mystery was solved at last.

The expression came into my mind again when I began thinking about the boundaries of Wiltshire. It is not that I have a particular desire to even them up by acquiring a little bit of Berks or Hants; but simply that perhaps like old George, I have, on occasions, a certain tidiness of mind and felt that in an attempt to turn this portrait into "one great whole", I ought to go round the edges, as it were.

At one time, I decided to entitle this tidying-up process "The

Frame of the Portrait"; but frames are usually square or oblong or round, and borders of counties go wandering about haphazardly, quite unlike any frame that I have yet come across, even for the most modern of pictures. Of course, like most things, there is a good reason for their supposedly inconsequential course. Originally, counties were created for judicial purposes and were made up from 'hundreds'; and hundreds were odd-shaped areas of land which are thought to have supported either 100 families (or ten tithings) or possibly 100 warriors. Therefore, a long time ago, when hundreds became grouped together to form counties to be governed by some overlord or ancient Saxon king (after a victorious but very bloody downland battle), his little dominion had a somewhat erratic border.

When I think that these curiously shaped dominions may soon be fused into larger unitary areas for judicial and administrative purposes, I feel I have another very good reason for wanting to take a good look at my native boundary of Wiltshire before it possibly melts away under modern methods of government. If I possessed unlimited time, I should dearly love to march with my boundary (or a little inside it), but only in the ordinary sense of the word. Yet this would be quite impractical, for not only would it be something that could only be done during summer (and more than one at that), but if I literally tried to follow the meandering line on the map, there are too many woods, rivers, ditches, and pieces of personal property wherein I might so easily become trapped. Therefore, I shall have to be content not to march with my boundary but perhaps jump it in helicopter fashion, stopping at the places which appeal to me most in the northern, eastern, southern, and western extremities of what I like to think of as 'my' personal kingdom, without having had the bother of winning a battle to get it.

I feel I should like to start with a piece of the county which, at the time of writing, seems most likely to lose its allegiance to Wiltshire and become affiliated to Bath and Bristol. Much of this area I have already covered, because the planners have their eye on quite a large chunk which would even include places farther south than Bradford and Trowbridge and might possibly appropriate the lovely Woodland Park at Brokerswood, near Westbury, where the public are free to wander at will. I hate to think of so much of the west and north-west of the county 'going', although

I realize that, looked at from a geological aspect only, the land nearest the present boundary here seems to have far more affinity with Somerset and Gloucestershire, while the towns have an un-Wiltshire look about them also. Bradford-on-Avon, for instance, is but a smaller Bath.

Travelling northwards in these parts there is an altogether different flavour about the county. The fields are smaller than those to which I am accustomed, and suddenly there are steep gorges occasionally crowned by hill-top villages such as Box and Colerne, which face each other across the By Brook, one of the many tributaries that flow down to join the Bristol Avon.

Box, like Bath itself, is as old as the Romans, but it is particularly well-known for the long railway tunnel beneath it which was one of the indefatigable Brunel's greatest achievements. It is to Colerne, however, that I am most attracted because of the way it stands up so majestically against the skyline, with the church tower of St. John the Baptist making an impressive landmark as it rises, over 550 feet, above the glorious landscape around it. A Saxon cross once stood near this church, which is alleged to have been erected to mark a stage of the journey when the body of St. Aldhelm was borne from Doulting to Malmesbury for burial, although now there are only fragments of the plinth which are preserved in the church.

As with Box, Colerne is a village of considerable antiquity. Its close proximity to the old unswerving Fosse Way made it favourable for Roman settlements and it is known that a large villa was sited on ground near by, which is now covered by an R.A.F. station. At one time the village was famous for brewing, as the surrounding land grew good crops of malting barley; but it was also a place that produced generations of excellent stone-masons and also, strange as it may seem, golfing addicts. The game was not then known as golf but 'stowball', and how much similarity there was between this and the more sophisticated antics now undertaken by today's champions, it is hard to say; but, nevertheless, the turf on Colerne Down was found to be highly suitable for this kind of game, as it gave the ball a quick rebound owing to the fact that it was very fine, although there was rock only 2 inches below the surface.

Possibly the natives of Colerne had an added incentive in days gone by for 'making their own amusements', as the place could well have been almost inaccessible in winter. The first bus to take the place of the carriers' cart to Bath, only started operating here as recently as 1920, when the sole car in the entire neighbourhood was one Ford 'Tin Lizzie'. Even today, local expressions are still much in use in Colerne, and it is not unusual to hear an aged inhabitant referring to his grandson as "oondermenting about", which means playing around and being mischievous; while to be greeted by the more commonplace "it be main teart z'marnin', zno", is simply another way of learning that there is a painful nip in the air.

By being cunning, it is possible to march or drive northwards again from Colerne, keeping just inside the Wiltshire boundary, without having to travel on any main roads. It is also possible to use much of the Roman Fosse Way itself for this journey, although only certain sections which have become ordinary tarred roads are suitable for motoring. I have never understood why modern road-makers have not made more use of the routes of their ancestors. I daresay they have very good reasons, but it sometimes seems a pity to create such havoc over the countryside when there is a ready-made direct route still in evidence, albeit sadly overgrown by thickthorn hedges. But then, I suppose, if these roads were used, we should by now have had something equivalent to the M4 running crossways down the north-western section of the county and completely spoiling all the nearby villages, especially that of Castle Combe, where the new motorway is already running far too close for comfort. As it is, a little way outside this village there is a very popular racing circuit where young men driving loud and alarming-looking motor-cars, or crouched over equally menacing motor-cycles, shatter the peace as they roar round and round on what seems to me like a pointless journey to nowhere.

It is not surprising, however, that Castle Combe itself, with all its picturesque stone houses, was once a film company's paradise and continues to be a tourist's dream; although I am hesitant to say this, because I realize any such remark is not helping it to be left alone in its secluded hollow, protected from the rest of the world by steep and wooded hills. There is little evidence of the Norman castle from whence the village acquired the first part of its name, but the combe remains utterly delightful all the year round, per-haps even more so in autumn and early spring when there are not so many sight-seers about.

The Fosse Way passes this village only a mile or so to the west and continues its direct approach to the north-western tip of Wilts. For half this length the county border bulges out uncertainly into the foothills of the Cotswolds, but both boundary and Roman road join forces near Easton Grey where they press northwards together through flatter, less interesting countryside. It is, however, just about here that I occasionally experience certain pangs of jealousy for two reasons. Firstly, this is because there is a most beautiful arboretum and silk wood which, although abutting on to Wiltshire territory, really belongs to the 'other side'; the second reason (which seems somehow more important) is that a few miles farther north still, Gloucestershire has taken unto itself the honour of possessing the source of the Thames.

To me, there are so many other tributaries (especially those which rise in my native county, such as the Kennet) which join this river as it "marches along to the mighty sea", that it could just as easily have been Wiltshire that started the Old Father off. He can be seen, all sculptured in stone, placed behind some railings in a remote field about half a mile west of the Thames Head Bridge* on the main Tetbury–Cirencester Road. In front of his secluded hideout there is a minute hollow in which a few stones can be found, but otherwise no sign of anything approaching a river at all. In fact, the absence of water at the time I visited him worried me no end, and when I next went to London I kept looking at the wide expanse of river rolling along underneath Waterloo Bridge and wondering how Old Father Thames could possibly have arrived there is such full-floodedness, if I may suggest such a word. But, as the song so rightly says, "He has no need to worry," and certainly he did not appear to have a care in the world, stuck down as he was under an ash tree in that Gloucestershire field by the courtesy of the Thames Conservators.

The Thames or Isis does not invade Wiltshire until just west of Ashton Keynes, where it is soon joined by several perfectly presentable Wiltshire streams, which help it to march with quite considerable distinction along or actually on the county's northern border. It then flows over this once again just south of Lechlade, seemingly bent on entertaining the younger generation at Oxford.

* This bridge spans an old waterway constructed in 1789 to connect the Severn Estuary with the headwaters of the Thames.

One little Wiltshire village that has great associations for me, which Old Father Thames misses by only half a mile, is that of Marston Meysey. I like its name, its inhabitants, its houses, and everything about it, but one house in particular I remember from my school-days. It is the most southerly of this very northerly village. At that time it was known as 'Green Fingers' and I can well remember the gorgeous assortment of rainbow-coloured flowers that greeted me when I was first taken there in 1936. It was then the home of Mr. Reginald Arkell, that well-known writer and poet with the whimsical and humorous touch, who wrote of the green-fingered young lady whom he married:

> I knew a girl, she was so pure,
> She couldn't say the word 'manure'. . . .

Evidently in 1936, although Reginald Arkell had not long been in possession at Marston Meysey, his lovely actress wife had found time to ensure that their first summer would, at least, be full of colour.

I went back to the village a little while ago. I had not been there for a very long time and I wondered whether, like Jefferies, it might be a mistake lest, to quote the words of his sympathetic contemporary, Stevenson: ". . . although the wandering fortune of my life should carry me back again . . . that will not be the old I who walks the street." And, of course, it was not the old I who stopped outside 'Green Fingers' and wondered who was living there now.

I knew that Elizabeth and Reginald Arkell were both dead but, quite irrationally, I think I still expected to find their garden full of flowers, even though I had been stupid enough to come in winter-time. I was just going to pass on (having been brought up never to stare at other people's houses too long), when the most wonderful thing happened. The present owner had evidently seen me spying out the land and came right out to ask if he could help, just like that. His name was Colonel Reeve, and it turned out that his wife was a relation of the Arkells. Somehow, before I knew anything else, I was inside 'Green Fingers' again and, although it was not the old I sitting down and drinking a cup of coffee, the present I suddenly felt extraordinarily pleased to be there.

We started talking about all the Arkells and it took a little time because they are a great family. Most of them were farmers or brewers and Arkells Ales is a very popular sign in this part of the world. Reginald, himself, was a Gloucestershire man, but there is a cousin of his still living at Highworth who has devoted much of his life towards the successful administration of Wiltshire, besides being a former High Sheriff of the county. This splendid character recalls with glee the time when he became Sir Noël Arkell, but only because it happened during the middle of the 1937 heat-wave. When Reginald later introduced him to his friends he used to say, "Meet my cousin, Noël. When he was knighted the local paper came out with a heading, 'Hottest night for twenty years'."

Before I left Marston Meysey, the Reeves suggested that they should take me across to see Miss Trinder at the post office next door, because she had known the Arkells for so long and had been so fond of them both. Once again, I did not regret coming back. Miss Trinder sat in her little front room (it was fortunately early closing day at the post office) and smiled. "Just to think of it," she said. "I can mind the day your father first came here. You see, when Mr. and Mrs. Arkell first moved in, it took a bit of time for them to get a telephone, so as I was next door I took all messages, like. Well, one Sunday morning, I remember as if 'twere yesterday, your father rung up an' asked if 'twould be a nuisance for me to ask Mr. Arkell if he could drive up to Marston Meysey for tea that day. Well, Mr. Arkell sent back word to tell Mr. Street to come and bring as many others as he likes. An' what d'you think? Later that afternoon Mr. Arkell brings your father over to thank me, special like. I can see 'im standing on the doorstep now. Big chap. 'Lor' bless 'ee,' I says, "twere a pleasure.' Fancy that now, an' here you be."

But then a certain sadness crept into Miss Trinder's reminiscences. Her affection for the Arkells went very deep. She continued, "Mrs. Arkell was a great gardener, you know, and Mr. Arkell, well he just loved the garden too. When he came down from London he used to go out and stand down by the stream and sometimes he used to say to me, 'Miss Trinder, I'm a Gloucestershire man. If I could make that little bit of water go round the front of my house, I'd be living in my native county.' 'Twere on the border, you see." It was the old, old story all over again. I do hope the planners-that-be will give enough thought to this business of 'local pride'.

I was sorry to leave Marston Meysey, but I no longer minded about the absence of any flowers to greet me this time. I had met the Reeves and Miss Trinder and their memories were clear and bright and that was all that mattered. I drove over the Thames again at Castle Eaton. The Old Father was spreading himself a little now. The waters of my native county were giving him a boost, as well as others from Gloucestershire such as the stream which ran round the back of 'Green Fingers'. I knew by the time he reached Inglesham and passed close to its tiny medieval church so beloved by William Morris, that Father Thames would be grand enough to have a photograph of himself in one of the Wiltshire guide-books, showing how splendidly attractive he had become for recreational purposes. And on he would go, past Oxford where he would soon be met by Brother Thame, past Reading where the Kennet would join him, and on, and on. . . .

I suppose I ought to face it. The words in the song are right, and if I might be permitted to paraphrase them slightly:

> 'My' kingdom may come; 'my' kingdom may go,
> But whatever the planners agree,
> Old Father Thames keeps on rolling along
> Down to the mighty sea.

All the same, I do wish I could have said he started off in Wiltshire.

East

To leave Inglesham and march with Wiltshire's eastern boundary, right down to Nomansland in the south, is a long, long way. In fact, it is far too long a journey to be undertaken at any one time with proper appreciation, whatever method of transport is adopted. But for those who want to enjoy a broad view of the county and bowl along in a high, wide, and handsome fashion, much of the route is 'just the job' (to use an old cattle-dealer's favourite expression).

After reaching Highworth, the valley of the Thames seems far behind and, in front, like some spectacular backcloth to the Swindon scene, the high Marlborough and Berkshire Downs beckon insistently, so that it is almost impossible for a traveller not to begin hurrying in order to get up on top of them as quickly as possible. According to present proposals, the boundary of Wiltshire might bulge farther east just around here to incorporate a little of Berkshire's Vale of White Horse. It would be but a small

Longford Castle
The former Bristol High Cross at Stourhead Gardens

area in comparison with what my county might lose on its north-western side, but presumably Wiltshire will have to be content with an extra little bit of good productive farmland by way of compensation.

At least one good thing which former planners have done in this part of the world is that, contrary to expectation, they have used the old Roman Ermin Way for a beautifully straight diagonal road across the north-eastern section of the county; and to travel along this on top of the downs from Wanborough to Baydon is to put oneself, both physically and metaphorically, 'on top of the world'. I am not sure exactly what it is about the Wiltshire Downs, but they always make me feel glad; glad that I am on them and glad that they are there for me to be on. Mountains are all right, but they are a bit too steep and the valleys in between them therefore become too shut in. The downs are so much more open and friendly, and on the road to Baydon the countryside around just stretches away for miles and miles; while poised at pleasing intervals in the undulating distance is the most gorgeous array of 'proper objects', none other than 'Mr. Capability's' clumps. No wonder Richard Jefferies loved this part so much, and considered that the view looking down over Aldbourne from Baydon one of the finest he had ever found.

Baydon is, in fact, the highest village in Wilts. It stands more than 750 feet on the very edge of the Berkshire border. It is worth a visit for the view alone, but it is also a particularly interesting place for other reasons. Close to the village lies Finche's Farm where Sir Isaac Newton spent many a summer, although unfortunately it was not a Baydon apple that happened to gravitate on to his head. The farmhouse and buildings are very old and now belong to Mr. and Mrs Day, whose main concern at present seems to be the proximity of the M4, which is going to spoil much of their holding. Mr. Day also tells me that Baydon can lay claim to being the village from which steam-ploughing originated, and that it is possible to find underground tanks where water was kept for this purpose.

Baydon is also a very horsy place. Although Mr. Fred Winter trains just over the border at Lambourn, Baydon has its own racing stables and gallops where Mrs. Lomax's horses are very much in evidence. Just to add to the sporting flavour, the last time I visited Baydon, the Craven and Vine Hounds were meeting in

N

Old Wardour Castle

the village and all the locals were out in force. Many people assert that life in modern Wiltshire is governed by the horse, the pig, and the motor-tyre. I do not go along with that completely because I feel the gun, the cow, corn, and the army ought to come into the list somewhere, while even sheep are regaining their popularity; but certainly the horse does loom quite large throughout the county, and young Pony Club equestriennes (because it is always the girls who are keenest) would appear most admirably to live up to Sir John Betjeman's charming verse:

> Oh wasn't it naughty of Smudges?
> Oh, Mummy, I'm sick with disgust.
> She threw me in front of the judges,
> And my silly old collar bone's bust.

At a discreet distance I followed some of these young enthusiasts as the hounds moved off, and it took me back thirty years to the time when I, too, would have been trotting along in high anticipation after a meet of the Wilton Hounds. Just for a moment I felt I should quite like to have been looking down on Aldbourne from a horse instead of skulking inside a motor-car; but then realization of both age and the length of time since I had undertaken such a hazardous pursuit, made me come to my senses, and I left my more courageous brethren streaming away towards Liddington with naughty little Smudges fairly kicking up the dust.

Aldbourne is an attractive place, despite the fact that the main road from Swindon to Hungerford passes through it. The village has a pond and a green, but its singular attraction for me is the fact that inside the pleasant old Church of St. Michael there are two fire engines called Adam and Eve. They are wonderful contraptions, dating from the end of the eighteenth century, and are accompanied by delightful instructions both for use and maintenance. After earnest pleas for the liberal application of neats-foot-oil and tallow, there is a delicate afterthought telling the locals how to adjust the flow for watering their gardens to make it fall "like gentle flowers". Possibly Aldbourne and Baydon gardens needed the assistance of Adam and Eve more than other Wiltshire villages, because the nearest lowland is a few miles farther south at Ramsbury.

It is hard to think of this little town on the Kennet once being the centre of a diocese with ambitious Bishop Hermann casting envious eyes on Malmesbury, which would have been a much more splendid place from which to conduct his bishopric. Little is known of the cathedral church at Ramsbury from which sulky Hermann did his best to escape and eventually succeeded, firstly by going to Sherborne and then to Old Sarum where both his previous sees then became united. It is to be assumed that a later edifice at Ramsbury embodied the one with which Hermann was dissatisfied as, when the present church was restored in 1891, a number of highly important Anglo-Saxon carvings were found. They can be seen today in the north-western corner of this well-buttressed flint and stone building.

Behind the organ in Ramsbury parish church lies the famous Darrell chapel. The Darrell family was very well-known in these parts, although it is unfortunate that its notoriety has always been chiefly connected with one member of it, 'Wild' Darrell, a man with a most unsavoury reputation. Towards the end of the sixteenth century this lawless character came into possession of the family home at Littlecote Manor, a few miles south-east of Ramsbury. It is a long low Tudor mansion set in ancient parkland by the River Kennet. Much of the south side of the house is of mellow brick, with stone dressings running up to gabled eaves and roofed by Cotswold stone. Of its kind it is just about perfect, but there is a certain "*Je ne sais quoi*" about it which, although I appreciate its undoubted beauty, makes me glad that I do not have to live there.

Even if I had never known the story of 'Wild' Darrell, I still think that I should have the same feeling about the place. I do not believe in ghosts; I have never experienced anything that could remotely be described as supernatural; and I was quite affronted when the late Ruby M. Ayres once told me that I was the first person who would be likely to see some headless apparition floating down the stairs. Nevertheless, on the day I was taken round Littlecote in the depths of winter when the house is not normally open to the public, I felt extremely cold on the haunted landing in spite of the permanent central heating.

Like all really good spine-chilling stories, the 'Wild' Darrell episode took place one 'dark and stormy night' in 1575. Among all his many other escapades, 'Wild' Darrell had now made a certain unknown woman pregnant. It would seem that she may have been a rather special inamorata because when she was about to give birth, a midwife, known as Mother Barnes from Shefford in Berkshire, was called upon with the promise of a high reward if she would attend the confinement. Her mission was unusual, to say the least, because she was blindfolded all the way to Littlecote and not allowed to see where she was until she found herself actually in the bedroom of Darrell's mistress. However, she did her job well, delivered the child, wrapped it in her apron, and then went out on to the landing, where she found Darrell and asked him for some clothing for the infant. Whereupon, good Mother Barnes was asked to cast the child into the roaring fire that was conveniently burning thereon. When she besought Darrell to let her keep it and bring up as one of her own, he refused and was then said to have performed the horrible deed himself. Mother Barnes was later able to identify Littlecote as the place to which she had been brought because, according to some accounts, she was astute enough to cut a snippet of the bedcover before being taken away blindfolded as before.

Some kind of charge was brought against Darrell, but he appears to have escaped justice and it is thought that the fact a distant cousin of his was Attorney General at the time probably had much to do with this. At all events, when Darrell died through a hunting accident in the park (and here again the baying of phantom hounds is said to be heard by the psychically orientated) he possessed no heir and left the property to this said cousin, Sir John Popham. Perhaps it is wisest not to delve too deeply into this doubtful and murky little saga and enjoy going round Littlecote as it is today, because it is one of Wiltshire's prize exhibits.

Since 1922 the place has been in the possession of the Wills family, who live in but a part of it, and it would be quite impossible to enumerate here the priceless treasures which may be seen in the rest of the house, such as the unique collection of seventeenth-century fire-arms, the wall paintings in the Dutch parlour, the Cromwellian chapel, and the coat of arms in a certain bedroom proclaiming that "Queen Elizabeth I slept here". It is really necessary to go to Littlecote and take a good long look, although perhaps it might be just as well not to linger too long by the haunted landing and bedroom.

If I were to say that within half an hour of leaving Littlecote I was having lunch at Wilton, I should probably be accused of being a liar or possessing a private helicopter. Neither of these accusations, however, would be justifiable because I was, in fact, doing exactly that, except that this particular Wilton was not my home town near Salisbury, but a tiny village just south of the Kennet and Avon Canal near Great Bedwyn. This business of places sharing the same name in the same county is very confusing, and in Wiltshire we have at least two Wiltons, two Bishopstones, and four Charltons. I deplore such a state of affairs but I cannot see what can be done about it, because no right-minded village or town is going to give up its birthright, as it were.

Moreover, I am happy to say that this smaller Wilton (postal address, near Marlborough) is extremely pretty. The only unfortunate feature about it seems to be that letters are continually being sent to its larger namesake. Little Wilton (because that is how I think of it) has some charming old houses, and the ducks disporting themselves on the village pond make a picture almost identical with one I remember in a story-book as a child. Near by there is also a very much larger pond or lake known as Wilton Water, which rises from a natural spring and acts as a feeder for the canal. The steam engines which used to pump the Wilton Water for this purpose were made by Boulton and Watt and are now quite unique in the country. They may still be seen on any Sunday at the Crofton Pumping Station by the canal, although electricity took over their job in 1958.

As with my home town, the inhabitants of Little Wilton give the impression that they are very proud of the place. Mine host and his wife at the Swan Inn make the most delicious sandwiches from locally home-made bread; all the gardens are neatly tended, and it is obvious that this is a village to which much care and thought is given. It must be admitted, however, that in this respect, certain outside influences may be at work. Little Wilton happens to be in the odd easterly bulge of Wiltshire. It is also within a mile of a fast train to Paddington. Therefore this makes it easily accessible as a week-end paradise for Londoners, while the surrounding countryside is a happy shooting-ground for the pheasant-conscious tycoon. At present, it still appears to be truly rural, but it seems likely that Little Wilton is in danger of becoming overrun and thereby losing what I feel to be the 'battle of the bulge'.

I should be sorry to see this happen because this little corner of Wiltshire is really lovely and parts of it are strangely remote. Just south of Wilton, for instance, is the tiny hamlet of Wexcombe. Fortunately, no one drives straight through the place because the road only goes to a track leading up to the downs. When I was quite small I was once brought here by my father to see 'The Wizard of Wexcombe'. This was none other than the inventor, the late Mr. A. J. Hosier, who was responsible, among other things, for that great innovation, the movable open-air milking machine or 'bail'. During the farming depression of the late 1920s and early 30s this became an established feature of downland farming, heralding a system of dairying which is still carried out today and is now becoming very popular again. I know that my father was always sincerely grateful to Mr. Hosier both for his friendship and his ingenuity, because owing to these two factors he decided to switch from arable farming to grass and was consequently able to survive that desperate period.

Although 'switch', perhaps, is not the right choice of verb. Such a revolution was complicated and took time; moreover, my father's initial struggles at introducing cows to an out-door milking machine at 4.30 a.m. were fraught with hazards, aptly described in his own words:

> I can visualize it all quite distinctly. Two bobbing lights moving to meet each other, as their carriers ran in a futile attempt to stop the cattle. Dark shapes of cows on the skyline streaming away between the lights, with their tails waving in high derision. The vapour of breath in the lantern-light . . . the squelch of one's rubber boots, the tumbles on the wet grass, sodden efforts to relight one's lantern . . . the sound of bad language floating up from all sides through the wet dark, and over all the rain, the persistent steady rain of Southern England, which not only dampened us physically, but which sapped all our courage and endeavour.
>
> And then just as we had almost decided to wait for daylight, a final attempt succeeded, and we started the engine and started milking.

Yes, and started climbing out of the farming depression too, thanks to tenacity of purpose and Mr. A. J. Hosier, whose descendants can still be found farming at Wexcombe, while the firm of Hosier Equipment Ltd. flourishes at Collingbourne Ducis not far away.

But for present-day travellers, and especially those who want to march with the boundary along the high, wide, and handsome route, they should now climb up to the Chute Causeway via

Marten or Oxenwood as this, to me, is one of the most lovely drives in all Wiltshire. I cannot understand why it is so comparatively little known, because it is possible to travel nearly 900 feet in a glorious semicircle for at least 5 miles, looking down on a natural amphitheatre to the east and what seems like the whole of Wiltshire to the west.

Chute Causeway is a deviation on an old Roman Road from Winchester to Marlborough. Those ancient warriors did not always march straight as a bow-string, and near Chute they made one of their rare exceptions which is now tarred, deserted, and utterly beautiful. Moreover, at the southern end of it, on a slightly lower level, lie all the Chute villages (and there are quite a few of them) which hide themselves in a singularly attractive fashion among the remains of what used to be the Forest of Chute; although I could wish that St. Mary's Church, in the one which is called 'Chute Forest', was not quite so desolate and abandoned. It was only built at the end of the last century for the nearby mansion, which is now a preparatory school, but services are only held there during summer as the church at Upper Chute serves the whole parish. St. Mary's is the only church in Wiltshire that I have come across which is so obviously out of use, and the overgrown and ivy-covered churchyard saddens me, perhaps the more so because I have been particularly struck by the well-kept appearance elsewhere, especially the artistically arranged vases of fresh flowers to be found in the most unlikely and remotest places of worship.

After the Chutes, the county boundary turns sharply inward again to Ludgershall and Tidworth. In fact, it bisects the latter town from east to west, North Tidworth being in Wiltshire and South Tidworth remaining in Hants. Both are, of course, entirely military-dominated and the buildings and barracks have overshadowed much of the surrounding beauty, although not entirely, especially in South Tidworth, where the Officers' Club at Tidworth House stands in a magnificent setting worthy of the Tattoo which takes place there.

Except for the natural sentinel known as Beacon Hill, the border of Wilts as it points southward again remains uneventful until the Winterslow villages are reached, lying well to the east of the River Bourne. Here I feel almost back on home ground once more. Salisbury and that welcoming spire are only 5 miles away, but the land round about still seems subtly different from my native valley and downs. I think of it as half-and-half country. It belongs to the Plain yet much of it actually lies within the northern extremity of the Test basin. It is scrubby countryside scattered with stray fir trees, an indefinite link in that long chain of erstwhile forests, this time joining that of Chute to Clarendon.

But the area is certainly not without renown. It has produced many men of letters, one of them of the present day, that well-known writer on all country matters, Mr. Ralph Whitlock, who hails from the village of Pitton. As for former times, Sir Stephen Fox was born at Farley; Sir Benjamin Brodie, Queen Victoria's serjeant-surgeon, began his life at Winterslow Rectory in 1783; while the famous essayist, William Hazlitt, used to lodge at the Winterslow Hut, an old coaching inn on the main London road, which is better known today as 'The Pheasant'.

Hazlitt's first wife had property at Winterslow, and for many years they lived there in a small cottage where their friends, Charles and Mary Lamb, are said to have visited them. But the marriage was not a happy one and when the couple parted Hazlitt had become so fond of the neighbourhood that he removed to the Winterslow Hut to write in solitude. Doubtless today he would not have found such peace and quiet as when the sole excitement was the arrival of the Exeter Mail Coach on its journey to London; although even this event was livened up considerably on a certain October night in 1816, when one of the coach's leading horses was attacked by a lioness who had escaped from a travelling menagerie *en route* to Salisbury fair. The beast was eventually captured by the heroic efforts of its owner and assistants, but the incident bestowed more than a little publicity on the Hut, which the present-day 'Pheasant' still fosters by way of pictures portraying the scene.

Other more recent Winterslow characters who, although not men of letters, were leading lights in their own particular profession and people to whom communications addressed "Truffle Hunter, Salisbury Plain" would be delivered automatically by the post office, were the late Mr. Eli Collins and his son, Alfred. My father once took the latter to Broadcasting House, where he captivated all England by his account of the truffle-hunting industry as carried on at its headquarters at Winterslow with the aid of truffle-hunting dogs.

My father's report on the broadcast went as follows:

Occasionally I asked a question, but, once started, Mr. Collins free-wheeled easily on the subject of truffles, until I had to break in with, "I'm sorry, Mr. Collins, but we'll have to stop. It's just on six o'clock, and the news is to follow."

"Be we done?" he asked. "Why I bain't but jist nicely started. I could talk to you fur long enough."

He could have done just that, and all of it would have been good. Here is an example of his admirable style. I asked him how large truffles were.

"All sizes. I've a vound 'em as small as a number four shot." And then, I could almost see him thinking that such a comparison was rather beyond the grasp of town listeners, and hunting for something easier, "An' as large as a Jaffa horange."

I defy anyone to write lines like that or anyone to argue that it was not broadcasting of the highest class.

Alas, Mr. Alfred Collins died at a good age in 1953 and with him truffle-hunting in England became extinct.

Before leaving this district it would hardly be fair not to refer to another industry undertaken by English China Clay Ltd. which, however, is very far from being extinct. At the village of East Grimstead this company has quite extensive works that have been the centre of much controversy. Although the area seems to have had more than its share of 'digs', as several Roman villas have been discovered hereabouts (to say nothing of unearthing the ancient palace of Clarendon in the nearby woods), it must be remembered that any large-scale commercial excavation of a rather special kind of chalk, is an extremely messy business. In order to extract stuff that is chiefly used as coating material on paper, the roads near the source of the raw product not only become coated themselves, but are heavily frequented by lorries. Fortunately, the present excavations are adjacent to the main Salisbury–Southampton railway line which E.C.C. hope to be able to use so that, with an accommodating spirit on both the side of industry and the local populace, the present conflict may well be resolved.

East Grimstead is only 5 miles from Nomansland but, as I said at the beginning of this eastern march, it seems a long, long way. As any kind of marching with the southern boundary will be but half the length of this one, I feel it is only fair to end just a little short of target at an outpost on some high ground belonging to

the National Trust, which is known to all and sundry as Pepperbox
Hill. This is because of a brick hexagonal building erected in the
seventeenth century by a member of a local family called Eyre,
who was so envious of the fine towers of Longford Castle below
(and they do look rather gorgeous from here) that he decided to
have a higher tower on his own land from which he could look
down on his neighbours. It is thought that the gentleman concerned was probably Gyles Eyre, who died in 1655, and whose
memorial tablet in Whiteparish church describes him as "a man
much oppressed by publick power". Although this strange edifice,
with its bricked-up doors and windows, is also known as Eyre's
Folly, posterity seems to regard it with benevolence and I, for one,
feel that Gyles Eyre knew a good spot when he found it. Somehow
I cannot help feeling a certain sympathy towards this man who has
left 'his mark' where we now stand looking out over the Odstock
Downs, the cathedral-dominated city of Salisbury, the Plain, the
wooded estate of Clarendon sheltering the three villages of Alder-
bury, Whaddon, and West Grimstead, the New Forest, and even,
on clear days, the shipping in Southampton Water backed by the
Isle of Wight beyond.

South

Nomansland was, and almost still is, a place that seems to belong
to no one in particular. Its postal address is Wilts, yet Nomans-
landers have to go to Hants to be buried; while they are alive,
their drinking water comes from Christchurch but their drains
simply seem to go to ground; if they want to make a new gateway
opening on to any unenclosed wasteland their application goes to
the Forestry Commission, and if they themselves want to go anywhere at all they have to go over a cattle grid.

At Nomansland it is really possible to *see* the boundary of
Wiltshire in a physical sense. The frontage of the village shop, for
instance, is at a curious angle because the shop itself is in Wilts, but
anyone with his nose pressed against the windows would be in
Hants. The Lamb Inn next door is in Wilts, but the patrons who
ascend or descend its front steps are in Hants. It is, to say the least,
a little confusing, especially as Nomansland does not appear to
have had much documentation of any description.

The only person in the village whose memory is backed up by
any kind of written history is Mrs. Riddett, the 81-year-old

proprietress of the village shop. She possesses a slender booklet written by a Mr. Livens in 1910 which gives certain interesting information. It describes the place as an extra-parochial strip of wasteland on the north border of the New Forest. It also instructs the reader about the correct pronunciation of the name with the accent on the last syllable, because 'land' was the all-important thing by which people lived and died.

It appears that sometime during the eighteenth century a gipsy by the name of Willett decided to settle down here, presumably in order to be within easy reach of the forest deer. So long as he kept just outside the borders he would not be interfered with, because this particular land belonged to nobody. Using clods or sods he built himself what was referred to as a "clotten" house, with trodden earth for the floor. Perhaps he made a more elaborate home than usual, because Mr. Livens also touches on the stories which allege that, in those days, any dwelling within the forest itself which had been erected during a single night so that smoke issued from the roof before dawn, gave its builder some kind of tenuous proprietorship to the site.

However, ingenious Mr. Willett would appear to have got the whole thing worked out on an even better basis. To the south he had the whole of the New Forest for his larder; to the north he had a splendid view of Wiltshire for the good of his soul. It is hardly surprising that in a short space of time he was joined by other squatters whose names were, and still are, typical of these parts: Moody, Dibden, Giles, and Shergold. Mostly they were single men who arrived to peg out just such an estate as they cared to take possession of in the wilderness, but in the natural order of things Nomansland soon became Nowomansland also. Families were founded and slightly more respectable occupations than poaching were undertaken, such as faggoting, gravel-digging, charcoal-burning, and, of course, cattle-rearing aided by the grazing rights permitted to 'borderers'.

Today, Nomansland is a pretty place, particularly in summer, but I have to admit that on face value alone it belongs to the New Forest. It is as unlike Wiltshire as the proverbial chalk is from cheese. To leave it and march with the boundary in a slightly north-westerly direction is to pass through high heathery open countryside that is strikingly different from that which is usually found in my native county; it is as if nature suddenly decided to change to a darker complexion and even to tinge the sky on the horizon with the same bluish-purple hue. It is not until one has passed Redlynch or perhaps Lover (pronounced Low-ver and not the way that might spring to mind) and arrived at Downton, that Wiltshire appears to reassert itself once more. In fact, Mr. Ralph Whitlock refers to Downton as the gateway to the chalk, to Wiltshire, and to Salisbury Plain.

It is also thought to have been the gateway for the Saxon warrior, Cerdic, who many people believe came pushing his way up the Avon Valley in the year 519 to fight a decisive battle at Charford, a mile or so south of Downton over the Hampshire border. Although there are other claimants for the site of this battle, it can reasonably be assumed that this would have been just the place for the invaders to challenge the downland defendants, who might well have come roaring down from their fortifications on nearby Clearbury Rings to meet them.

Downton itself also possesses some ancient earthworks known as The Moot, which occupy the garden of an old house. Because of the lay-out it is thought to have been a Saxon meeting-place; although there is no confirmation about its exact origins because the Bishop of Winchester began building a castle in the vicinity during the twelfth century, and his enthusiastic plans are said to have considerably altered the existing lie of the land.

Apart from the impressive flint and stone Church of St. Lawrence, the building which seems to dominate Downton today is the large creeper-covered Tannery, which appears to be a rather unique survivor of the times when there were many more such establishments about. The Downton Tannery concentrates on leather for the soles of shoes only and, as there is now a swing away from the synthetic kind, I am happy to say that sole leather, as produced at Downton, is enjoying a come-back. The tanning liquid used here is an infusion made from the bark of the mimosa tree which comes from South Africa, although I regret that the curious dark-looking concoction inside the Downton Tannery does not appear to have much connection with the yellow flower that arrives to cheer our English winter.

In a parkland setting on the northern fringes of Downton, there is an exceptionally fine example of Georgian architecture, formerly known as Standlynch House. This large brick and stone building was designed in 1733 for a city banker, but in the early nineteenth century the whole place, together with its estate, was presented by a grateful nation to the heirs of Lord Nelson and appropriately rechristened Trafalgar House. Until quite recently, the admiral's descendants still lived there commanding, from their little wooded eminence, a splendid view over a long stretch of the River Avon.

From Downton the county boundary zig-zags doubtfully west-ward over tracts of downland countryside that might well be thought of as a typically debatable kind. This is because much of it comes within the parishes of Martin and Whitsbury, which have always been slightly uncertain as to whom they owe their allegi-ance.

During the last century these two rather charming villages were transferred from Wiltshire to Hampshire, but in the 1930s there was a definite movement afoot to entice them back to their original fold. This, however, was resisted owing to a successful campaign on the part of the hard-up farming fraternity now residing in Hants. One can hardly blame these particular farmers for wanting to maintain a *status quo*, because during the agri-cultural depression of that time the newly formed Milk Marketing Board paid a few halfpence more per gallon for milk coming from Hampshire (which was in their South-eastern Region) compared to Wiltshire (in their Mid-western one). Therefore, the attractive village of Martin, which was used by W. H. Hudson as a prototype for Winterbourne Bishop in *A Shepherd's Life* and where he met Caleb Bawcombe, the son of his immortal character, Isaac Bawcombe, unfortunately still belongs to the 'other side'.

Apart from the main Salisbury to Blandford road which crosses the southern boundary of Wilts at Swayne's Firs, the other smaller roads leading up to the downs in this district all seem to peter out into grassy tracks. Consequently, there is sometimes a rather deso-late atmosphere about the area, especially as it abounds in eerie reminders of our ancestors' activities, not simply in the shape of earthworks and examples of their strip lynchet way of farming, but also in the formidable names given to specific features. There is the Giant's Grave, Gallows Hill, and Grim's Ditch,* the latter forming the actual boundary itself. Even the wood known as

* Thought to be the southern barricade against Saxon invasions.

Great Yews has a slightly awe-inspiring ring about it, and some-times makes the lone walker glad to return to the safety of the Ebble Valley that runs parallel to the downs below their northern slopes. Yet, even here, the little village of Odstock is haunted by the memory of a gipsy's curse which is still strong enough to scare its present-day inhabitants.

At the beginning of the last century the son-in-law of a certain gipsy stole a horse but pinned the blame on his father-in-law, Joshua Scamp, a man with a good reputation far removed from that which might have been expected from anyone with such a name. But poor Joshua eventually paid the penalty and was hanged in Fisherton gaol in 1801. Few people, however (and least of all the gipsies), believed him to be the guilty party and he appears to have been granted burial in Odstock churchyard. Soon, he came to be thought of as a tribal hero and for years afterwards the gipsies paid an annual pilgrimage to his grave, although un-fortunately these visits degenerated into drunken brawls which the rector, not unnaturally, tried to prevent. One year, the vagrants became especially enraged when they found that someone had cut down the briar growing where Scamp lay buried. Immediately they retaliated by ransacking the church, cutting the bell-rope, overturning the tombstones, and retiring to a neighbouring inn where they drank themselves silly. As a final insult, the gipsy queen returned to the churchyard at nightfall where she gave vent to a variety of curses.

Her first victim was the rector, who she prophesied would not be preaching in twelve months time. She then cursed the churchwarden, Farmer Hodding, saying that bad luck would dog his footsteps for two years. The sexton, James Hackett, next came in for the chilling information that he would be dead and buried before she returned to Odstock again; while two half-gipsies who had taken the opposite side in the affair were told they would die "sudden and quick". She ended by laying a curse on the church door, vowing that whoever locked it should also lie in his grave before the passing of a year.

The terrified inhabitants of Odstock were then left to witness all these things being brought about. The rector had a stroke; Farmer Hodding went bankrupt; James Hackett died from heart failure while working on the roads. The two half-gipsies mysteriously disappeared, and what were thought to have been their skeletons were subsequently found in a grave on Odstock Down (although in this instance their fate may have been settled by the gipsies themselves).

Nevertheless, there was still the curse on the church door to be reckoned with, and it remains to this day. Two men have locked it within the last fifty years, one accidently and the other intentionally. Both departed this life within twelve months. The key is now said to have been thrown into the River Ebble and Odstock church door is never locked. The present vicar suggested that it might be secured when repairs were being carried out to the organ not long ago, but his proposal was met with embarrassed but determined opposition. Neither will anyone take on the job of trimming the briar now growing again on Joshua's grave. Memories die hard in Wiltshire and the likelihood of having a new key made for Odstock church is extremely remote.

Remote is also perhaps a suitable word with which to describe the remaining extremities of South Wilts, because the lonely bare downs above Odstock, Coombe Bissett, and Bishopstone soon become gripped by the equally mysterious tentacles of Cranborne Chase. Edward Hutton regarded Wiltshire as a county that was once hemmed in by more forests than any other and therefore much dominated by ancient Forest Law.

At one time, Cranborne Forest (as it was known when belonging to the Crown) spread over a considerable part of Wiltshire, Hampshire, and Dorset. In fact, it stretched from Salisbury in the east to Shaftesbury in the west, and from Wilton in the north to Christchurch in the south. The Abbess of Wilton is said to have bitterly protested against the hunting rights which were claimed on her lands in the Nadder Valley, and especially the toll which was levied upon anyone using Old Harnham Bridge in the Midsummer Fence Month, when travellers might disturb the does that were fawning. As an undeniable mark of forest tyranny, a pair of horns used to be set up on the bridge fifteen days before and after Midsummer Day as a warning that cheminage must be paid.

King John was particularly fond of hunting in Cranborne Forest and the village of Tollard Royal owes the superior second half of its name to the fact that, as Earl of Gloucester, he held a knight's fee here in right of his wife, Isabella, from whom he was divorced. His much-altered hunting lodge, which once acquired the distinguished epithet of King John's Palace, but which is now known quite simply as King John's House, still seems a curiously tangible reminder of those royal visits which took place over 700 years ago. As a child, my imagination was also fired by the references I often overheard to something called the Larmer Tree which stood in the Larmer Grounds near by. I knew nothing of the history of Cranborne Chase and can remember hopefully thinking there was a llama residing on the borders of South Wilts. Even now, the word often mystifies people and needs a little explanation.

The most knowledgeable authorities say categorically that it means "the pool where the rushes grew", and certainly there is a deep watery hollow near today's Larmer Tree.* Other theorists, however, think that as 'mere' was the old word for 'boundary', the first syllable most likely denoted a certain kind of tree, probably a laurel. At all events, some kind of important landmark evidently existed here in days gone by which subsequent generations have fostered, because not only was this the place where Wiltshire met Dorset and where the three parishes of Tollard Royal, Tollard Farnham, and Farnham joined forces, but it was also where King John met his huntsmen and where Chase Courts were held. During the last century this celebrated spot was honoured by a wych elm that unfortunately came to grief in the winter of 1894, although, with the aid of some ivy, a portion of its bark has now successfully attached itself to the oak tree that has been planted in its stead.

The twentieth-century Larmer Tree now stands looking slightly forlorn in the Larmer Grounds, which consist of 6 acres of pleasure gardens laid out by that famous archaeologist and ethnologist of the last century, General Pitt-Rivers. For many years these gardens were open to the public and drew sightseers from far afield. Teas could be bought; a local band played on Sundays, and it seemed as if the general genuinely wanted others to enjoy the pleasure he himself derived from the Larmer Grounds, long before such a thing as the more commercialized 'country house industry' came into being.

Although General Pitt-Rivers has been called the father of British archaeology, he was passionately interested in the lives of people both past and present. It is said that he did not excavate

* Larmer was spelt both Lavermere and Lauermere in former times.

Longleat viewed from Heaven's Gate

merely in order to collect 'finds'; he dug to 'find out' how our
ancestors went about their everyday living. It is to him that the
Pitt-Rivers Museum at Oxford owes its existence and this is where
many of his specimens are housed, although it is unfortunate that
the fine collections in his more personal museum, just across the
border at Farnham, is now closed to the public, and it is to be
hoped that this may either be reopened or the specimens seen
elsewhere.

Today General Pitt-Rivers' grandson still lives in King John's
House at Tollard Royal, but the original family home at Rushmore
Park is now occupied by Sandroyd School. It would appear that
preparatory schools have a certain 'penchant' for setting themselves down in the ancient forests of Wiltshire, and I trust the
little boys of Sandroyd appreciate this particular one as much as I
used to when arriving for Pony Club rallies that were held at
Rushmore during the 1930s. This was at the time when the Master
of the Wilton Hounds, Colonel Llewellyn-Palmer, lived in the
house, and I can well remember being examined on the 'points
of the horse' by the benevolent colonel and also instructed, not
only on how to ride but on the equally important accomplishment of how to fall. The lesson about automatically tucking
my head down and rolling up into a ball is something which
I often think is neglected in a would-be rider's education,
and one for which I have had good occasion to be more than
grateful.

Both Tollard Royal and the Chase itself are on high ground but,
a little farther north, the wide-open countryside of Win Green,
Winklebury, and White Sheet Hill rise to even greater heights of
more than 900 feet. They could perhaps be thought of as the happy
digging-ground of General Pitt-Rivers, for I can imagine him
being overjoyed at discovering the little Saxon cemetery on
Winklebury and burrowing away on White Sheet, or possibly just
stopping to gaze at the panorama surrounding Win Green from
where, like its Pepperbox counterpart in the south-east of the
county, he could occasionally catch a glimpse of the Isle of Wight
in the distance. And if he stayed a little too long of an evening on
top of these darkening hills, he could be guided by the tolling of
the church bell in the village of Berwick St. John crouching in a
hollow beneath the three of them. This custom has only ceased
quite recently but it originated over 200 years ago, when a certain

o

The loveliest landmark of all

kind-hearted rector of Berwick left a legacy in his will for the church bell to be rung for fifteen minutes at eight o'clock every winter's night, to help any lost travellers up on the lonely downs.

Win Green is another possession of the National Trust and I cannot think of anywhere else in Wiltshire where quite such spectacular scenery can be seen when looking in every direction. I think it is the 'all-roundness' of the views from so many Wiltshire downs that makes it such a unique county. This particular gigantic green pyramid sports a small wooden pillar box in which contributions may be placed for the upkeep and replanting of the rather weather-beaten clump of beech trees growing on top of it. It seems well worth while dropping a little something inside to help preserve such a splendid 'proper object' that stands like a sentry box or, to be more in keeping with this chapter, marches like a sentry with the southern boundary of Wilts.

South-west

From the windy heights of Win Green to the sheltered depths of Wincombe is only a matter of a few miles, yet in this short, steep, and somewhat perilous journey there are so many changes of scene that Wiltshire appears to be acting like a quick-change artist. The River Nadder rises in Wincombe Park and, curiously enough, it is here that the valley is at its widest. The fan-shaped headwaters of the Sem, added to those of the Don which rise near the 'down-head' villages of Donhead St. Mary and Donhead St. Andrew, all help to give the extra boost needed to enable the main stream to force itself down the narrowing passageway between the downs to be joined by the Wylye at Wilton.

Wincombe, to me, is rather a special place because not long ago it was the home of our greatest living historian, Sir Arthur Bryant. Peaceful and secluded, yet surrounded as it is by so many memories of our contentious past, Wincombe seems just the right place for the writing of history. Not far away are the lovely old ruins of Wardour Castle, a fortress that has witnessed more than its share of strife, but which has now settled down to a quiet old age under the protection of the Department of the Environment.

Wardour came into the possession of the Arundell family in the sixteenth century when it was bought by Sir Thomas Arundell, husband of Margaret, the sister of Queen Catherine Howard. A later Sir Thomas, a grandson of the first, pursued a most distinguished career in which he acquired the titles of Count of the Holy Roman Empire and Baron Arundell of Wardour; but it is the brave and beautiful Blanche, a daughter-in-law of the said baron, who achieved lasting fame for her valiant efforts to defend Wardour against the Roundheads when her husband was fighting elsewhere. In 1643, with only a small band of fifty men and women to assist her, she withstood a force of 1,300 Parliamentary troops for five days and only came to surrender on what she considered to be honourable terms. Unfortunately, Cromwell's men then broke faith with their pledges, plundered the park and ransacked the castle while Lady Blanche, deprived of all her possessions and with only the clothes she stood up in, was forced to leave her home and be housed by charity. For a year the rebels garrisoned the battered remains of Wardour under the command of Colonel Ludlow, until Lady Blanche's son, young Lord Arundell, after a long siege, forced him to surrender, albeit blowing up a large part of his ancestral home in so doing.

About a mile away from these picturesque ruins stands new Wardour Castle, a somewhat austere Palladian-type mansion designed for the eighth Lord Arundell by James Paine and now-adays open to the public when the young ladies of Cranborne Chase School depart for their summer holidays. Both Old and New Wardour lie in the most lovely parkland which comes within the parish of Tisbury and where, among many of her kith and kin, the gallant Lady Blanche lies buried.

Another ardent Royalist from these parts was Christopher Wren's father, who was appointed rector of East Knoyle in 1623. It was he who designed the plaster work in the chancel of the parish church representing biblical scenes surrounded by cherubs, scrolls, marigolds, and Tudor roses. It is an unusual type of artistry and one which unfortunately was later quoted against him at his trial by the Commonwealth authorities. His young son, Christopher, was born in a room above the village shop at East Knoyle, where the family had been forced to seek temporary lodgings owing to a fire at the rectory. Neither of these buildings is now in existence, although the present post office and stores proudly trade under the name of 'Wren's Shop' and on a little patch of green at the other side of the road there is a plaque marking the great man's birthplace with the words:

In a house near this spot
was born on 20th October 1632
Sir Christopher Wren
Architect, Mathematician, Patriot,
The son of the Rector of this Parish.

It is strange that although Christopher Wren was recognized as a genius in almost all branches of learning by the time he was 24, architecture was not among them. It was not until a few years later when Charles II, having been reinstated, appointed him Assistant to the Surveyor-General, that he really came into his own in this field; so that when Old St. Paul's was destroyed by fire it was Wren who was immediately called upon to build what was to be his greatest creation. As this magnificent new cathedral rose from the ground, Wren was regularly hoisted to the top of the works in a basket in order to witness his ideas coming to life.

Another building near his birthplace which also seems to reach to the sky, albeit in a slightly less exalted style, is a house standing on top of a hill overlooking East Knoyle and which, appropriately enough, is named 'Clouds'. This was built by Philip Webb at the end of the last century for the Wyndham family and only just completed when it was burned to the ground, so that it had to be entirely rebuilt in 1893. Although it is now an institution and no longer a family home, there remains a certain sadness about 'Clouds' for anyone acquainted with a little of the Wyndham family history.

Some of this history reveals itself in the little parish church, where there is a particularly lovely east window given by members of both Houses of Parliament in honour of George Wyndham, whose early death in 1913 deprived England of a brilliant national figure, so deeply involved in all political issues that many people had good reason to believe Parliament was being run at 'Clouds'. Then by the chancel arch there stands a tablet dedicated to the five grandsons of Madeline Wyndham (among them George Wyndham's much-loved only son), who lost their lives in the First World War. But as if this were not tragedy enough for one family, the tender age and exceptional promise of the youngest member must have made his loss perhaps the hardest to bear.

Edward Wyndham Tennant, the son of Lady Pamela Glen-conner (one of the three graces), was only 19 when he was killed at the Battle of the Somme. He was an idealist, a poet, and a passionate lover of England, made manifest by his poignant lines "Home Thoughts in Laventie" which ended:

> I saw green banks of daffodil,
> Slim poplars in the breeze,
> Great tan-brown hares in gusty March
> A-courting on the leas;
> And meadows with their glittering streams,
>   and silver scurrying dace,
> Home—what a perfect place!

In Salisbury Cathedral there is an unusually touching memorial to this heroic young poet on which is written:

> When things were at their worst he would go up
> And down in the trenches cheering the men.
> When danger was greatest his smile was loveliest.

Shortly before he died he wrote to his mother, "I have the feeling of Immortality very strongly. I think of death with a light heart and as a friend whom there is no need to fear. To-morrow we go over the top. . . ." Edward Wyndham Tennant was never to visit the Wiltshire 'Clouds' again.

The Wyndham family is still remembered with affection at East Knoyle, especially by the older generation. This is perhaps best illustrated by the fact that the recently retired postmaster, Mr. Burton, whose own family has held the same position in the village for a combined number of 107 years, has named his new home 'Wyndhams'. It would seem that, together with 'Wren's Shop', history is being kept very much alive in this secluded corner of Wilts.

After passing close to East Knoyle, the county boundary points almost due west towards Mere and Zeals. Mere possesses one of the finest old churches in the county and is a small town which, as might be expected from its name, stands near the combined meeting-place of Dorset, Somerset, and Wiltshire, although it is the latter village which marks the exact nodal point. Barely a mile to the north of Zeals lies Stourton and the famous mansion of

Stourhead with its even more famous gardens, in which the River Stour begins its southbound wanderings into Dorset.

Since before the Norman Conquest, there has always been an estate here at the southern edge of the old Forest of Selwood. Originally it belonged to the Stourton family, and in 1448, a former High Sheriff of Wiltshire, Sir John Stourton, was created the first Lord Stourton by Henry VI. Over 100 years later the eighth baron came to an untimely end in Salisbury market-place, where he was publicly hanged in a halter of silk for the murder of two men, a father and son by the name of Hartgill. It appears that these two gentlemen had enraged the hot-headed nobleman in more ways than one, but chiefly because they had supported the claims of people who stood to gain material benefits in preference to himself.

Although the heirs of the bad baron managed to retain his title, it would seem that such a sinister event put a slight damper on the family fortunes because little more was heard of the Stourtons until 1714 when, for reasons unknown, the estate was sold to the trustees of Mr. Richard Hoare, son of the goldsmith, Sir Richard Hoare, and founder of the bank of that name. Somehow I cannot help wondering whether the Stourtons wanted to get away from a place where one of their ancestors ordered the bodies of the two Hartgills to be thrown into a vault in front of the house. Although I have no evidence whatsoever for suggesting such a possibility, I still feel it was sensible of Richard Hoare's younger brother, Henry, on buying the property outright from the trustees in 1720, to begin making drastic changes at Stourton. Not only did he pull down Old Stourton House and rebuild a new one in a completely different style on another site, but he also broke with tradition by rechristening it Stourhead.

But it is to his son, another Henry, that greatest credit must be given for the creation of the gardens and that well-known landmark called Alfred's Tower, a high outpost on the county border which is supposed to mark the spot where King Alfred set up his standard before his victory over the Danes at Ethandune in 879.

Henry Hoare II, who seems to have been such a great landscape gardener that he was able to devise many a 'proper object' without any assistance from Capability Brown, bequeathed the Stourhead property to his grandson, young Richard Colt Hoare, who was soon to become equally famous in his own right as an eminent

antiquary and county historian. He collaborated with William
Cunnington in writing the ancient history of Wiltshire and was
personally responsible for the first volume of a *History of Modern
Wiltshire*.

Sir Richard Colt Hoare is said to have opened 379 Wiltshire
barrows during his travels round the county, but his research
methods have come in for one or two criticisms. Owing to his
popularity it has been asserted that digging operations were often
held up while he himself was kept conversing at the houses
of whomsoever had offered him hospitality during his travels;
moreover, General Pitt-Rivers considered that Sir Richard committed the unpardonable sin of burying his skeletons too quickly
without measuring them and that he only once gave a description
of one saying, "it grinned horribly, a ghastly smile, a singularity I
have never before noticed". This, according to the General, was
enough to give any lover of antiquity a more than ghastly smile
himself.

Nevertheless, Sir Richard's work, which resulted in his mammoth tomes, made it far easier for his successors to find their way
among the maze of prehistoric monuments with which Wiltshire
is so generously endowed. His books would perhaps make heavy
reading now (both mentally and physically), but of their kind they
are unique productions and it seems fitting that Sir Richard's own
effigy may be seen in Salisbury Cathedral seated on one of the
Stourhead library chairs.

The estate remained with the Hoare family until the late Sir
Henry Hoare, whose only son had died of wounds received in
action in 1917, gave the greater part of it, including the house and
gardens, to the National Trust in 1946. The following year Sir
Henry and his wife died within two hours of each other, after
devoting their long lives to the management and improvement of
their home.

But their efforts have certainly not been wasted. Today Stourhead can claim to be one of the most beautiful places in Europe.
The house, with its priceless works of art, is one of the first great
buildings that sprang up from the English landscape in the new
Georgian style, and set a kind of official stamp on the Palladian
victory over the so-called 'Mannerist' style of Wren; while the
gardens, with their little temples and grotto half hidden in the
trees that surround the lake, give this part of Wiltshire a romantic,

if Continental flavour. But to me, this latter influence does not intrude or seem out of place. Basically, Stourhead is still English because it is lush and green. There are none of those dry dusty cactus-covered borders to be avoided, as in the more formal French and Italian gardens. Perhaps Stourhead is a perfect example of getting the best of both worlds. Wiltshire has adopted the Pantheon and the Temple of the Sun with grace and sensitivity, and I am glad that, according to John Britton, the second Henry Hoare "at an advanced age had the heartfelt satisfaction to hear his own creation universally admired and to see a barren waste covered with luxuriant woods".

But this could surely have not been as beautiful then as it is today. I have never ceased to wonder at the large-heartedness so characteristic of people such as the creator of Stourhead gardens. He lived with a vision and was prepared to work towards its more tangible existence, knowing that he himself might never see it at the height of its perfection. Or maybe he never thought that at all? In days gone by there was a stronger belief in immortality and the atmosphere at Stourhead seems to be full of this particular quality. In the little Church of St. Peter the Stourtons and the Hoares lie buried, yet somehow they still seem to be with us in the gardens, marching in perpetuity with the south-western boundary of Wilts.

Although it is sometimes hard to leave Stourhead, whenever I finally turn northwards along the road to Maiden Bradley, I always experience a strong sense of being drawn towards home. On my left I know the statue of King Alfred on his tower is keeping a firm stand by the Somerset border; on my right I am very aware of the high Deverill Downs that seem to be backing him up; but in front of me, although I know it is now necessary to travel farther north if I am to march full circle with Wiltshire's boundary, I feel compelled to slow down as usual by a little thatched cottage on the road near Kilmington in front of which there is a bold blue and white sign saying: "River Wylye". It is the same-sized sign that is repeated many times as the road crosses and recrosses the river in "my" valley, but this particular one seems by far the most important because it marks just a very small trickle at the Wylye's source.

It is said that the name 'Wylye' means 'tricky stream', and it would appear that there is every justification for such an appellation as far as its wanderings in the Deverill countryside are concerned; although strangely enough, the river never used to be called the Wylye at this point at all, but was known as the Deverill. Just to add to the confusion, according to local folklore, the Deverill was really the 'Dive-rill', because a duck once swam down it and dived underground like the stream itself on a long tortuous subterranean journey to Kingston Deverill, where they both surfaced in splendid condition. The duck's adventures seem a little hard to credit, but there is apparently no doubt that this is how the tricky Wylye originally began its life, although it would seem to have made up for such devious conduct in its subsequent open-hearted and pleasantly mature course.

There is a great temptation for me now to skirt round Maiden Bradley and turn eastwards to follow this course but, in order to keep faith with the south-western boundary, I must continue northwards at least as far as Heaven's Gate, even if this is still a little short of where the proposed 'take-over bid' from Bath and Bristol may one day monopolize so much of the north-west of the county.

Maiden Bradley itself is an attractive village that is entered after the road has cut, almost like a small mountain pass, between two high hills, Long Knoll and Little Knoll. The former lies like a gigantic lion facing westward, as if it were helping King Alfred to keep a wary eye on Somerset. In the twelfth century, the place became famous for its leper hospital, founded by Manasser Biset, a steward to Henry II. This was later accompanied by a priory which continued long after the hospital had ceased to function, leprosy having become far less common. Although both these establishments have almost been forgotten, there is still a tangible reminder of their existence in the presence of Priory Farm, situated a little to the north of the village.

At the Dissolution of the Monasteries, the priory and lands around it were granted to Sir Edward Seymour, whose descendants, the Dukes of Somerset, have always made a home at Maiden Bradley. In the church there is an elaborate memorial to a later Sir Edward, Speaker of the House of Commons in the reign of Charles II. He was a knowledgeable but evidently arrogant gentleman who, when his carriage once broke down at Charing Cross, is said to have commandeered the one behind it, telling the ejected owner that he could hardly expect to ride when the Speaker of the House was walking.

Maiden Bradley was the home of another proud man of exceptional ability. In 1617 Edmund Ludlow, the soldierly Parliamentarian, was born at Newmead Farm, just east of the village. The Ludlows, who had been influential in the county for over two centuries, were convinced republicans, although Edmund eventually quarrelled with Cromwell, opposed the election of his son, Richard, favoured the installation of the Long Parliament, and refused to support the recall of Charles II. He ended his days in exile on the Continent, where he occupied them by writing his memoirs which have been considered the best contemporary source of knowledge of that long unhappy period.

Less than 2 miles to the north of Maiden Bradley is the lovely spread-out village of Horningsham on the southern fringe of Longleat Park, with which it is inextricably associated. When Sir John Thynne planned his vast mansion here in the second half of the sixteenth century, he is alleged to have imported a number of Scottish masons to help with its construction. Tradition holds that because they were all staunch Presbyterians and had nowhere to carry out their Sunday worship, Sir John founded the Meeting House at Horningsham, claimed to be the oldest dissenting chapel in the country. However, no documentary evidence has ever been found for this and authorities now firmly assert that the present building only dates from 1700.

Longleat has already been sketched into this 'portrait' elsewhere, although any of Wiltshire's stately homes really need whole chapters to themselves if justice is to be done by them. The house, like so many of its contemporaries, began its life as a religious establishment that passed, at the Dissolution, to Sir John Thynne. This wealthy knight appears to have been a great favourite with the Protector, Duke of Somerset, and it is said that Sir John made use of the same architectural plans for Longleat as the Protector intended to use for the great palace which he had hoped to build at Savernake. It seems quite possible that this may have been the case because Longleat has often been referred to as the most magnificent house in England. Successive generations have added, rebuilt, and remodelled the *tout ensemble*, but it is to the third Lord Weymouth (created the first Marquess of Bath in 1789) that special credit must be given for the beauty of the grounds. He it was who called in Mr. Lancelot Brown, labelling him for ever 'Capability', the word that the great landscape gardener was always using with such enthusiasm. Although I feel that my favourite part of these grounds, Heaven's Gate, is so amazingly natural that Capability may not have had much hand in the celestial view, yet at the same time I am aware that he possibly had a clever, if slightly more earthly one, in the immediate foreground.

Without really knowing it, I believe I have been trying to get to Heaven's Gate since I first started marching with the county boundary; and it certainly seems a splendidly suitable place at which to end. I last went there in the winter when snow was on the ground and it was utterly deserted. There was mist in the parkland below me, although the sun was doing its best to break through. It was so quiet that a drip from one of the beech trees sounded like a pistol shot. I could see across into Somerset, but the valley was still shrouded. And then, just as if a spotlight was beginning to play on a darkened stage, Capability's foreground came on the scene. Little clumps of strategically placed trees arrived out of nowhere. The First Act was beginning; the little stream they call the Long Leat was being lit up, and I knew for sure why this hill above it was called Heaven's Gate.

Then suddenly, like all good theatrical productions, something really startling happened which made a shiver go down my spine and brought me right back to earth. There was a noise, a terrible noise, like no other noise that anyone could possibly expect in the heart of the Wiltshire countryside. It was not a bull bellowing or a horse neighing, or even the Marquess's circular saw whining in the woodland behind me. It stopped. I waited. It started again, loud and insistent, and I realized what it was. Somewhere, waiting in the wings below me, there was a lion wanting his breakfast.

It was probably very silly to decide to leave the auditorium at this point. After all, I had arrived by a legitimate route and I knew the lions of Longleat were well-fenced in; yet at the same time that roar was uncomfortably near. Home and the security of the Wylye Valley seemed more than unusually attractive. I had had my fill of heaven and somehow a lion at its gate was a little more than I had bargained for.

XVIII

BACK TO BASE

I AM a great one for going home. I believe my roots must be as deep as mine shafts by now. I suppose it is cowardice but I really do dislike leaving the security of my native county, and even a well-confined lion on the borders is enough to send me scurrying back to base along the banks of the Wylye. As for wanting to go farther afield or flying overseas to literally foreign parts, well, I just feel the agony of sitting strapped down in one of those nerve-racking machines, waiting for it to make up its mind whether to risk leaving *terra firma*, is simply not worth the eventual disappointment at the other end, especially when this is compared with the Wiltshire countryside back home.

The Wylye Valley was looking simply beautiful on the morning I left Heaven's Gate. I always said it was at its best in winter, when for some unknown reason many non-moonrakers want to leave it. Of course, this does not mean I should like it to be winter all the time, because naturally I enjoy seeing the changes rung. Each season bestows its own particular blessing on the Wylye and usually has enough good sense to know just when to bow out. This seems to me to be a great asset, as there is nothing worse than a guest who hangs on and on.

Although there was snow on the ground on this particular morning I knew it would not last long, because it was the beginning of March and spring would soon be stealing down the 'back' road, touching up all the little villages and making the farming community sowing-conscious. Already there were two men tinkering about with a new-fangled machine in some farm buildings near Sutton Veny. Soon they would all be 'at it', right the way down the valley, seeing the seed safely into the ground.

They would bring out their harrows, cultivators, drills, rollers, and all the rest of the paraphernalia connected with such an important operation.

It reminded me of a certain occasion which I loved during my childhood, when one of the weeklies (I think it must have been *Punch*) took my father up on a sentence he had written in a farming journal. He had said something to the effect that: "after spring sowing I always like to roll down every field". As he was such a large man it gave us all a glorious picture of him; but of course he was quite right. Farmers do roll down their fields soon after sowing and in a few more weeks they would be doing just that, all the way from Kilmington to the outskirts of Salisbury or, at any rate, seeing that someone else was doing the rolling for them. It was almost as if I could feel the warming-up process beginning, what with the sun making the road all slushy and the promising-looking catkins hanging in the hedgerow.

I should like to have hung around a little longer myself, but I had two appointments that day at Wilton which were both important. First of all I was going to visit the people who now live in the house where I was born, and later I was to have lunch with an elderly aunt. I was having a real day out, or perhaps it could simply be called a sentimental journey; but whatever it was, it was very enjoyable travelling along through Tytherington, Corton, Boyton, Sherrington, Stockton, and Wylye, thinking about everyone revving up for spring.

On my left, between Wylye and Hanging Langford, I caught a glimpse of my present home across the meadows, with the downs behind it. In a month or two when the trees came into leaf it would be hidden from view, but this morning it stood there winking at me through the bare branches, with the Wylye meandering (quite sedately now) through the garden. On my right lay the steeper slopes leading up to Grovely Woods, where once I used to ride almost daily, sometimes searching out the earthworks known as Grovely Castle or visiting the old park where the remains of a cluster of little houses went proudly under the name of Grovely Village.

I knew every inch of my present journey now; Hanging Langford, so called because it lies below a steep or hanging hill; Little Langford, because it is only a handful of houses with the tiny Church of St. Nicholas set down, as if by chance, in the middle of a meadow; Great Wishford, where they would soon be "keeping thic hankshent custom up on girt Oak Apple Day"; and then I was on the last lap, just over two miles of twisting lane to Ditchampton Farm.

I am glad no one has altered the name of the house, even though there is no longer any land to go with it. When my father left in 1951, because so many of the fields were being commandeered as housing sites, the remainder of the farm became incorporated with others on the Earl of Pembroke's Estate. I know he was glad that, as an entity, it had 'picked up sticks', as it were, at the same time as he did. The actual buildings have now been taken over by Grovely Riding School and even this, to me, seems quite a happy solution, because this morning I could see the head of a brown pony looking uncommonly like my precious Toby, peering out from the same loose box that once belonged to him.

During recent years, the farmhouse itself has changed hands more than once and I had not been inside it since my parents left. Now, here it was, looking the same and not the same, browns where there were greens, greens where there were reds; the oak floor in the drawing-room darkened by countless more polishings; my father's study devoid of his mammoth desk; my one-time lavender-coloured bedroom all bright and contemporary-looking as befits the young man who now inhabits it; another bathroom next to my parents' bedroom and an entire 'new look' to the old one where, once upon a time, I seem to remember pieces of flannel being warmed in front of a gas-fire, preparatory to covering my chest after it had been rubbed with camphorated oil. Back they all came, dim memories from the 1920s, not so dim from the 30s, a little confused in the 40s after the house had been altered and I was away from home much more.

And then the garden—there was just the same pungent smell to greet me round the corner by the potting shed; I could still see our signatures scratched in the cement in the pool that my mother created with such pride; a little way away stood the walnut tree I gave my father during the last war, looking quite mature now and even leaning a little as if the years were really creeping up on it. All the important things were still there, but what seemed equally important was the fact that it was so obvious that the present owners, who have now bought the place outright, love Ditchampton Farm and are taking most excellent care of it. I

thanked them and left with promises to come again, happy to
feel it was still the sort of home anyone would want to come
back to.

I was a little on the late side arriving for lunch with my aunt. I
should have known, really, that an expedition of this sort always
takes longer than expected. I made my apologies but, for all her
77 years, she is a forbearing lady. My aunt is also an excellent cook.
I was hungry by then; it seemed quite a time since I had been
listening to that lion wanting his breakfast; I tucked in for a while
and then, for no reason at all, I suddenly thought of asking her
something that had been puzzling me since I was a child, so I said,
"Aunt Edith, you've been a Wiltonian all your life. Who exactly
was Jimmy Kirby?" I cannot imagine why I had never thought
of asking her before because she came straight back at me with,
"But my dear, don't you *know*?"

"No," I replied, rather shamefacedly. "I often wondered, but
he just seemed to be someone the drowner's wife used to say was
always in a 'klit'."

My aunt pushed back her chair and smiled. "Jimmy Kirby was
a cooper," and then, as I looked slightly nonplussed, she qualified
her statement by adding, "You know, my dear, he made barrels.
Well, one day he was asked to make an outsize barrel for a publican
who lived a little distance from his inn. I suppose the idea was that
then he would be able to keep a good supply of liquor available
without having to be seen for ever going to the pub to get it.
Jimmy Kirby made him a beautiful barrel and trundled it down
to his house early one morning when it was still dark. The trouble
was that it was so big he was unable to get it through any doorway,
and as it got lighter everyone who passed by saw Jimmy standing
outside with his barrel, scratching his head and wondering what to
do. He was, as they say in Wiltshire, in a complete 'klit', and all
Wilton was laughing about it." And with that, we both broke
down and laughed together.

"Thank you, Aunt Edith," I managed to say at last. "You've
made my day. I can't think why I never asked you before."

"Perhaps it's just as well you've got around to it," she replied,
sobering up a little. "I shall be 78 in May and there can't be all
that many people in Wilton who know about Jimmy Kirby
now."

I looked at her. There was not a grey hair in her head, and if she goes on cooking or "lining the inner man" as she calls it, in the same way as she had just lined mine, I see no reason why she should not be good for a 100, especially as all true Wilsaetan are a 'race apart'.

The sun was still shining when I left her standing on the doorstep of her little cottage in South Street; in fact, it felt really quite warm on the corner by the one-time Misses B. & M. Winters. It was such a good day that I decided to play my luck, so I went back towards Ditchampton, only this time I took the path by our old farm that leads to Grovely Woods. Half-way up I turned round and saw the whole of Wilton spread out sharp and clear below me like a child's model toy. In the foreground lay my old home and then, one by one, I could pick out the other landmarks in my life. There was the tall chimney belonging to the Felt Mills where I watched my grandmother doing her washing; behind it, I could just distinguish the Carpet Factory where my uncle used to live; a little patch of shining water marked the exact spot in the Wylye where I learned to swim; over to the right was the tower of Wilton Church which I once climbed with such trepidation; close by lay Wilton House, my working headquarters in the war; and beyond all this stretched the city of Salisbury, backed-up by Harnham Heights, whereas guarding the entire scene stood my focal point of Wiltshire, the spire of Salisbury Cathedral radiant in the afternoon sun.

I looked at my watch. It was only 3.30 p.m. I could be there within half an hour. It almost seemed inevitable that this was where I was going to complete the day's journey and, perhaps at the same time, put the final touches to my *Portrait of Wiltshire*. The drive took just a little longer than usual because I had forgotten about it being market-day in Salisbury. The traffic was thinning slightly, but there was still the usual 'madding crowd' around the Poultry Cross and plenty of stall-holders in the market-place who were not yet content to 'call it a day'.

There they all were, busy doing their Tuesday trading as their predecessors must have done seven centuries ago. Maybe the scene before me looked very different compared to what it was like during the time when my home town did its best to thwart the up-and-coming prosperity of its immature rival; yet here was Salisbury market still going strong, a symbol of one of those twin forces that have so successfully nurtured the city throughout the ages, Trade and the Church. As I went on towards the latter, I could not help thinking that although some of W. H. Hudson's words may now seem rather dated, there are others which still hold good: "Business is business, and must be attended to, in fair or foul weather, but for business with pleasure we prefer it fine on market-day . . . the mere sight of it exhilarates like wine."

It certainly was fine today, and exhilarating. It was a joy to go round the market-place and turn the corner into Milford Street past the Red Lion Hotel. I did not actually see Mrs. Thomas on the pavement wearing one of her gorgeous hats, but I felt she might well have been inside taking tea at the Chelsea Tea Rooms that belong to the same establishment. It was still sunny by the time I reached the Close, although the shadows were beginning to lengthen. It was very quiet and peaceful, exactly like getting home after a party. Only the regular habitués seemed to be about. I could see Mr. Quine, the Chief Security Officer, striding purposefully along on what I felt sure was important Close business, such as a missive for Dr. Elsie Smith. I noticed our family solicitor emerging from the offices he has occupied in Bishop's Walk for as long as I can remember. I caught sight of a clerical figure on his way to the Theological College. It was pure Trollope perhaps, but it was also quite delightful.

The Cathedral itself enveloped me with a warmth which that author could scarcely have envisaged. Central heating has recently been installed and its impact, especially on the uninitiated, is enormous. Those arriving for the annual carol service, complete with rugs and hot-water bottles, have had to relegate them, albeit shamefacedly, to the stone floor beneath them. Nowadays, whenever it is particularly nippy along the High Street, the Cathedral is about the best place in which to warm up. I realize that this is not exactly a creditable reason for entering such a sacred building, especially when our worthier ancestors regularly attended divine service under arctic conditions; yet nevertheless a literally warm welcome does make it easier for less commendable souls such as myself to linger about its interior far more often.

But I am at a loss to say just what it is about Salisbury Cathedral and the Close that has always attracted me so much. It is not simply a question of religion or beauty. I think it has more to do with age and continuity. It seems to tell a story about the district I was brought up in. It was built from its stone and it holds so many

P

memories from the past. Maybe it is like a much-loved picture-book, with a spire on the cover and no end of splendid types illustrated inside.

I could see old William Longespée's tomb from where I was standing, the gallant warrior who actually laid one of the Cathedral's foundation stones and was the first man to be buried therein. On my left, was a tribute to that younger hero of the First World War, Edward Wyndham Tennant, who "gave his earthly life to such matter as he set great store by: the honour of his country and his home". Behind me lay an effigy of Longespée's own son and close to him another miniature stone figure under which the heart of Bishop Poore is thought to have been interred; while I knew that all around me there were countless tombs and memorials to men and women of the same name, claiming to have derived their descent from the original intrepid creator of this great building.

Then I looked towards the shrine of St. Osmund, the bishop who completed that first Norman Cathedral at Old Sarum and who created the 'Sarum Use', a form of service that became famous throughout the country. His is a unique monument in which there are curious apertures where pilgrims used to thrust their afflicted limbs in the hope of obtaining healing. Close to it lies the famous Lancastrian soldier, Robert, Lord Hungerford; while on the opposite side of the nave is the tomb of the first Lord Hungerford, who fought at Agincourt and assisted in executing the Will of Henry V. In the south transept there is a memorial to Sir Robert Hyde, Lord Chief Justice and cousin of the famous Earl of Clarendon. Somehow, I have always felt grateful to the Hyde family because so many of its members did their best to protect the Cathedral during the Cromwellian period. Likewise, I have the same kind of feeling towards those other men whose memorials grace the north transept, Richard Jefferies, Colt Hoare, John Britton, and the first Earl of Malmesbury, each of whom in his own individual way seems to have earned the special tribute paid to him.

I wandered down the north choir aisle and went inside the tiny chantry chapel of Bishop Audley, glad to think that its interior had recently been refurnished as a memorial to genial Bishop Lovett who confirmed me many years ago. Farther along I stopped beside the grand monument to Sir Thomas Gorges and his wife, the indefatigable builder of Longford Castle, and then looked at the new window above it commemorating a less worldly character, the Bemerton poet-parson, George Herbert. Across on the other side of the Lady Chapel I saw the marble slab that once marked the actual grave of St. Osmund and, next to it, the family tomb of that 'good' Warden of Savernake Forest, the Earl of Hertford, husband of Lady Catherine Grey and son of Protector Somerset. Farther westwards, behind the Radnor family pew, there is an even more elaborate edifice, lit up to show the brightly coloured effigies of Sir Richard and Dame Katherine Mompesson, whose descendants built the most distinguished Queen Anne house in the Close. Here they all were, a galaxy of moonrakers, long since dead yet remembered not only with pride but often with more than a little affection also.

Many of them, of course, were bishops—the bridge-building Bingham, college-building Giles, scientifically minded Seth Ward, and the later-day Bishop Wordsworth and nephew of the poet, who founded the well-known school of the same name and gave the slope on Harnham Heights to the citizens of Salisbury. It seemed that all around this lofty building men and women were honoured in one way or another. In every corner or niche the present included the past. In the choir an old plaque was discovered and subsequently reinstalled by the sixteenth Earl of Pembroke to commemorate the last resting-place of one of the family's most beautiful countesses. On this has been written those immortal lines that have sometimes been ascribed to Ben Jonson and sometimes William Browne:

> Underneath this sable hearse
> Lies the subject of all verse,
> Sidney's sister, Pembroke's mother. . . .

Similarly, in 1946, the Freemasons of the city decided that it was high time the Cathedral's first Clerk of the Works, Elias de Dereham, was better recognized. This has resulted in a very pleasant-looking Elias, standing proudly with his tools of office against one of the pillars.

But it is not altogether necessary to be rich or famous to have a place in Salisbury Cathedral; other less exalted men and women are also remembered. There is the archdeacon's wife who was buried here on her fiftieth wedding day, and the seventeenth-century oculist whom Pepys once visited in the hopes of regaining his failing sight, who has been given the delightfully human epitaph:

> Beneath this stone extinct he lies
> The only doctor for the eyes.

Then there are even simpler inscriptions such as to another valiant doctor during the years of the plague, to a present-century Clerk of the Works, to those who lost their lives in a terrible railway crash at Salisbury station in 1906, and, of course, to those who died while fighting for their country. As I left the Cathedral I noticed the colours of the erstwhile Wiltshire Regiment proudly adorning the wall by the North Door, and the song to which those moonrakers used to march came suddenly into my mind. Although perhaps it was not quite the right occasion, somehow I found myself humming it as I walked across the green. By the time I reached the car-park I was really beginning to get well under way:

> The Vly, the Vly,
> The Vly be on the turmut. . . .

And then the Chief Security Officer came round the corner. "Good-evening," he said, "lovely day it's been."

"Lovely," I answered, hoping he had not heard my strange little solo. I knew him quite well, but all the same it was embarrassing to think he might have caught me singing "The Vly" in the Close, of all places.

"Have you finished your book on Wiltshire?" he asked, as he came towards me.

"Just about," I said, somewhat taken aback, "but how ever did you know that I was writing one?"

He held up an authoritative hand. "In my job you get to know about these things. I trust you've given pride of place to the Cathedral and the Close."

"I think so. I've begun and ended there, anyway," I told him.

"Ah," he replied slowly, "I thought you might. I guessed you'd do the 'round trip'."

I looked across at the Cathedral and upwards to the spire. It towered above us, dark against the evening sky. Soon, its friendly night-light would shine from the top and the Close would settle down to sleep, irrespective of what the noisy city of Salisbury was getting up to. I turned back towards this patriarchal figure before me who looked almost as if he might have been rounding up his flock at sundown, as in days gone by. I still did not know exactly why this particular part of Wiltshire meant quite so much to me and I felt rather like the small girl who expressed the same predicament with the words, "How do I know what I feel until I see what I say?" So I simply said, "Yes, I always like making a 'round trip'."

And then I wished the Chief Security Officer "Good-night."

INDEX

Purbeck marble, 22
Purton, 171
Pyt House, Tisbury, 56

Q

Queensberry, Duchess of, 80
Quine, Mr., 16, 225

R

Raceplain, 36–8
Races, Salisbury, 36–8
Radnor, Earl of, 68
—— Dowager Countess of, 79
Radnor family, 227
Ramsbury, 179, 194–5
Rank, J. V., 37
Rawlence, the Misses, 51
Reading, Berkshire, 165, 192
Redlynch, 204
Reed, Grace, 63
Reeve, Lieut-Col. and Mrs., 190–2
Reform Act, 1832, 43
Reformation, The, 22, 24
Rembrandt, 52
Rennie, John, 96–100
Return of the Native, The, Thomas Hardy, 78
Richard I, 39, 144
Richard III, 25
Richard of Farleigh, 21
Richards, Sir Gordon, 37
Riddett, Mrs., 202
Rider, Mr., 154
Ridgeway, the, 81, 156
Roads: A4 through Marlborough, 127, 134, 138
  A36 through Wylye Valley, 66, 86
  M4 across North Wiltshire, 134, 156–63, 168, 188, 193
  Ridgeway, 81, 156
  Roman, 43, 128–9, 187–9, 193, 199
Robbins, Mr., 134
Roger le Poer, Bishop, 42, 101, 179
Roman Occupation, 43, 79, 100, 187, 201
Roundheads, 211
Roundway Down, 101
Rowde, 101
Royal Albert Bridge, Saltash, Cornwall, 167
Royal Artillery Foxhounds, 66
Rushall, 99
Rushmore Park, 112, 209
Russell, Lord Hugh, 67, 78
—— Lady Hugh, 67

S

St. John family, 171–3
St. Nicholas, Hospital of, 40

St. Paul's Cathedral, 57, 212
Salisbury, Ela, Countess of, 106–7, 136
Salisbury (New Sarum), 14, 18–47, 53–5, 58, 67–8, 70–1, 76–7, 84–6, 89, 99, 105–6, 114, 130, 141, 179, 199–200, 202, 221, 224–9
—— Black Death at, 29
—— Black and Grey Friars at, 29, 86
—— Common Cold Research Unit, 34, 41
Salisbury and South Wiltshire College of Further Education, 29
Salisbury Cathedral, 14, 17–28 31, 35, 37, 39–40, 63–4, 100, 106, 155, 165–6, 179, 213, 215, 224–9
Salisbury Cathedral Close, 20–7, 53, 63, 141, 225–9
Salisbury Journal and Devizes Mercury, 137
Salisbury Museum, 34, 79
Salisbury Plain, 17–18, 23, 31, 45, 55, 67, 69, 71–83, 85, 98–100, 103–5, 141, 174, 200, 202, 204
Salisbury Station, 35, 167, 228
Salter and Co., 87–8
Sandell, Richard, 14, 100, 104
Sandroyd School, 209
Sanscrit, 161
Sarah Arnot roses, 109
Sarisberie (Norman name for Salisbury), 18–19, 28, 43
Sarsen stones, 73–7, 125–7
Sarum, New, *see* Salisbury
—— Old, *see* Old Sarum
Saunders, David, 83
Saunders, Peter, 182–3
Savage Club, 52
Savernake Forest, 96, 100, 134, 142–51, 160, 165, 218, 227. *See also* Ailesbury family; Esturmy family; Seymour family
—— Tottenham House and Park, 147–51
—— Wardens of, 142–51, 227
Savernake Forest, a History of, the Marquess of Ailesbury, 15, 142, 148
Saxon Invasion, 46, 72, 79–80, 94, 100, 204–5
Scales Bridge, 99
Scamp, Joshua, 206
Searisbyrig (Saxon name for Salisbury), 18
'Seftum Pudding', 182
Sem, River, 210
Severn Bridge, 62
Severn Estuary, 189
Seymour, Sir Edward, *see* Hertford, Edward Seymour, Earl of
—— Sir Edward, *see* Somerset, Edward Seymour, Earl of Hertford and Duke of
—— Sir Edward (Speaker of the House of Commons), 217
—— Lady Elizabeth, 148